Lessons My Father Taught Me

Michael Reagan

WITH
Jim Denney

Humanix Books
www.humanixbooks.com

Humanix Books

Lessons My Father Taught Me

Humanix Books, P.O. Box 20989, West Palm Beach, FL 33416, USA
www.humanixbooks.com | info@humanixbooks.com

Library of Congress Control Number 2016931039

Cover photo: Getty Images 53379287
Interior design: Scribe Inc.

Humanix Books is a division of Humanix Publishing, LLC. Its trademark, consisting of the words "Humanix" is registered in the Patent and Trademark Office and in other countries.

ISBN: 978-1-63006-053-4 (hardcover)
ISBN: 978-1-63006-054-1 (ebook)

Printed in the United States of America

10 9 8 7 6 5 4 3 2 1

Contents

Introduction

The Greatest Man
I've Ever Known

ON JUNE 5, 2004, Ronald Reagan died after a decade-long battle with Alzheimer's disease. He was the fortieth president of the United States and the first American president to die in the twenty-first century.

He was my father.

After a state funeral at Washington National Cathedral on June 11, our family accompanied the casket back to California aboard Air Force One. We rode in the funeral motorcade to the Reagan Library in Simi Valley, California, where the final service and interment would take place.

As I looked out the window of the limousine, I saw that the streets were lined with thousands and thousands of well-wishers—a vast sea of people who loved, respected, and mourned my father. Many of them had banners or American flags in their hands. Others had their hands over their hearts. Some wept openly. Countless men and women in uniform saluted.

That amazing outpouring of love gave all of us in the Reagan family a huge sense of strength and comfort. We were lifted up by their prayers and their love.

Our motorcade reached the top of that hill where my father's library stands. There, seven hundred invited guests came to honor his memory and say farewell. People Dad had known since his Hollywood days mingled with leaders who had shaped world events.

The Air Force Band finished playing "Battle Hymn of the Republic" as the sun was setting toward the west. Then I stood and spoke from my heart "Good evening," I said. "I'm Mike Reagan. You knew my father as governor, as president. But I knew him as Dad. I want to tell you a little bit about my dad—a little bit about Cameron and Ashley's grandfather—because not a whole lot is ever spoken about that side of Ronald Reagan.

"Ronald Reagan adopted me into his family in 1945. I was the chosen one. I was the lucky one. And in all of his years, he never mentioned that I was adopted, either behind my back or in front of me. I was his son, Michael Edward Reagan.

"When his family grew to be two families, he didn't walk away from the one to go to the other. He became a father to both families—to Patti and then Ronnie, but always to my sister Maureen and myself.

"We looked forward to those Saturday mornings when he would pick us up. We'd sit on the curb on Beverly Glen as his car would turn the corner from Sunset Boulevard, and we would get in and ride to his ranch and play games—and he would always make sure it ended up a tie. We would swim and we would ride horses or we'd just watch him cut firewood. We were in awe of our father.

"As years went by and I became older and found a woman I would marry, Colleen, he sent me a letter about marriage and how important it was to be faithful to the woman you love, with a PS: 'You'll never get in trouble if you say "I love you" at least once a day.' And I'm sure he told Nancy every day 'I love you,' just as I tell Colleen.

"He also sent letters to his grandchildren. He wasn't able to be the grandfather that many of you are able to be because of the job that he had. So he would write letters. He sent one letter to Cameron and said: 'Cameron, some guy got ten thousand dollars for my signature. Maybe this letter will help you pay for your college education.' He signed it, 'Grandpa,' then added, 'PS: Your grandpa is the fortieth president of the United States, Ronald Reagan.'

"Those are the kinds of things my father did.

"At the early onset of Alzheimer's disease, my father and I would tell each other we loved each other, and we would give each other a hug. As the years went by and he could no longer verbalize my name, he recognized me as the man who hugged him. So when I would walk into the house, he would be there in his chair opening up his arms for that hug hello and the hug good-bye. It was truly a blessing from God.

"We had wonderful blessings of that nature—wonderful, wonderful blessings that my father gave to me each and every day of my life. I was so proud to have the Reagan name and to be Ronald Reagan's son. What a great honor.

"He gave me a lot of gifts as a child. He gave me a horse. He gave me a car. He gave me a lot of things. But there's a gift he gave me that I think is wonderful for every father to give every son.

"Last Saturday, when my father opened his eyes for the last time, and visualized Nancy and gave her such a wonderful, wonderful gift—When he closed his eyes, that's when I realized the gift that he gave to me, the gift that he was going to be with his Lord and Savior, Jesus Christ.

"Back in 1988, on a flight from Washington, D.C., to Point Mugu, he told me about his love of God, his love of Christ as his Savior. I didn't know then what it all meant. But I certainly know now.

"I can't think of a better gift for a father to give a son. And I hope to honor my father by giving my son Cameron and my daughter Ashley that very same gift he gave to me.

"It's the gift of knowing where he is this very moment, this very day—that he is in heaven. And I can only promise my father this: Dad, when I go, I will go to heaven, too. And you and I and my sister, Maureen, who went before us, will dance with the heavenly host of angels before the presence of God. We will do it melanoma- and Alzheimer's-free.

"Thank you for letting me share my father, Ronald Wilson Reagan."

Every fifth of June since my father's funeral, unless I'm away on business, I make a point of visiting my father's grave at the Ronald Reagan Presidential Library. I think about his life and I say a prayer of gratitude—and I read the inscription in my father's own words: "I know in my heart that man is good. That what is right will always eventually triumph. And there's purpose and worth to each and every life."

I have traveled across America, giving speeches and meeting thousands of people. Again and again, people tell me how much they love and miss my father. Some share stories of meeting him. Others tell me what his presidency meant to them. I never tire of hearing people talk about my dad or receiving the hugs they wish they could give to him. I'm always reminded of the many hugs my father and I shared whenever he and I were together.

I've often said that Ronald Reagan was the greatest man I've ever known—and one of the greatest men the world has ever known. I've spent my whole life studying him, absorbing the lessons he taught me, trying to follow the example he set. Dad was not a perfect father, but he truly loved his children. He and my mother divorced when I was three, so I only got to see him every other weekend—but he would pack as much fun and relationship-building as he could into those weekends.

Dad would take me to his ranch, and we'd do chores together, he'd tell me stories and talk to me about life. Did I understand everything he was trying to teach me? Did I appreciate his wisdom and experience? No, not at the time. But years later, I remembered many of those lessons, and they finally made sense to me.

The lessons my father taught me have made all the difference in my marriage, my family, my professional life, my friendships, and my faith. In the next few chapters, I'll share those lessons with you and show you how my father's values and wisdom impacted my life—and changed the world.

Thank you for letting me share with you the lessons my father taught me.

1

Love Your Family

I OWE MY LATE SISTER Maureen a debt I can never repay. I owe her ninety-seven cents.

That's how much Maureen paid to bring me into the Reagan family. She was three years old when she accompanied Mom and Dad to Schwab's Pharmacy—yes, the famed Schwab's Pharmacy at Sunset and Crescent Heights, where actress Lana Turner was discovered and where Harold Arlen sat at the lunch counter and wrote "Over the Rainbow."

While Mom and Dad were browsing in the aisles, Maureen strode to the counter, opened her little pink purse, and dumped a pile of coins on the counter—ninety-seven cents.

The pharmacist peered over the counter. "What do you want, little girl?"

Maureen said, "I want to buy a brother."

My mom and dad—Jane Wyman and Ronald Reagan—witnessed this exchange. Mom hurried over and told Maureen to put her money back in her purse. To Mom, the incident was embarrassing. After her first child, doctors had told Mom she should not get pregnant again. To her, the whole issue of a baby brother was private family business.

Returning home, Mom and Dad talked it over. They had accepted the idea that Maureen would be an only child—but they hadn't consulted with Maureen. Maybe she really did need a sibling to play with. So they decided to adopt.

I was born in Los Angeles on March 18, 1945. My birth mother was an unmarried aspiring actress named Irene Flaugher. Three days after my birth, Ronald Reagan and Jane Wyman adopted me as their son and brought me home from the hospital.

When they showed me to Maureen, she was indignant. "I don't want a *little* brother—I want a *big* brother like my friends!"

"Well," Mom said, "Michael was the only brother available. You're going to love him very much."

A nurse had come from the hospital to help care for me. When Maureen saw the nurse, she ran up the stairs to her room, snatched her piggy bank off the dresser, and threw it on the floor. She grabbed up the money from the shattered piggy bank—all ninety-seven cents of it—then ran downstairs and dumped the coins into the nurse's hands.

"What's this for?" the nurse asked.

"Keep it," Dad said. "She wants to have a part in bringing Michael into the family."

That's how I came into the Reagan family. Maureen paid the price of my admission, and I'll never be able to repay that ninety-seven-cent debt.

Alternating Saturdays with Dad

Mom and Dad met in 1938 while costarring in *Brother Rat*, a comedy about cadets at the Virginia Military Institute. They were married on January 26, 1940, at the Wee Kirk o' the Heather in Glendale, California. Their first child, Maureen Elizabeth Reagan, was born January 4, 1941. I was born four years later.

When I was two years old, Mom became pregnant again. The pregnancy was unplanned, but not unwanted. As soon as Mom knew she was pregnant, she wanted that baby very much and was determined to carry the baby to term.

But on June 26, 1947, just six months into the pregnancy, Mom went into labor and gave birth to a daughter, Christine, at Queen of Angels Hospital. Christine only lived for nine hours. It was the greatest heartbreak of Mom's life—and she had to go through it alone. When baby Christine died, Dad was at another hospital, Cedars of Lebanon, with a serious case of viral pneumonia.

The death of a child often takes a devastating toll on a marriage. One day in May 1948, Dad came home and Mom stunned him with the news that she wanted a divorce. Dad was a devoted family man, and the notion of divorce had never entered his thoughts. He knew Mom was grieving, but he had no idea his marriage was in jeopardy. I was only three at the time, so I didn't understand what was happening. But Maureen understood, and remembered. Years later, she recalled, "It just never occurred to him, no matter what their problems were, that he and mother would get a divorce; it was so foreign to his way of thinking, to the way he was brought up."[1]

I think Mom had decided that there was only one thing she could do to escape the painful memories after Christine's death: she had to go back to work. She immersed herself in her next role in a film called *Johnny Belinda*. She played a young deaf-mute woman, Belinda McDonald, who is raped and gives birth to a little boy named Johnny. It's a powerful motion picture, and Mom gave the performance of a lifetime. The film was nominated for a dozen Academy Awards, including best picture, and Mom won an Oscar and the Golden Globe Award for best actress.

(Incidentally, my mother handled the divorce with consummate class and discretion. She never said a word about my father in public or in private. After Dad was elected president of the United States, publishers offered my mother a number of lucrative book deals if she would dish some dirt on the first divorced president. She didn't give those offers a moment's consideration. In fact, when she was starring in *Falcon Crest* on television in the 1980s, she had a written agreement with the studio to participate in any interview about the show, but if the interviewer brought up her marriage to Ronald Reagan, she would instantly walk out. From the divorce in 1948 until my father's death in 2004, she never said one word about him and their marriage. A few days after his death, she did issue one brief yet touching statement: "America has lost a great president and a great, kind, and gentle man.")

After the divorce, I saw my father on alternating Saturdays. Maureen and I would go outside at ten o'clock and sit on the curb in front of my mother's two-story mansion at 333 S. Beverly Glen. We'd watch and wait, and soon we'd see Dad's red station wagon turn from Sunset Boulevard onto Beverly Glen. Then I'd yell, "He's here!"

I was practically quivering with excitement when Dad arrived to pick us up for the weekend. Those days with my father were very important to me, because they were so much fun—and so rare. For a little boy, having to wait two weeks to see your dad is like waiting an eternity. When I was with my father, I didn't want to waste a moment.

We'd drive out to Yearling Row, Dad's ranch in Northridge, in the San Fernando Valley, where he raised thoroughbred horses. Conditions at the ranch were primitive. The only structure was a one-room caretaker's shack. Dad and his ranch foreman, Nino Peppetone, stayed in that shack on weekends when they worked with the horses.

While Dad and Nino put the horses through their paces, Maureen and I played with the goats or fed the chickens. At lunch time, Dad would open a picnic basket and we'd sit on the grass in the shade of an oak tree, talking and watching the clouds' shadows move across the Santa Susana Mountains.

In 1951, Dad bought a new ranch near Malibu, adjacent to the 20th Century Fox movie ranch where *M*A*S*H* and *Planet of the Apes* were filmed. It became the new Yearling Row. It was four hundred acres of meadows and hills enclosed in a white fence that Dad built with his own hands. During our Saturdays at the ranch, I helped Dad dig the post holes for the fence, and I helped him repaint that fence many times over the years. The Malibu ranch had separate houses for the family and the foreman, and a swimming pool.

As Maureen grew older, she spent some of those weekends with her friends. So sometimes it would just be Dad and me at the ranch, or I might bring one of my friends along. My friends liked being with my father because he made everything fun. None of my friends were ever nervous around Dad. During the drive to the ranch, we'd play car games like Beaver—we'd shout out "Beaver!" whenever we saw a wood-paneled station wagon. The person with the most sightings by the end of the trip was the winner. Dad was the referee and scorekeeper, and somehow he managed to make every game end in a tie.

When we got to the ranch, there were usually some chores to do, but there was always plenty of time to run and play. The ranch was a great place for a game of hide-and-seek, which we played on horseback. My friends and I built forts out of hay from the hay barn. I can close my eyes and recall the earthy smell of the horses, the dust in my nose, the feel of the tall grass brushing against the legs of my blue jeans, and the dry-oak scent of the wood my father cut and split. I remember bouncing on the passenger seat of the Jeep as Dad drove us around on rugged dirt trails or off-road.

On late afternoons, after Dad had finished his chores, we'd ride horses or jump into the pool. Dad had one rule around the swimming pool—no running. To enforce that rule, he required that whenever Maureen and I were hurrying around the deck, playing tag, we had to stop at each corner and dip the toes of one foot into the pool.

Dad had taught me to swim when I was three years old. I have no memory of it, but Dad told me the story. We had a pool at our home in Trousdale Estates, and Dad was determined to "drown-proof" me, so I'd be safe around that pool. Mom had gotten me swimming lessons at a place where they put an inflatable life jacket on me and taught me some rudimentary water skills. Dad didn't think much of that approach. He figured that if I fell in the pool by accident, I might not be wearing a flotation device. So he told Mom I didn't need the life jacket anymore.

"You're out of your mind, Ronnie," Mom said. "Without that life jacket, he'll sink to the bottom."

Dad didn't say a word. He just took off my life jacket, carried me to the pool, and—as Mom watched in horror—dropped me in.

Years later, after Dad told me that story, I asked him, "What did you expect me to do?"

"Well," he said, "you swam, didn't you?"

It's true. I can't remember a time when I didn't know how to swim.

Dad was an amazing swimmer. As a youth, he had worked as a lifeguard on the Rock River near his hometown of Dixon, Illinois. Because he was such a strong swimmer, Dad could hold his breath underwater forever. His swimming prowess came in handy when he played in the pool with Maureen and me at the Malibu ranch.

The pool water came from a well, and the water was green and rust brown with minerals. Dad would dive down into that murky water, and Maureen and I would try to find him. We'd thrash all over the pool and have to come up for air five or six times while he hid at the bottom. Sometimes we'd think he was *never* coming up—and then he'd pop up in the far corner of the pool. We'd play that game until it was time to head home.

At the end of the day, Maureen and I would flip a coin to decide whether to drive home via the Pacific Coast Highway (PCH) or through the San Fernando Valley. The PCH was a spectacular drive, and we'd stop at the Foster's Freeze by the Malibu pier for ice cream cones. The Valley road was lined with orange groves, apple orchards, and fruit stands, and if we went that way, we'd stop at a fresh cider stand on Ventura Boulevard.

On Sunday mornings, Dad would take Maureen and me to his mother Nelle's house in Los Angeles. Nelle had moved from Illinois to California in 1938. She'd drive us to Sunday school in her old Studebaker then bring us back to her house for Sunday brunch.

My Irreplaceable Dad

In late 1949, Dad met an actress named Nancy Davis. They dated for about a year before Dad introduced her to Maureen and me. Soon, he was bringing her on our weekend trips to the Malibu ranch.

Later, when Maureen and I were alone, we'd talk about Dad and Nancy, and what it would be like if the two of them got married. By that time, Mom had sent Maureen and me to Chadwick, a private boarding school, so for most of the year I didn't have much of a home life. I didn't even get to see Maureen very much because she was four grades ahead of me. (I didn't know then that I would spend most of my early years in boarding school and my summers at summer camp; only when I became an adult did I realize that because Mom was a working actress and a single mother, she really had no choice.) At night in the dorm, I'd lay awake, imagining how it would be if Dad and Nancy got married. In my childish naïveté, I pictured myself moving in with them, escaping from boarding school, and finally having a normal home life like families on television.

Dad never raised his hand to us and rarely raised his voice. He had an unusual parenting style: he wouldn't spank or scold— he'd tell a story. He spoke in parables—and he hoped you would connect the dots and get the point of the story. My father was the kind of guy who, if you asked him for the time, would tell you how the watch is made. That was his approach to parenting— and as we will later see, he approached politics the same way.

I didn't fear my father, but I respected him. I frequently disobeyed him behind his back, but I never defied him to his face. When he caught me doing something wrong, he'd give me that Ronald Reagan frown, and I'd instantly feel guilty. I almost never went to him with problems because our time together was too brief and I didn't want to say anything to upset him. I also knew that Dad and Mom had an understanding, and I was afraid that if I shared something with Dad, he'd feel obligated to report it to Mom.

At Chadwick, I appeared in a school play just before Memorial Day weekend. I had to wear a monkey costume, which was hot and made me feel sick. After the play, Dad and Nancy drove me home. I sat in the backseat of Dad's convertible and felt sicker and sicker until I turned around, leaned over the backseat, and threw up. My stomach contents ended up in that recessed area that the car top folds into. I'm sure that when Dad discovered the mess, he figured out who did it—but he never said a word to me.

When Mom wasn't working, she'd bring me home for the weekend. Sunday evenings, when I returned to Chadwick, we had a tradition: Mom would take me out for dinner at the Brown Derby, and I would order my usual avocado cocktail. (My mother was a longtime friend of the Brown Derby owners Bob and Sally Cobb—the originators of the Cobb salad—and she wrote the foreword to Sally Cobb's memoir and recipe book, *The Brown Derby Restaurant: A Hollywood Legend*).

In the late 1950s, Mom was very busy with a weekly drama series on NBC, *Jane Wyman Presents*. On weekends when she was working and Maureen and I couldn't go home, Dad would bring Nancy to Chadwick for a visit. I lived for those visits and reveled in our time together. As the visit was coming to an end, I'd feel a sense of melancholy setting in. When I watched Dad and Nancy drive away, the loneliness was almost unbearable.

Dad and Nancy were married on March 4, 1952, at the Little Brown Church in the Valley, a chapel in Studio City—but their marriage didn't change my life the way I hoped it would. I continued going to boarding school, and I didn't move in with Dad and Nancy. My father did the best he could to stay involved with Maureen and me. In fact, no one ever worked harder at staying involved with the children of his first marriage than Dad. And while it was hard for me to live in a home without my Dad, he was there on the weekends without fail. He tried hard to be a good father to all four of his children.

In November 1952, when I was seven, Mom also remarried. She had been dating a Hollywood bandleader, Fred Karger. Fred had composed the music for such films as *From Here to Eternity*, *Magnificent Obsession*, *Gidget*, and a string of Elvis Presley movies. One day, when his daughter Terry was visiting with us, our housekeeper, Carrie, called Maureen, Terry, and me together and gave us all handfuls of rice—then she told us to wait on the front porch. We said, "What's this all about?" Carrie said, "You'll see."

A few minutes later, Freddy and Mom pulled up in his black 1956 Thunderbird. Mom got out of the car and said, "Good morning, children. Meet your new father!" That was Mom's tongue-in-cheek way of announcing that she and Fred were now married—they had eloped to Santa Barbara. We didn't need to "meet" Fred—he had been coming around for more than a year. Maureen and I already knew Fred very well, and we liked him. Fred was a good guy.

As Fred and Mom approached the front door, Carrie signaled us to throw the rice. As they walked through the door, Fred asked, "Where's the toothache medicine?" (Translation: Where's the scotch?) We told him, "You know where it is, Fred. Same place it's been every other time you come here!"

My mother and Fred were married for three years and then divorced in December 1955. They married again in March 1961 and divorced in March 1965. Fred and Mom were two people who loved each other but couldn't live with each other.

Fred's daughter, Terry, is still a dear friend of mine today. I kid her and call her my stepsister twice removed. (Terry and Marilyn Monroe were best friends, and she's writing a book about their friendship.)

Now it did bother me somewhat that Mom said that Fred would be my "new father." I already had a father, and no one could replace him. As it turned out, Fred didn't try to replace my father. My relationship with Dad continued pretty much as before, and he still came by every other Saturday to take us to the ranch.

On trips to the ranch, I watched Dad and learned from him. I'd see him working with his hands, cutting wood or fixing fences—and I admired his strength. He taught me how to ride horses and how to shoot a gun. He taught me not to lie or cut corners or take the easy way out. When I asked questions, he always had an answer that made sense.

I studied him in those unguarded moments when he didn't know I was watching. I made sure his deeds matched his words. I measured myself against the example he set, and I realized I had a lot of growing to do. I wanted to be like him, and I wanted him to be proud of me.

Dad seemed to understand that I was dealing with a lot of confusion and conflicting loyalties because of the divorce and remarriages. I often say that a divorce is where two adults, a mom and a dad, take everything that's important to a child—home, family, security—and smash it to pieces. Then they walk away and expect the child to put it all back together. Well, I wasn't putting things together very well—and my father could see that.

One day, Dad did something amazing: he invited Fred to come out to the Malibu ranch. Looking back with an adult perspective, I can see what a wise gesture that was. Dad wanted to show me that he and Fred could get along. So Fred joined us for a day of hiking, riding, and four-wheeling around the ranch. Seeing Dad and Fred having a great time together made me feel happier than I had felt in months.

Later, as Fred and I drove home together, he leaned over and said, "Let's not tell your mother how much fun we had, OK?"

"Why?"

"Well—it would only upset her."

So I agreed, and I said nothing to Mom about our day.

Blinded by the Divorce

I loved my dad—but sometimes I wondered if he really loved me. He didn't do the things with me that other kids got to do. He never took me to a baseball game, a football game, or Disneyland. And the irony is that Dad helped open Disneyland—but he didn't take me. On July 17, 1955, Dad was one of three celebrity emcees Walt Disney chose to host a live ABC telecast of Disneyland's opening day. The other two were Art Linkletter and Robert Cummings.

I was ten years old at the time, and I would have loved to be at Disneyland on opening day. But I was home with Mom, watching the Disneyland special on television along with the rest of America. (However, in June 1959, my mother took me to Disneyland for the opening day of the Matterhorn Bobsleds—one of the best memories of my boyhood.)

I once kidded my father and said, "Hey, Dad—remember that day you and Art Linkletter and Bob Cummings opened up Disneyland?"

"Well, yes."

"At any time that day, did you think, 'I should have brought the kids'?"

"Well . . . no. It didn't occur to me."

"I didn't think so."

I was kidding—but I was also hurt. To Dad, opening Disney-land was a job. He was working, he was performing in front of the camera. He didn't take his children to the movie set or the TV studio, so why should the Disneyland telecast be any dif-ferent? But all I could see were the happy kids jumping aboard the Disneyland railroad, or running through the Fantasyland castle. And I couldn't help wondering why I wasn't one of those kids.

I'm glad I learned to understand my dad's thinking as I grew older. A lot of "Beverly Hills brats" never understood why their parents made the choices they did. Many of them stayed angry with their parents, or used their parents as the excuse for their failure in life, or spent everything they had on therapy, booze, and drugs, or wrote bitter, hateful tell-all books.

Dad did everything he could to show me he loved me. To him, taking me to the ranch was the equivalent of taking me to a foot-ball game or a theme park. He assumed I'd understand that he couldn't go out in public without being mobbed. But I didn't understand at all—not until I was much older.

In my early twenties, hoping to win Dad's approval, I became a powerboat racer. I was inboard rookie of the year in 1966, out-board world champion in 1967, and I set five world records in the 1980s. I raised almost $2 million for charitable causes, includ-ing Cystic Fibrosis, the 1984 Olympics, and the Statue of Liberty Foundation.

In 1969, while racing in the Speed Classic Circuit at Offats Bayou near Galveston, Texas, my twenty-foot Raysoncraft boat exploded, throwing me forty feet in the air. A rescue boat fished me out of the bayou, and I was fortunate to be alive.

Dad called me the next day and said, "Michael, you might consider selling boats instead of racing boats—it's a lot safer." A couple of years later, I took his advice and got a job selling boats.

Once, when I was in my late twenties, Dad called me at Har-rison Boat Center, where I sold Sea Ray boats. He asked me to come to his office in Los Angeles because he needed—are you ready for this?—*parenting advice.* My brother Ron was a teenager at the time, and he was rebellious and angry. "Mike," Dad said, "you're closer in age to Ron than I am, so maybe you can tell me what his problem is."

On my way to Dad's office, I wondered, *What do I say?* I had a good idea what the problem was, but how should I tell Dad? I remembered how he always used stories and object lessons to make his point with me. I decided to use an object lesson to help him understand Ron's problem.

Arriving in Dad's office, I said, "I think I can help you with this. Take a piece of paper and draw a line down the middle."

He looked at me as if to say, *All right, where is this leading?* Then he took a piece of paper and drew the line.

"Okay," I said. "On the left side of the line, write the word 'Football.' On the right side, write the word 'Baseball.'"

And he did.

"Now," I said, "under 'Football,' write down the number of times you've taken Ron to a football game. Under 'Baseball,' write the number of times you've taken him to a baseball game."

Dad frowned at the paper; then he looked up at me—but he didn't write anything. He couldn't. "Michael," Dad said with a stricken expression, "you're right. I've never taken either of you boys to any games."

"Well, that's the problem," I said. "Dad, you need to sit Ron down and explain why. You've always taken us to the ranch to do what you wanted to do—and don't get me wrong, we like going to the ranch. But a boy Ron's age likes football and baseball like other kids do."

"Thank you, Michael. You've given me a lot to think about."

Dad didn't make excuses. He listened. He genuinely wanted to be a good father to all of his kids—from *both* marriages.

Fathers and sons make each other proud. But fathers and sons also disappoint and misunderstand each other. That's why we need to honestly face the past, including our failures. When fathers and sons can tell each other the truth, seek each other's counsel, and truly forgive each other, they make the bonds of love even stronger than before.

It took a lot of years for me to see how hard my father worked at being a father to all of his children—to Maureen and me, as well as to Patti and Ron. It took me a long time to gain an adult perspective on my childhood losses and hurts. It took me a long time to really understand how much Dad loved me and how many sacrifices he made for me.

Most of the questions I had about my relationship with Dad weren't answered until very late in our relationship. In fact, I never even told him I had these questions about our relationship until 1988, the last year of his second term as president. What made those issues finally come into focus for me—and for him? I wrote a book.

The process of working on my first book, *On the Outside Looking In*, forced me to look back over my life and to take a good, hard look at my childhood. It forced me to reexamine many of the immature attitudes and assumptions I had held since I was a boy. And it forced Dad and me to finally talk about issues we had never discussed before.

During the process of writing that book, I visited Dad and Nancy in the residence quarters of the White House. We had dinner together, then Nancy retired for the evening and my father and I had a chance to talk. Dad recalled that conversation sometime later when he wrote the foreword to the paperback edition of my book:

> It was a conversation we should have had years and years ago; too much had been left unsaid on both our parts—but the important thing is that we finally did have the chance to open up to each other, Michael to unburden himself of years of doubt and self-recrimination, I to say things I always assumed he knew.

Traveling back in my mind to Michael's babyhood, seeing again his impish, angelic smile and recalling his unlimited energy, I now realize that many adopted children do see themselves as different. . . . As a parent then, I didn't know how Michael felt inside. To me, he was my adorable little son, and from the moment he first smiled at me, I never recalled he was adopted. I loved him as I did my other children.

We, as parents, must always strive to communicate with our children, to let them know there is nothing they cannot tell us, to let them know our love will always be with them. . . .

Michael, whatever happens, always know I love you.[2]

I know, Dad. I really do know.

My father tried to show his love for me by spending as much time with me as he could. Sure, it would've been great fun to sit in the stands with him and watch a football game—but would that have been better than the times we spent bouncing around the ranch in his Jeep? Could I learn more about life from thrill rides in Disneyland—or by watching him cut wood and train his horses at the ranch?

Dad proved his love to me again and again throughout my life. I'm glad I finally grew up enough to see it.

Love Is Spelled "T-I-M-E"

The U.S. Census Bureau reports that twenty-four million children in America—that's one-third of all American kids—live in homes without their biological father.[3] That's twenty-four million kids who, at this very moment, are suffering the same insecurity and uncertainty I felt throughout my early years. That's twenty-four million kids who are going to bed without daddy reading to them and tucking them in at night, who have no male role model in the home, and who are not being taught how a man should treat a woman or how a father should love his kids.

Adults look at divorce and remarriage through grown-up eyes. They don't stop to think about how this all looks from a child's perspective. As moms and dads, we often get so caught up in our "needs" and our "rights," in our arguing and defending ourselves, that we don't stop to consider the frightened little child huddled in the corner.

Dad didn't understand everything I was going through, but he tried. I know he worked hard at making it up to my sister and me. He never forgot his first family after he remarried and started a second family.

Here, then, are some lessons I have learned from being the son of Ronald Reagan:

Love your family. And remember, love isn't just a feeling—love is a verb, an action word. Dad demonstrated his love for Maureen and me through his actions, by spending as much time with us as he could, by going out of his way to visit us at boarding school, and by being a friend, guide, and mentor to me.

Love means understanding—and Dad worked hard at understanding his kids. Looking back, I realize how hard Dad tried to understand me and what I was going through—just as he tried to understand my brother Ron. True, Dad didn't realize how much I wanted to be at Disneyland on opening day—but he understood the conflicting loyalties I felt, and he put me at ease by inviting Mom's new husband, Fred, out to the ranch.

And family love is a two-way street. As children, we need to love our parents by understanding them—and yes, forgiving them. Mom and Dad made many sacrifices for me that I just wasn't aware of. I went to school with Bob Hope's kids and Bing Crosby's kids, and we were all going through the same issues.

We all hated being at boarding school, and we wondered if our parents really loved us. We didn't know that all the actors and actresses in the Hollywood community talked to each other at cocktail parties and asked each other questions like, "Where are you sending your kids? Oh, that's a fine school. We'll send our kids there, too."

When I became an adult, I was able to look back and realize that Mom didn't send me to boarding schools because she didn't love me. She sent me to the best schools because she loved me very much. Mom worked very long hours in a demanding industry, so she sent me to some excellent schools—but I didn't want to be in the best boarding schools. I wanted to be with my family. That's understandable. But the decisions my mother made were also understandable, once I became an adult.

We can sit and stew in our childhood anger, blaming our parents for all our problems. We can use them as an excuse for our own failures. Or we can choose to understand and forgive them, and we can thank them for the sacrifices they made out of their love for us. I'm glad I was able to understand, forgive, and appreciate my parents before it was too late. When I forgave my mom and dad, my eyes opened wide and I could see their greatness and I could feel their love—and I finally knew how fortunate I was to be the son of Ronald Reagan and Jane Wyman.

Say "I love you" out loud. My father came from a generation in which men didn't say "I love you" to their kids. Dad told me he envied the freedom I had to show affection to my son Cameron and my daughter Ashley. In his day, fathers didn't spend "quality time" with their children, and they didn't give hugs to their sons. Late in life, he managed to overcome those inhibitions and became a man who could express affection without embarrassment.

People can change. How about you? I know you love your family—but does your family know it? Have you told your kids you love them? Have you shown your love through your hugs, your touch, your words of affection and affirmation? If you are not telling your children you love them, if you are not giving them hugs and affirmation, you should ask yourself who *is* giving them the love they need. Trust me, if they aren't receiving love from you, they will find it someplace else. Don't wait—tomorrow might be too late. Tell your kids you love them, and show them you mean it.

Listen to your family. I'm grateful that when I was ready to talk to my father about those childhood issues, he was willing to listen. He even came to me and asked me for help in understanding my brother Ron. Dad was a good listener, and that's why he was a great leader and a great father. When I would ask Dad questions, he'd always look me in the eye so that I knew he was listening and taking my questions seriously.

Listening is a learnable skill. A lot of people who think they are good listeners really aren't. If your kids are talking to you and you're looking at your phone and checking your texts or social media, you're not really listening. You have to put the phone down and really give them 100 percent of your attention. Give them a nod, a smile, an arm around the shoulder, and some verbal feedback so they'll really know you're hearing them. And please, turn off the phone during meal times and family times.

Make time for your family. Dad had a busy schedule when I was growing up. He didn't "find time" to spend with me—he *made* time. He set aside as much time as he possibly could so that he could be a strong and loving influence in Maureen's life and mine. In the eyes of a child, *love* isn't spelled l-o-v-e. It's spelled t-i-m-e. If you want your children to know you love them, spend time with them.

Dad wasn't a perfect father, but he was a good father, and he understood the importance of spending time with his kids. It's impossible to put a price tag on the memories I have of all the weekends I spent at the ranch with my father. Looking back at those happy times, I realize that they spell l-o-v-e—a father's love—in my life. I wouldn't trade those memories for all the gold in the world.

I remember the day my father left office, January 20, 1989. I was at home in California, sitting with my wife Colleen and watching television. On the screen, Dad stood at the door of the presidential helicopter, Marine One, delivering a final salute and a wave. Then he stepped inside. Soon he would board the presidential airplane for his last flight from Andrews Air Force Base to California. I thought of how intense and all-consuming my father's schedule had been during the eight years of his presidency and how little I had seen him during his White House years.

As I watched Marine One carry my father off the White House lawn and into the sky, I came to a decision. I turned to Colleen and said, "I've done my last weekend, Colleen. I will never give another speech or do another event on the weekend unless you approve it. I will be at home with you and the kids every Saturday and Sunday. Weekends are family time. That's my promise to you."

Why did I make that promise to Colleen at that particular moment? On one level, I was so proud of my father and all he had accomplished as president. But at the same time, I was keenly aware of all that his presidency had cost our family. Everyone in the Reagan family had sacrificed. Everyone had paid a price during the eight years we had shared Dad with the world.

Being a politician is a good news / bad news proposition. The good news is that you won the election—and the bad news is that you won the election. As soon as you win, your life is not your own. People start tugging at you. Events take over your life. You must speak at this fund-raiser, attend that dinner, and preside over those meetings. There's an old political adage: if the party had wanted you to have a family, it would have issued you one when you signed up.

People often ask, "What were the best times you ever had with your father?" I answer, "The times before he got into politics. After he entered political life, he just didn't have as much time as he used to."

Another question people often ask is, "Why are Ron and Patti so liberal? Why are your brother and sister so different from you and your dad?" It's a good question, and I have thought about it a lot over the years. The fact is, Ron and Patti both loved our father, yet they never voted for him. As I often say when I speak to adoption groups, if Ronald Reagan had not adopted me as his son, he would have been the only conservative in the family! My sister Maureen, with her support for the Equal Rights Amendment, was more of a moderate Republican than a conservative. Nancy was always trying to get Dad to moderate his positions and move to the political center. Of all his family members, I was the only one who was truly a Reagan conservative.

I was born in 1945, so I got to spend more than twenty years with my father before he ever campaigned for political office. I was able to spend weekends with him at the ranch, ride horses with him, shoot ground squirrels with him, go swimming in the pool at the ranch, and spend all those hours in the car with him, talking to him or listening to him sing patriotic songs. Dad would have the car radio tuned to Chuck Cecil's *Swingin' Years*, and I'd keep switching it over to The Beach Boys. Those were great times with Dad—and Maureen had four more years of those times than I did.

It was different for Patti, who was born in 1952, and Ron, born in 1958. Patti was thirteen when Dad got into politics and Ron was about seven. Both were at a vulnerable age when the Republican Party took their father away from them. Instead of weekend trips to the ranch with his children, Dad was attending political luncheons and cocktail receptions. His new family consisted of his staff, his advisers, and his constituents. He did what he could to spend time with his children, but the reality is that a political career is all-consuming. Who suffered? Patti and Ron.

So it's understandable that Patti would be liberal—because in her mind, the conservatives, the Republicans, took her father away from her. The party of "family values" robbed her of time with her father. And it's understandable that Ron would be a liberal and an atheist, because who were Ronald Reagan's biggest supporters? The Moral Majority—conservative Christians. It's not hard to see why Ron might blame Christianity for taking his father from him.

I'm who I am, in no small part, because of the things that happened to me as a child—both the good things and the bad things. And you, the person reading this book, are shaped in many ways by the things that have happened to you when you were a child. That doesn't mean you have no free will. That doesn't mean you can't change, can't grow, can't be healed of old wounds. It simply means that the events of your past still affect you in the present— and will continue to influence you in the future.

When I was growing up, I was separated from my parents by divorce and boarding school. When Ron and Patti were growing up, they were separated from their parents by the Republican Party, Christian conservatives, and politics. And they were angry. And they refused to vote for my father because *they didn't want him to win.* The country wanted a president, not a dad— but Ron and Patti wanted a dad, not a president.

This is my theory about our family dynamics. I haven't discussed this theory with Ron and Patti, and I don't know if they would agree. I can only say that this is the truth as I see it. It becomes easier to understand our family when we look at some of the wounds each family member suffered in their childhood. It becomes easier to forgive, easier to stop being angry, and easier to accept one another.

Dad was aware of the toll that politics took on our family life. He believed in what he was doing for America, but he understood that the demands of his political life stole time from his family. I remember how, during the 1980 campaign, he made a point of picking up the phone and calling Maureen and me at various times just to stay in touch. Dad's example spoke to me and convinced me that I needed to be more protective of the precious time I have with my wife and children.

So on January 20, 1989, as I watched Marine One take my father away from the White House and into the mists of history, I turned to my wife and made a solemn promise to honor our family. And she will tell you that I kept that promise. I can probably count on my fingers the number of times I have given a speech or made a personal appearance on a weekend since I made that vow. The few times I was away on a Saturday or Sunday, I did so with Colleen's blessing and approval. If she had said no, I would not have gone.

I want my wife and children to always know that I love them. I want them to never have any doubts. The first lesson my father taught me was one of the most crucial of all: *love your family*.

2

Work Hard,
Work Smart

WEEKENDS AT THE RANCH with Dad revolved around work.

There was plenty of time for fun and play *after* our chores were done. But chores came first—and Dad always made chores seem like part of the fun. I've never known anyone who took more pleasure in splitting firewood or painting a fence post than my father. He loved to work, and he taught me to take satisfaction from a job well done.

Dad majored in economics at Eureka College in Illinois, so he was well acquainted with the classic works on free market economics, such as Friedrich Hayek's *The Road to Serfdom*. He had a clear understanding of how work creates wealth and the importance of creating incentives for work and disincentives for laziness and dependency. He believed that the government should get out of the way of people who want to create wealth by their labor—and he passed those values on to me.

Our Saturday drives up the Pacific Coast Highway to the Malibu ranch were often like a classroom on wheels for me—and Dad was the teacher. I would pepper him with questions, and he'd always have the answers. One Saturday morning, when I was about nine years old, I asked my father for a raise in my allowance. At the time, I was getting a dollar a week, and I wanted two.

"Michael," Dad said, "when I get a tax cut, I'll raise your allowance."

"A tax cut? How much do you pay in taxes?"

"The government takes most of what I earn—as much as 91 percent."

"Ninety-one percent! What does the government do with all that money?"

"Well, the government does a lot of good things—and some that are not so good. Some of that money goes to buy tanks and airplanes to defend our country. Some goes to build highways. Some goes to a program called welfare."

"What's that?"

"Sometimes, when people are down on their luck, they need a helping hand. And there are people who are disabled and can't work for a living, so the government helps them out. And some people are able to work, but they don't want to—and the government pays them, too."

"But you shouldn't have to work hard to support people who don't want to work."

"True, Michael—but when the government pays you *not* to work, why work?"

That was my introduction to the confiscatory tax rates of the pre-Reagan era. Until my father got some tax relief, there would be no raises for me. That conversation took place in 1954 or so. Nearly a decade later, in January 1963, President Kennedy announced his plan to cut spending and slash tax rates in order to boost the economy. Though President Kennedy was assassinated in November, his successor, Lyndon Johnson, pushed through the Revenue Act of 1964, which honored JFK by cutting tax rates by about 20 percent across the board.

By that time, I was a nineteen-year-old high school senior. What did Dad do after he got his tax cut? He remembered the promise he had made to me a decade earlier: "Michael, when I get a tax cut, I'll raise your allowance." It's true—he raised my allowance from one dollar a week to five. He kept his word.

That's when I learned that tax cuts benefit everybody—the rich, the poor, the old, the young. Little did I know that Dad would one day be elected president and would slash those top marginal rates even further, to 28 percent. And in the process, he would revive a dying economy.

Even though this is a book about the lessons my father taught me, my mother was a great teacher as well. Like Dad, Mom taught me about the importance of a strong work ethic. All my rich friends—the brats of Beverly Hills—we're getting ten-speed Schwinn bikes. It wasn't their birthday, and they didn't earn their bikes by doing chores—they just had their bikes handed to them for the asking. I knew my mother could afford to buy me a bike, so I went down to Hans Ort's Cyclery in Beverly Hills and picked out a shiny blue bike. Then I went home and asked Mom to buy it for me.

Mom said no.

I asked why.

She said, "I build men. I don't build boys. How badly do you want that bike?"

I told her I wanted that bike more than anything.

"Well," she said, "you're going to have to get a job and earn it."

"But I'm only ten years old."

"That's old enough to deliver newspapers." So Mom checked the classified ads and found a job for me, selling newspapers in front of the Good Shepherd Church in Beverly Hills on Sunday mornings. So my mother lent me the money for the bike, and I signed a promissory note that she wrote out—and there I was, ten years old, in debt to my mother for my ten-speed bike. I paid her back, little by little, Sunday after Sunday, with the proceeds of my newspaper job.

As any child would, I went to my father and tried to enlist his help so I wouldn't have to keep that job and pay my debt. But Dad said, "Nope, it's in your mother's hands, and I'm not interfering."

I wasn't happy about it at the time, but today, I'm glad that Mom taught me that lesson. I'm glad I learned at an early age that the world doesn't owe me anything, and if I really want something, I have to earn it myself. As Mom said, "I build men. I don't build boys."

Muscles and Brains

When I was at the ranch with Dad, he would often pay me to help them with his chores. He knew better than to pay me by the hour. Instead, he paid me by the chore. He wanted me to associate getting paid with being productive. He didn't want me to think I could get away with collecting my pay for just clocking in and clocking out.

I enjoyed working alongside my dad. I wanted his nod of approval and his "Good job!" even more than I wanted the money. Sometimes the jobs could be unpleasant, like mucking out the horse stalls and chicken coops. But on the whole, I was eager to do anything Dad asked of me, because I was eager to please him.

He taught me at a young age the importance of doing a job with care, pride, and excellence. One of the most important jobs I helped with was clearing the fields of large rocks. We would go through the fields and load large stones into the Jeep or onto a flatbed trailer pulled behind a tractor. He told me it was important not to miss any rocks because he didn't want his thoroughbreds to stumble and break a leg. He'd use the stones to build equestrian jumps to train his horses.

One of the worst chores at the ranch involved painting the long white fence that encircled the property. I can't tell you how many board feet of fence I painted over the years—sometimes with Dad and sometimes with Richard Jackin, the son of Dad's ranch foreman. By the time Richard and I would finish painting for a day, we'd be covered in paint—it's a hot, unpleasant chore. But that's how we made our spending money. After work, Richard and I would ride horses all over those hills, where the cities of Thousand Oaks and Westlake Village and the Sherwood Country Club are today. Richard Jackin and I remain good friends after all these decades.

Fast-forward to 1984, the night my father accepted his party's nomination for a second term as president. That night, ABC's *20/20* featured a special interview with my father—and in the course of that interview, he talked about those white fences and his son Michael. The interviewer was newsman Tom Jarriel, who had ridden with me in my Scarab racing boat when I set the world record between Ketchikan, Alaska, and Seattle, Washington, raising $250,000 for the Cystic Fibrosis Foundation. So Jarriel knew me, and one of the questions he asked Dad was, "When did you know that Mike was going to make it in life?" Dad said:

> Well, Tom, I can tell you the exact moment I knew Michael would make it. We had white fences at the Malibu ranch, and he'd make extra spending money in the summer by painting those fences. I'd pay him ten cents for the rails and fifteen cents a post. One day, I drove by the main entrance and I saw two young boys painting the fence. I didn't know those boys, so I stopped and said, "I'm Ronald Reagan, and this is my ranch. Who are you fellows? And where's Michael?" They said, "He's at the beach. He's paying us seven cents a foot to paint the fence." So Michael had subcontracted the job to these boys, and he was making money while relaxing at the beach. That's when I knew that Michael would do all right in life.

Dad believed in the importance of hard work—but he also believed in the importance of working smart. When he saw those two boys painting the fence, he knew I had the makings of a good businessman. He believed that the way to get ahead in life was to use your muscles—and your brains.

One of Dad's most-quoted lines was, "I've heard that hard work never killed anyone, but I say why take a chance?" A funny quip—but growing up with him, I knew better. Ronald Reagan believed in hard work. He worked hard at everything he did, whether it was mending his fences, making a movie, giving a speech, campaigning for office, or governing the country. And Dad worked hard to instill that Protestant work ethic in his four children.

Dad believed that some of the hardest and most important work we do is brain work. He believed in continually improving the mind. He was personally committed to the principle that education begins in school and continues throughout life. That's why, after graduating with a degree in economics, he continued to study the writings of free market economists, from Adam Smith to Henry Hazlitt to Ludwig von Mises. He had a large personal library in his home, and when I lived with Dad and Nancy in my teen years, I often saw him reading books, underlining passages, and making notes in the margins.

My father proved that you don't have to go to Harvard or Yale or some other Ivy League school to become president of the United States. But I would offer one suggestion as we make our decision at the polls: whoever we vote for should—like my father—have a degree in economics.

The historic success of Reaganomics during the 1980s didn't just happen. It was an economic revolution Dad set in motion after years of personal study and hard work. He had a team of great free market economists advising him, including Arthur Laffer and Milton Friedman, and he knew exactly where he wanted to take the country. The miracle of the Reagan Eighties was the direct result of years of preparation Dad invested in his economic plan.

Many people assume that, because my father could deliver a speech so naturally and effortlessly (at least, he made it *look* effortless), he simply had a "gift" for public speaking. Few people realize how hard Dad worked to make his speeches seem so "effortless." He spent countless hours preparing his speeches and honing his message in front of countless audiences. I lived with Dad and Nancy when he was a traveling ambassador for General Electric (GE). He wrote his own speeches, and he filled hundreds of index cards with talking points. He developed his own system of abbreviations so he could squeeze a lot of ideas into a single card. Then he practiced each speech until he no longer needed his notes.

Once, when I was eleven or twelve, I looked in the second drawer of Dad's big desk at his home in Pacific Palisades, California. That drawer contained stacks and stacks of note cards for his speeches, all in his own neat handwriting, wrapped in rubber bands. During that time, when Dad was hosting General Electric Theater on television, he kept up a grueling ten-week travel schedule every year, going from one GE plant or civic club meeting to another, sometimes giving as many as a dozen speeches in a single day.

Those years of hard work and preparation are the reason his speeches looked "effortless." I saw the hard work he put into becoming the "Great Communicator." And I saw what a powerful medium of influence and persuasion public speaking can be. That's why, to this day, I work hard at my own public speaking, and I continue to give fifty or sixty speeches every year.

Acting, public speaking, and leadership are essentially brain work. Yes, all three professions are physically taxing and can leave you physically spent at the end of the day. But whether you are emoting in front of a camera, delivering a passionate speech to an audience, or making decisions and chairing meetings all day, brain work is hard work—physically, as well as mentally and emotionally.

Always Working, Always Writing

Dad enjoyed physical labor as much as he enjoyed brain work. He could have been a great carpenter as well as an actor and president. He was, above all, a builder. If you go to Rancho del Cielo, his ranch in the Santa Inez Mountains near Santa Barbara, you'll see the ranch that Ronald Reagan built. You'll see the fence he put up with his own hands. You'll see the roof that he tiled, the doors he hung, the fireplace he built, and the boat dock he constructed with his own hands. Whenever I went with Dad to the Northridge ranch or the Malibu ranch or Rancho del Cielo, he was always maintaining, improving, working. He carried out every task with care, patience, and pride.

Dad bought Rancho del Cielo in 1974, near the end of his first term as governor of California. After he left office, he hired two men as his personal assistants—Dennis LeBlanc, a member of Dad's California State Police security detail, and Barney Barnett, a retired highway patrolman who had been Dad's driver when he was governor. LeBlanc and Barnett continued to work with Dad, doing everything from scheduling and advance work for his speeches to helping Dad rebuild and remodel the ranch property.

LeBlanc recalled that throughout each day, Dad was always busy, always working—and much of his work was writing:

> He was constantly writing. . . . A lot of the time it was on a legal pad, where he'd write things out longhand. Other times it would be taking speeches that he wrote out longhand, and then putting it on 4 by 6 cards. . . .
>
> We drove up to the ranch from Los Angeles and back down the same day many, many times for the next two

years. Either Barney or I would drive, and Reagan would sit in the backseat with his legal pad, writing. . . .

When we got to the ranch, we put in eight or nine hours of work. We ripped out walls and really gutted the place. . . . Then we'd drive back. He would be writing in the backseat. . . .

Ronald Reagan never slept on planes when he was traveling. It was the same way when I was with him in the station wagon. It was like—you're wasting time if you are sleeping. You know, everyone's got things to do. And his thing to do when I was with him was his writing.[1]

Dad cultivated an image of a chief executive who delegated everything and took a lot of naps, and I believe he did so because that image lulled his opponents into underestimating him. While they were laughing at him and calling him an "amiable dunce," he was running rings around them and enacting his agenda. Whether he was working with his hands or working with his mind, Dad always worked hard. Everyone who was close to him attests to his intense work ethic.

I remember taking Colleen and Cameron to visit Dad and Nancy at their Pacific Palisades home shortly before Dad took office in 1981. General Electric had built that house as a showcase in 1956, when Dad was a spokesman for GE. In 1980, when Dad ran for president, the Secret Service rented a small house below the main house to use as a security command post during the campaign. At taxpayer expense, the Secret Service built a stairway that cut through the ivy and connected the Secret Service house to the Reagan home, so agents could reach the house quickly. I was visiting the home one last time because I had spent much of my adolescence in that home, and it would be sold after the inauguration.

Dad and I took a walk around the house and yard, and he pointed to the Secret Service house below, and the stairs that led up to our house. "See those stairs?" he said. "What do you suppose it cost to build that stairway?"

"Dad, I have no idea."

"Well, I just saw the bill for those stairs. The General Services Administration charged the Secret Service twenty-five hundred dollars to build those steps a year ago, and they're charging another thousand dollars to rip them out. My driver, Barney, and I could have done that whole job for less than five hundred dollars with plenty of lumber left over. The federal government wastes too much money. Those steps are typical of all the waste in government, and I'm going to put a stop to it."

When I look back on that conversation, I think it says a lot—not only about my father's view of government waste, but also about his work ethic. He would have gladly gone down to the lumber yard, come back with a load of boards and nails, and he and Barney would have done the whole job for a fraction of the cost. And you know what? He would have enjoyed every moment of that project. Dad just loved to work.

His work ethic kept him in incredible shape for his age. After he was shot, Dad had a weight room set up in the family quarters of the White House. He wanted to stay in shape—and he knew that a person's muscles tend to atrophy during a hospital stay. He worked out almost daily and ended up adding two inches of muscle to his chest. Riding horses, chopping wood, and mending fences at the ranch undoubtedly contributed to his excellent physical condition and longevity.

Many times when Dad and I were together, he'd jab my belly with his forefinger and say, "You should be working out, Mike." Then he'd invite me to throw a punch at his rock-hard abs and say, "You've gotta stay in shape."

The American Government versus the American Work Ethic

My father often talked about an experience he had while in college during the Great Depression. His father, Jack Reagan, was a federal relief administrator in Dixon, Illinois, and Jack shared an office with the supervisor of county relief programs. Dad sometimes dropped by Jack's office, and he was dismayed to see the fathers of many of his classmates standing in line, waiting for handouts.

Jack Reagan knew that dependency on government handouts was killing the pride and dignity of those men, so he came up with a plan of his own. Every morning, on his own initiative, Jack Reagan would leave home early and drive around to different parts of the county, asking if anyone had temporary work available. Then he'd go back to his office, and when men came in for their handouts, Jack would tell them where they could find work.

My dad was often present when Jack gave those men the news that there was a job waiting for them. The men would actually stand taller because they *wanted* to work—they didn't want to be dependent on handouts.

But a few weeks after Jack started finding jobs for these men, something changed. Jack would offer a lead on a job to a line of waiting men—and there were no takers. The men would just look at the floor, unable to make eye contact, unwilling to take the job. Finally, one of the men explained why.

"Jack," the man said, "I know you're trying to help, but the last time you found work for me, the man of the welfare office took away my relief check. He said I had a job. It didn't matter that the job was temporary—I wasn't eligible for welfare anymore. I can't afford to do that to my family. I can't take any more jobs."

In the depths of the Great Depression, there were jobs to be had—and no takers. The government had made sure that those unemployed men stayed on the dole, not on a payroll. The government killed the incentive to work.

That experience helped shape Dad's view of government. He knew that the best "program" for lifting people out of poverty is a job—a private sector job. And he saw how government policies undermined the hard-working American family.

As a result of government interference in our lives, working families spend more on taxes than they spend on food, shelter, and clothing *combined*.[2] Many American moms and dads have to work extra jobs just to pay their taxes—and time spent away from the family is time robbed from children, time that can never be repaid once a child has outgrown those formative years. The crushing tax burden translates to more children who are not hugged, nurtured, read to, and prayed with as they should be. One of Dad's economic advisors, Arthur Laffer, explained Dad's economic philosophy this way: "When you tax something, you get less of it, and when you subsidize something, you get more of it. You know, we tax speeders to get them to stop speeding, and we tax cigarette smokers because we want them to stop smoking. And then we come along and tax people who work, and especially people who work very productively and make a lot of money. Do we do that to stop them from working and stop them from being productive?"[3]

My father thought it was outrageous that the government taxed American ingenuity, hard work, and productivity while subsidizing idleness and irresponsibility. He was not about to subsidize laziness in his own family—and he certainly didn't want the government to subsidize laziness in his own family, including his son, Michael.

You have to understand, my father went to Eureka College then he paved the way for his brother Neil to also attend Eureka. He made arrangements for Neil to attend college on a scholarship—a scholarship based on financial need. So in Dad's mind, Neil was receiving a "poor person's scholarship"—and he told Neil, "You're going to have to pay this scholarship back when you get out of school and start working." To Dad, a scholarship was a form of charity.

Fast-forward to 1963. I was in my senior year at Judson School, a K–12 boarding school in Scottsdale, Arizona. I had led the Judson football team to a state championship and was named player of the year by the *Scottsdale Press.* So Arizona State wanted to offer me a football scholarship.

I came home for the Christmas holidays, and as I walked through the door, Dad said, "Do you know somebody named Kush?"

"Kush?" I said. "As in Frank Kush? The football coach at Arizona State?"

Dad said, "Yes, I believe it was Frank Kush."

"Why are you asking?"

"Well, Frank Kush called me. He said he wanted to offer you a scholarship to play football next year at Arizona State."

"What did you tell him?"

"I told him to give it to some young man who truly needed it. I could pay for your education, and you didn't need a scholarship."

My heart sank. "Dad," I said, "you and I need to talk about the difference between a scholarship and welfare."

I can laugh about it now, but at the time, I was boiling mad. Dad had thrown away my football scholarship! I later learned that, having gone through the Great Depression, Dad viewed scholarships as subsidies for poor people, like welfare or charity. I couldn't be angry with Dad once I understood his thinking.

(As an aside, in December 2013, I attended a banquet aboard the aircraft carrier USS *Ronald Reagan* in San Diego. It was a pregame event honoring the football teams of Arizona State and Texas Tech prior to the Holiday Bowl. Frank Kush, who had retired from coaching with a record of 176–54–1, was still working for ASU as a fund-raiser, and he was at the banquet. I was asked to say a few words, so I told my story about Frank's phone call to my dad, and the scholarship offer my father turned down. Then I turned to Frank and said, "Frank, is that what happened?" He laughed and said, "That's absolutely right.")

But that was my dad's view of hard work—and he felt that government, whether in the form of scholarships or in the form of welfare—tended to undermine the work ethic of the people it was supposed to help. Dad did not believe in subsidizing laziness. He believed that hard work was good for the soul and that work ought to be incentivized and rewarded.

In 1966, as Dad was gearing up to run for governor, I was toiling away in the industrial heart of Los Angeles, loading oil well equipment for Asbury Trucking for $2.85 an hour. From five in the evening until one thirty in the morning, I worked on the loading dock. I hated every moment of it, and I cheered Dad's political ambitions because I thought being the governor's son would be my meal ticket.

I remember, the night before the election, daydreaming about how cool it would be if everybody in California voted except me—and it came down to a tie, and exact fifty-fifty split between Governor Edmund G. "Pat" Brown and Ronald Reagan. I thought, wouldn't it be great to hold the deciding vote? I'd go to the Brown camp and I'd go to the Reagan camp and say, "Hey, I haven't voted yet, the polls close in an hour, and what can you offer me?" Because at that point in my life, I was looking at everything—including Dad's political career—in terms of what was in it for me.

On election night, I went to the victory party at the Ambassador Hotel and congratulated Dad. I was certain that my life was about to change. I asked Dad for a job in his administration.

"Michael," he said, "you might as well know right now— I don't believe in nepotism. You need to keep that job with the trucking company."

I left the victory party with my hopes dashed, thinking I should have voted for Brown. The Brown family, at least, believed in nepotism and cronyism. I had the misfortune of being a Reagan instead of a Brown.

When I returned to the loading dock, my coworkers were amazed I showed up for work the day after the election. Why was I still doing grunt work when my dad was the governor-elect? One of them said, "Tell us, Mike—do your parents love you?"

I wondered the same thing myself.

The answer, of course, was yes. In fact, Dad loved me enough to teach me the value of hard work. I'm grateful for his example of respecting hard work and defending hard-working families. I've tried to follow his example and teach those values to my own children.

Here, then, are some of the vital lessons my father taught me about the importance of working hard and working smart:

Working hard and working smart leads to success. Working smart is not a substitute for working hard. You must do *both*. All honest labor is honorable labor. It is honorable to work with your mind and honorable to work with your hands. My father did his share of both.

When Dad went up to Rancho del Cielo with Dennis LeBlanc and Barney Barnett, he did hard, physical labor, remodeling and refurbishing the original adobe farmhouse that was built in 1872. In the process, Dad got dirty and he worked up a sweat—and he had a great time. On the ride home, he sat in the backseat and did brain work—writing and working on speeches. My father was perfectly at home working hard *and* working smart.

Mike Rowe, the host of the Discovery Channel series *Dirty Jobs*, once said that the worst advice he ever received was posted on the wall of his high school guidance counselor's office. Seventeen-year-old Rowe was talking to his guidance counselor about his options for college. He noticed a poster on the wall that read, "Work Smart, *Not* Hard." He says that it's a terrible idea to tell young people *not* to work hard and to suggest that hard physical labor is demeaning. Rowe concludes, "I think often about the people I met on *Dirty Jobs*. Most of them were tradesmen. Many were entrepreneurs and innovators. Some were millionaires. People are always surprised to hear that, because we no longer equate dirt with success. But we should. . . . Why aren't we encouraging the benefits of working smart *and* hard?"[4]

Dr. Martin Luther King Jr. once expressed a similar notion: "If it falls to your lot to be a street sweeper, sweep streets like Michelangelo painted pictures, like Shakespeare wrote poetry, like Beethoven composed music; sweep streets so well that all the host of Heaven and earth will pause and say, 'Here lived a great street sweeper, who swept his job well.'"[5]

I'm glad there are still people in this country who are promoting the benefits of working hard and doing a job well. Actor John Ratzenberger, who is remembered for his role as Cliff Clavin on *Cheers*, plus a series of memorable voice parts in Pixar animated films, is the cofounder of the Nuts, Bolts & Thingamajigs Foundation, which goes into schools and teaches the fast-disappearing trades of woodworking and metal shop. Even more important, they are teaching the American work ethic, just as my father taught me.

Yes, it's important to "work smart"—but most successful people will tell you that the point of working smart is not to create more leisure time, but to free up more work time. Michael Moroney, in *Entrepreneur*, observes:

The problem with the working hard vs. working smart dichotomy is that all too often we frame the choice as one in which we can only choose "hard" or "smart." The question we should be asking is, why aren't we doing both? . . . Smarter work affords us more time, but that saved time doesn't mean anything unless we put it to optimal use.

Top CEOs have reported an average wakeup time of 6:15 a.m., with many rising before 5:00, and most worked at least two hours at home after dinner. In some cases, they regularly turned in eighteen-hour workdays. Many of these industry leaders credit their success to working while others aren't.[6]

Contrary to the way his detractors have portrayed him, my father, Ronald Reagan, was one of the hardest working men I've ever known. He worked hard and smart, and he respected both muscle work and brain work. That's why he was lenient with me when he caught me using the "Tom Sawyer" approach to fence painting. He wanted to encourage my creativity and initiative without discouraging my willingness to work hard.

My late brother-in-law Roger Stearns was an executive with Verizon. When he saw people procrastinating or sitting and doing nothing, he'd say, "How will you ever finish if you never get started?" I think that's a question we all need to ask ourselves whenever we feel lazy or unmotivated.

America is still one place in the world where we can start with nothing and achieve success through the work of our own hands and brains. Our hard work and smart work creates wealth and leads to success. One of the most important lessons my father taught me is that if you are able to work smart and willing to work hard, there's no limit to what you can accomplish.

Support the free market economy. Every election day, from local races to national elections, vote for candidates who believe in economic freedom. Demand that your elected representatives support lower taxes, less regulation, smaller government, and greater freedom. Read about free market economics and study the writings of Adam Smith, Friedrich Hayek, Henry Hazlitt, Ludwig von Mises, Arthur Laffer, and Milton Friedman.

Preach free market economics to your friends and neighbors and learn how to defend the principles of freedom in your Facebook posts, your blog posts, your letters to the editor, and your conversations over the back fence. Defend hard work and productivity. Become a vocal advocate for freedom.

I have two friends, Karel and Sandy, who escaped from Communist Czechoslovakia in 1986. They spent a year in a refugee camp before coming to the United States. The Czech government tried them in absentia, and Karel (pronounced "Karl") was sentenced to twenty-five years in prison; Sandy was sentenced to twenty years. Their crime: stealing property of the Czech government. What property did they steal? Their one-year-old son; under the Communist system, children belonged to the state.

They arrived in America with the clothes on their back, plus a few clothes in a bag they brought with them. When they got to Los Angeles, they saw how Americans dressed—and they threw their bag of clothes in the trash. Within a week, Karel got a job at the Disneyland Hotel, working in the kitchen. His wife Sandy worked nights and stayed with their one-year-old child during the day, learning English by watching soap operas.

Karel would come home and speak Spanish because that was the only language he heard at work and he thought it was the national language. Sandy said, "No, no, English is the national language." They decided to learn both.

Karel once said to me, "Michael, most Americans don't understand the country they live in. They don't understand how wonderful America is. You can come to this country with the clothes on your back, not knowing the language—and if you're willing to work hard for twenty-six years, you won't have to worry about the next twenty-six. There's no other country in the world where you can do that. It's too bad that Americans, born in freedom, don't appreciate what they have here."

My father appreciated the freedom we have here in America, and he tried to preach the wonders of America to everyone he met. Sometimes we don't realize how much America means to us until we see our country through the eyes of immigrants—immigrants like my friends Karel and Sandy.

Teach the American work ethic to your children. Be a great example to your kids, as my father was to me. Let them see you enjoying the work you do, both at home and in your profession. Instead of grumbling about your tasks, plunge right in and whistle while you work. Show your children that hard work can be enjoyable—and that hard work pays.

Have your children do chores right alongside you. Give them praise and affirmation for working hard and doing their chores well—just as my father praised and affirmed me. Help your children to understand that wealth is created through hard work, including brain work. Whenever they talk about their dreams and goals in life, help them understand that it takes focus, perseverance, and hard work to achieve those dreams.

I will always remember my days at the ranch, watching Dad as he worked, seeing how his muscles flexed as he swung his ax and how the sweat beaded on his brow as he worked with his horses. My father taught me the value of hard work, and I'm thankful for his example every day of my life.

3

Speak the Truth, Live the Truth

URING DAD'S ACTING CAREER, it was sometimes said that Ronald Reagan played Ronald Reagan on the screen. And there's a lot of truth to that.

In his first film, *Love is On the Air*, my father—who had just left a job as a radio announcer—played (what else?) a dashing young radio announcer. In the years that followed, he played a series of different roles, but most were variations on the real Ronald Reagan. He might be portraying the dedicated Secret Service agent Brass Bancroft in *Code of the Secret Service*, or the lighthearted ladies' man Alec Hamm in *Dark Victory*, or the athletic George Gipp in *Knute Rockne, All American*, or the carefree playboy Drake McHugh in *Kings Row*, or the crusading district attorney Bert Rainey in *Storm Warning*—but all of them came across as quintessentially Ronald Reagan.

I'm not saying Dad lacked range as an actor. Any actor who can successfully portray Gen. George Armstrong Custer in *Santa Fe Trail* and an epileptic scientist in *Night unto Night* is no one-dimensional actor. But every actor's range has limits, and my father knew he had exceeded his range after accepting the role of an organized crime boss in the 1964 drama *The Killers*.

It was Dad's final film role, and he accepted it against his better judgment after his agent, Lew Wasserman, talked him into it. (Wasserman was a manager of the talent agency MCA; when he merged MCA with Universal Studios and Decca Records in 1962, he created the powerful entertainment conglomerate MCA/Universal.)

In every other role Ronald Reagan played, he could create the character by tapping into some aspect of himself, some inner truth. But how could he find within himself the qualities of a vicious mobster—a man without a conscience, a man who would kill you as soon as look at you? If you watch that film, you can't help feeling that there's something fundamentally wrong about the scene in which Dad's character, Jack Browning, strikes Angie Dickinson's face, sending her reeling.

Dad regretted making that movie. Why? Because his character was a mask, not a revelation of truth.

I visited with Angie Dickinson at a Hollywood event a few years ago, and she said, "Do you know why your father was so bad in *The Killers*? It's because he had to play an evil character, and your dad was a good guy—he couldn't relate to the character. No one as kind and decent as your father could ever be convincing playing a cruel gangster."

"Well, Angie," I said, "if it makes you feel better, the whole movie was terrible."

She laughed and agreed that it was—and she affirmed my belief that acting is about finding and expressing an inner truth.

Both of my parents, Ronald Reagan and Jane Wyman, saw acting as a process of revealing truth. Mom would stay in character for days during a film production to preserve the truth and integrity of her character. Mom and Dad both believed that the camera was merciless in detecting insincerity and fakery.

Great actors know that acting isn't just a game of "let's pretend." I've been in actors' workshops and I appeared in six episodes of Mom's television drama *Falcon Crest* (I played the concierge at Mom's spa—and by the way, I was terrible!). I've done enough acting to develop a deep respect for the skills and accomplishments of my parents. The goal of acting is not to present an illusion to the camera, but to reveal *truth*.

That was also Dad's goal in his political career—revealing truth. All too many politicians think that their job is to conceal the truth. But if you want to succeed the way my father succeeded, if you want to do some good in the world, then you need to deal in the truth, the way my father did.

I often speak to political gatherings, and I say, "If you want to do well in politics, take an acting class. Get involved in an actor's workshop. Do some community theater. Learn how to reveal your inner truth and become comfortable being who you are in front of an audience." Acting is great preparation for a career in politics because acting teaches you a deep respect for the truth.

People called my father the Great Communicator. But do you think he woke up one morning with the ability to give speeches, the ability to believably play a role on the stage? No. He had to learn those skills. When he went to Eureka College, he took acting classes, and those classes taught him how to be himself in front of an audience or in front of a camera. There are a lot of politicians, such as Rick Perry and Mitt Romney, who are said to be natural, likeable, and easygoing in one-on-one situations—but turn on the camera and they turn into tense, unlikeable robots.

My father was often called "The King of the Bs." There were A-listers and B-listers, and Dad was among the best B-list actors in Hollywood. He was dependable, easy to work with, and he could give a director whatever was required in a single take. Plus he was an excellent horseman—and the studios paid an extra $25 a day to an actor who rode his own horse.

Ronald Reagan was a *good* actor. Had he gotten the roles he wanted, he would have been a *great* actor. Just look at his portrayal of George Gipp in *Knute Rockne, All American* (1940) or the tragic Drake McHugh in *King's Row* (1942). (Incidentally, his *King's Row* costar, Robert Cummings, prophetically said in 1942, "Someday I'm going to vote for this fella for president.")

My father approached every film role with a commitment to truth. And while many of his critics disparage the notion of electing an actor to be president of the United States, I think my father's early career uniquely prepared him for his crowning role as chief executive. In fact, Dad himself once made the same observation:

> Some of my critics over the years have said that I became president because I was an actor who knew how to give a good speech. I suppose that's not too far wrong. Because an actor knows two important things—to be honest in what he's doing and to be in touch with the audience. That's not bad advice for a politician either. My actor's instinct simply told me to speak the truth as I saw it and felt it.
>
> I don't believe my speeches took me as far as they did merely because of my rhetoric or delivery, but because there were certain basic truths in them that the average American citizen recognized. When I first began speaking of political things, I could feel that people were as frustrated about the government as I was. What I said simply made sense to the guy on the street, and it's the guy on the street who elects presidents of the United States.[1]

I watched my father give speeches long before he ran for governor or president, and he inspired me to become a public speaker in my own right. He was totally authentic. I think that was the greatest lesson I learned from him as a speaker: know what you believe and know why you believe it.

I can't write out a speech and deliver it from a script. But if you hire me to speak to your organization, I can get up and talk for fifteen minutes, half an hour, or an hour, whatever you need.

I won't use notes—I'll simply get up and talk extemporaneously and bring it all together in the allotted amount of time. I can do that because I know exactly what I believe, and I know exactly why I believe it.

After I delivered the eulogy for my father at the Reagan Library in 2004, Sean Hannity asked me if I had a written copy of my prepared remarks. I said, "I don't have any notes. I didn't prepare those remarks. I just spoke from my heart."

"No notes?" Hannity said. "The most important speech of your life and you didn't use notes?"

"No notes. If I didn't already know the subject, I shouldn't have gotten up to speak."

Great leaders, like Ronald Reagan, live the truth and speak the truth. A reputation for telling and living the truth creates *trust*, and leaders cannot lead unless their followers trust them.

The *Real* Ronald Reagan

More than once, as I was growing up, my father caught me telling a lie—and I heard a number of sermons on the importance of guarding my integrity. One story Dad told Maureen and me, a story that made a huge impact on both of us, took place in 1965 as he was considering a run for governor of California.

Justin Dart, the CEO of the Rexall Drugstore chain, invited Dad to his office for a meeting. Mr. Dart was influential in Republican circles. So Dad went to Mr. Dart's office and they talked about what it would take to get my father elected governor. Dad had long been acquainted with Mr. Dart. Almost three decades earlier, Dad had appeared in two motion pictures with Dart's wife, actress Jane Bryan—*Brother Rat* and *Brother Rat and a Baby*.

As their meeting came to a close, Mr. Dart pointed to a paper bag on his desk. "That's for you," he said.

Dad said, "What is it?"

"Take a look."

Dad glanced inside. The bag contained tens of thousands of dollars in cash. Dad said, "What's this for?"

"When you're running for governor," Mr. Dart explained, "you're not able to go out and make a living. So this is a little something for you and Nancy."

Dad closed the sack and *threw* it at Mr. Dart. Furious, he said, "Do you think you're going to own me? Do you think you can get favors whenever you want? I've changed my mind. If that's what being governor is all about, I don't want the job. I'm not running."

Dad stormed out, leaving the Rexall executive speechless.

It took three days for Mr. Dart to persuade Dad to return for a second meeting. As the two men faced each other, Dart apologized for suggesting that my father could be bought.

Dad heard him out, then said, "I've had a chance to cool off. I've decided to run—but I want one thing understood: if you ever need help from the governor's office, you'll go through the same channels as everybody else."

"I understand," Dart said. Then he said something that was a real eye-opener to my father: "I've never met a politician like you. They *all* take the money."

"That's just it, Mr. Dart," Dad replied, "I'm *not* a politician."

In the years that followed, Dad and Justin Dart grew to be good friends, and Mr. Dart was one of my father's strongest supporters. Why? Because Ronald Reagan was something rare in this world—an honest man in politics, a man of truth and integrity.

My father taught me to be a person who tells the truth and lives the truth. Like so many of the lessons he tried to teach me, I was slow to learn it. I'm still learning it. But as the saying goes, "More things are caught than taught." He taught me by his example, and that's why Ronald Reagan was such a good father and such a great leader.

Again and again, people ask me, "What was your father *really* like?" They want to know: Was Ronald Reagan the real deal? Was the private Ronald Reagan the same as the public Ronald Reagan? Was he authentic? Did he have integrity?

I'm here to tell you that my father, Ronald Reagan, was the same man whether he wore white tie and tails at a state dinner or blue jeans, plaid shirt, and cowboy hat on the ranch. He was the same man whether he was asking for your vote in a campaign speech or sitting across the table from you, offering you a handful of jelly beans. The public Ronald Reagan was seamlessly joined to the private Ronald Reagan.

When I watched my father give speeches on television, I saw exactly the same man who used to pick me up in his red station wagon, drive me out to the ranch, and teach me how to shoot a rifle and ride a horse.

The American people almost never saw my father lose his temper in public. The angriest I've ever seen my father was on February 23, 1980, three days before the New Hampshire primary. The Reagan campaign was footing the bill for a candidate debate, and my father wanted to debate *all* the GOP candidates, not just George H. W. Bush. The debate moderator, *Nashua Telegraph* editor Jon Breen had declared that it would be a two-man debate. Dad took the microphone and, over Mr. Breen's objections, made his case for including all the candidates. Finally, Breen shouted, "Turn off his microphone!"

My father leveled an if-looks-could-kill stare at Breen and thundered, "I am *paying* for this microphone, Mr. Green!" Yes, he got Breen's name wrong—but he made his point.

My sister Maureen and I were watching that event on television together—I believe we were at her house. When we saw Dad get angry, Maureen and I looked at each other in shock, because we had never seen him like that before.

"Well," Maureen said, "it's about damn time!"

That was as angry as I've ever seen my father. Believe me, I have given him plenty of reason to be infuriated with me, yet he was always patient and fatherly, more disappointed than angry.

So if you want to know what the *real* Ronald Reagan was like, I'll tell you: you *already* know. His public image and his private reality are one and the same. He didn't present a false persona to the public, as so many politicians do. He was *always* the real Ronald Reagan.

That's what it means to have integrity. That's what it means to live the truth.

The Importance of Trust

My father nominated the first woman Supreme Court justice, Sandra Day O'Connor. But very few people know the story behind that nomination. Justice O'Connor was elevated to the High Court because Dad kept a promise to my sister, Maureen.

During the 1980 primary campaign, Dad and Maureen were on opposite sides of an issue called the Equal Rights Amendment. Dad believed in equal rights for women, of course, but he believed women were already guaranteed full equality under the Fourteenth Amendment. He worried that the ERA, if ratified, might be interpreted in ways that would tear apart the fabric of our society. And he worried that if Maureen kept pushing the issue during the primary, he might lose the nomination.

So Dad's staff called Maureen into a meeting with Dad. Dad's top aides, Michael Deaver and Lyn Nofziger were in that meeting. They were searching for a way to convince Maureen to drop ERA as an issue before it began to erode his support with Republican women. So Deaver and Nofziger, along with Dad, sat down with Maureen and asked her, "What can we do to get you to stop supporting ERA—at least during the campaign?"

Maureen said, very pointedly, "If you can get your candidate to tell me that, if elected, his first appointment will be to nominate a woman for the United States Supreme Court—then I will stop talking about ERA during the campaign."

Dad said, "Deal." Maureen shook hands with Dad. My father made that pledge to Maureen, and she knew she could trust his word.

But in July, at the convention in Detroit, campaign officials freaked out when they saw Maureen handing out buttons to Republican women. Maureen was wearing one of the buttons, and it read—in *huge* letters—"ERA." At first, the Reagan campaign people thought Maureen had gone back on her word—but when they got closer they saw that underneath the big letters "ERA" was an inscription in smaller type: "Elect Reagan Anyway."

Dad won the election in a landslide. And on August 19, 1981, he nominated Sandra Day O'Connor to the High Court. He was a man of his word.

Ronald Reagan's critics and opponents called him a lot of things—but "dishonest" wasn't one of them. Mikhail Gorbachev squared off against my father in many tough negotiating sessions, and he endured a lot of blunt talk from Dad about the faults and failings of Soviet Communism. Yet Gorbachev called Dad "a man of his word."

And Democrat Senator John Kerry—who was an implacable foe of the Reagan administration, especially during the Iran–Contra investigation—said, "Even when he was breaking Democrats' hearts, he did so with a smile and in the spirit of honest and open debate."[2]

Dad's opponents knew that his word was his bond. His reputation for truthfulness and integrity enabled him to get a lot accomplished, even though the Democrats controlled both houses of Congress. For example, Dad made a pledge to Democratic Speaker of the House Thomas "Tip" O'Neill that he would not campaign against Democrat lawmakers who supported his signature legislation, the Economic Recovery Tax Act of 1981. Where did Dad make that pledge? At the White House.

Dad invited Tip O'Neill and his wife to the White House for dinner. Afterwards, O'Neill told his staff he would carry the legislation instead of opposing it. Someone asked, "What did President Reagan say that persuaded you to carry his legislation?"

"He never talked about the legislation," O'Neill said. "Instead, he talked about the greatness of America, the goodness of her people, and how he and I could work together to make America better for all. Soon we were telling Irish stories and drinking a glass of wine together, and I agreed to carry the legislation on the floor the House of Representatives. He promised he wouldn't campaign against any Democrat who voted for it."

As a result of O'Neill's support, ERTA passed. On August 13, 1981, Dad signed ERTA into law. In fact, Dad signed ERTA at Rancho Del Cielo, and the table on which he signed it is on display at the Reagan Ranch Center in Santa Barbara, operated by the Young America's Foundation. And yes, Dad kept his word to the Democrats.

Dad had a remarkable ability to win the trust of his opponents because they knew he told the truth. In June 1985, Dad gave a speech in the garden of Ted Kennedy's home in McLean, Virginia—a fund-raiser for the John F. Kennedy Presidential Library. The JFK Library had no living president to serve as the fund-raiser in chief. So the late president's children, Caroline and John, asked my father, President Reagan, to stand in for JFK and help kick off the fund-raising event.

Politically, Ronald Reagan and the Kennedys were adversaries. JFK's brother, Attorney General Robert F. Kennedy, had gotten my father fired from his job as host of General Electric Theater. Yet my father didn't let political differences poison his personal relationships. Though Dad had not supported John F. Kennedy for president, he admired President Kennedy's love of country, his service in World War II, his commitment to tax cuts and small government, and his call to all Americans to "ask not what your country can do for you; ask what you can do for your country."

So when John and Caroline Kennedy—President Kennedy's two children—invited my father to stand in for JFK at the Kennedy Library fund-raiser, Dad didn't hesitate. He gave the speech to kick off the fund-raising efforts for the JFK Library.

Years later, when it was time to dedicate the Ronald Reagan Presidential Library, Caroline Kennedy-Schlossberg and John F. Kennedy Jr. were in attendance. Their presence symbolized their gratitude at what my father had done in helping launch the John F. Kennedy Presidential Library. My father wasn't trying to get applause or recognition; rather, he was always trying to do the right thing. He brought Republicans and Democrats, conservatives and liberals, together, so that both sides could work together for the common good. He spoke the truth, and he lived the truth. As my father said, between nine and five, you can battle full tilt over politics—but at five o'clock, it's time to sit back, enjoy a glass of wine, and talk about the greatness of America and her people.

Just as Dad always kept his word to friends and foes alike, he expected people to keep their word to him. When he found out that someone dealt falsely with him—look out.

During the 1980 primaries, my father got terrible advice from his campaign consultants, Manafort, Stone, Black, and Sears. Campaign director John Sears told Dad not to campaign in Iowa or attend the candidate forums. This way, Sears said, Ronald Reagan would appear "above the fray" and would easily defeat George Bush in Iowa.

I couldn't understand that advice. I knew that Dad ought to be a "favorite son" in Iowa. He had spent five years as a radio announcer in Iowa before going on to an acting career in Hollywood. I thought he should build on his special relationship with the people of Iowa.

When I went to Iowa to campaign for my father, I discovered that Dad's campaign consultants were lying to him. They assured him that his support in Iowa was rock-solid and he was going to win easily. Yet everywhere I went, the people of Iowa were telling me they were supporting George Bush instead.

So I called Dad and told him, "You've got to come out to Iowa and campaign. George Bush is going to beat you if you don't."

"Well, Michael," Dad replied, "I just got off the phone with my campaign consultants, and they tell me I'm doing fine in Iowa. They tell me that if I come out and campaign like the rest of the candidates, it will reduce my stature."

"Your consultants are lying to you, Dad. I've been all over this state, and I'm chasing George Bush wherever I go. The grassroots folks are telling me you've forgotten your roots. They want to know why you're so aloof and disengaged. Dad, George Bush can't talk to these people like you can—he's not one of them. But George Bush is going to win because he's here and you're not. This weekend, WHO Radio, the station where you used to work, is hosting a big event and you're the only Republican candidate who won't be there. Dad, if you don't come out here, you're going to lose Iowa."

"Well, I'm paying my consultants for their advice. I think I ought to follow it."

"You mean John Sears? Dad, he's all over the local news in Iowa, and if you ask people who's running for president, they say, 'John Sears.' Dad, he's promoting himself more than he's promoting you."

"I'll look into it, Michael," Dad said—but I knew he was not persuaded.

Days later, George Bush beat Ronald Reagan, 32 percent to 30 percent, in Iowa. The pundits were saying that Ronald Reagan, the one-time frontrunner, was now in danger of losing the nomination. George Bush, meanwhile, came out of Iowa declaring he had "the Big Mo" (momentum).

Two weeks later, I was at home in California when the phone woke me up. I checked my clock. It was six thirty in the morning on the day of the New Hampshire primary. I answered the phone. It was Dad. I thought, *Oh no, what have I done now?*

"Michael," he said, "I want to read a press release to you. Subject to your approval, I intend to give this statement to the press in a few moments. You are probably the only one who will understand."

Subject to my approval? Why would a press release from Dad need my approval?

He read: "Ronald Reagan today announced that William J. Casey has been named executive vice chairman and campaign director of his presidential campaign, replacing John Sears who has resigned to return to his law practice. . . ."

Then I knew. Dad had just fired his campaign consultants.

When he finished reading, he said, "So Michael, what do you think?"

"Dad, I think it's great."

"Then I have your permission to release this to the media?"

"Yes, Dad, you have my permission."

"Turn on the television. This will be breaking news in a few minutes."

"Thanks for calling, Dad."

"Well, you're the one who was honest with me." It was Dad's way of thanking me for telling him the truth about Iowa. Dad valued the truth above all, and he hated being deceived.

Before hanging up, I asked, "Are you going to win in New Hampshire today?"

"Yes, Michael, we're going to win today."

And as he predicted, when the polls closed, Ronald Reagan had won more than half of the vote in a seven-way race. He then went on to win almost every primary in the country.

Lessons in Truth and Trust

From my earliest years of watching and learning from my father, and throughout his professional and political life, I saw that he valued the truth. He spoke it, he lived it, and he demanded it from his family members, associates, and advisers. His commitment to the truth made a deep and lasting impression on me.

Here are some of the lessons my father taught me about speaking and living the truth in every arena of our lives:

Focus on being worthy of trust. The American people elected Ronald Reagan president because he told them the truth and they trusted him. My father's political friends and political foes knew they could work with him because his word was his bond. In order to work together for the common good, we have to be able to trust one another. Trust is the glue that holds any family, any organization, or any society together. Trust is based on truth.

A few years ago, I was leaving the 24 Hour Fitness gym where I work out, and who should I see but actor Alec Baldwin. He is the quintessential Hollywood liberal—yet I never let his liberal activities get in the way of my enjoyment of his acting performances. I've enjoyed his work in many films and television shows, from *The Hunt for Red October* to *30 Rock*.

So I said, "Excuse me, Mr. Baldwin. My name is Mike Reagan, and my mother is Jane Wyman." He looked befuddled, and I could read the unspoken question in his eyes: *Why didn't he say his father is Ronald Reagan?*

I answered his unspoken question. "I thought it might be safer to say that Jane Wyman is my mother. I wasn't sure I'd still be standing if I said that Ronald Reagan was my father."

He laughed and shook my hand. I told him how much I enjoyed his work on *30 Rock*, and I added that my son Cameron has the actual teddy bear that was used in the final scene of *The*

Hunt for Red October—someone had given it to President Reagan, and he had given it to Cameron.

"Well," Baldwin said, "let me tell you something. You know that liberalism is in my blood—but I wish we had your father back."

I couldn't have been more surprised. "Really? But you were against everything my father stood for."

"That's right, but I've learned a lot since those days. I'm still liberal, but I miss your dad. I'm totally serious."

"Why's that?"

"A few nights ago, I was with some friends and we were talking about your dad. They were bashing him, you know? Then I said something that surprised even me. I told my friends, 'Say what you will, Ronald Reagan had a good soul.' Mike, what the world is missing today is someone with a good soul. I didn't agree with him. I still don't. But your father had a good soul."

Why would a political opponent like Alec Baldwin say that about my father? I believe it all comes down to the truth. Dad's opponents may not have liked what he said or agreed with what he said. But they believed that what he said came from his heart, not from some political calculation or attempt to deceive.

Dad's political campaigns were always rooted in truth and optimism. When my father ran for governor of California in 1966, his opponent was the Democratic incumbent Edmund G. "Pat" Brown. Governor Brown was leading in the polls when he made a disastrous decision. He filmed a campaign commercial in front of an elementary school class. He told two African American girls in the front row, "I'm running against an actor. You know who shot Abraham Lincoln, don'tcha?" When that ad came out on television, voters and political pundits were shocked and appalled. The premise of the commercial seemed to be, "Don't trust an actor because an actor assassinated Lincoln." Within hours, Dad surged into the lead and he never looked back. Dad defeated Brown by a 58 to 42 percent margin.

He made voters feel good about themselves and their country. When my father campaigned, it was always "morning in America"; it was always upbeat. Are there political candidates who make us feel that good today?

Over the years, I've encountered many people who said they didn't like my dad's politics, but they voted for him anyway because he made them feel good about America and good about themselves. Dad didn't talk about Republicans versus Democrats. He talked about all of us working together to make America great. I don't remember a time in my life when my father spoke ill of anyone. Never.

When people trust you to always tell the truth as you see it, then even if they disagree with you, they'll respect you. They'll know you have a good soul.

Defend historical truth. Dad never worried about political correctness or the slanders of his critics. His only concerns were as follow: What do the American people think? What is the truth they need to know? His uncompromising honesty gave him a lot of freedom to simply speak the truth as he saw it and let the chips fall where they may. It gave him the freedom to call the Soviet Union an "evil empire" and to demand that Mr. Gorbachev "tear down this wall." His advisors told him he should mute his rhetoric and soft-pedal the hard truth. But Ronald Reagan was committed to the truth, period.

My father honestly didn't care who got the credit for his achievements, such as restoring the American economy and ending the Cold War. But you and I should care deeply about whether he gets the credit. Why? Because historical truth matters. If American leaders and the American people are going to make wise decisions in the future, we need to know what has worked in the past. We need to know the political principles that always get results—and the ideological theories that always fail.

History tells us that the economic program we call Reaganomics—lower taxes, limited government, and greater economic freedom—always produces an economic boom. It worked during the Harding–Coolidge years of the 1920s, the Kennedy–Johnson years of the 1960s, and the Reagan Eighties. The U.S. economy has been ailing ever since we abandoned Reaganomics. And we abandoned Reaganomics because of historical and political amnesia. We forgot what works—and even Republicans have failed to stand up for the most successful economic turnaround in American history.

Historian Larry Schweikart, author of *A Patriot's History of the United States* (2004), uses a so-called Reagan test to determine whether a history textbook is truthful or unfairly biased. You simply open the textbook to any section that discusses the presidency of Ronald Reagan, and the way the authors describe Reagan's legacy tells you all you need to know about the book and its authors. For example, if the textbook gives Mikhail Gorbachev sole credit for ending the Cold War, you can bet that the book is equally dishonest on other subjects.[3]

We need to have a clear understanding of my father's principles and achievements in order to maintain our freedom, our prosperity, and our security for future generations. All Americans need to know the truth about the Reagan Eighties.

Be scrupulously honest in everything you do and say. In your family life, in your business life, in your conversations with friends and neighbors, always tell the truth. Always own up to your mistakes. Prove you can be trusted to always tell the truth. Your reputation is at stake. Let people know you stand for the truth.

When you overstate your case, you undermine your cause and your credibility. So stick to the truth, the whole truth, and nothing but. Absolute honesty is not only your best defense, but your best offense is well.

Sometimes I can't help being amazed when I look back over the lessons in integrity my father taught me. Again and again, he told me how important it is to tell the truth, to respect my family name, and to guard my integrity and my reputation. Again and again, whenever I had tried to get away with lying or cheating, he reminded me that a good reputation takes years to build but moments to destroy. These lessons are hardly new or profound, yet every generation needs to be reminded of the importance of speaking and living the truth.

What amazes me is that the man who tried to build in me a love for the truth was the same man who lived out a love for the truth on a world stage. Every lesson he tried to teach me, he exemplified in a magnified way when he told America the truth—and won America's trust.

4

Live to
Influence Others

W HEN I WAS A boy, I wanted nothing more than to be like
    my dad. More than anything, I wanted to be as rugged as
he was and to ride like he did. Above all, I wanted to shoot like
he did. Of course, there's more to shooting a gun than pulling
the trigger. The first thing Dad taught me was that there's no
such thing as an "unloaded" gun. A lot of people have been acci-
dentally killed by supposedly "unloaded" guns. He also taught
me to never point a gun in a direction that would cause injury
and never aim at anything I don't intend to shoot.

I learned to shoot with Dad's .22 semiautomatic. Later, he
gave me a .22 caliber Remington single-shot rifle and taught
me to use it. I couldn't have been more proud. After our chores
and before we went swimming, we'd drive around the ranch in
his Jeep and shoot ground squirrels.

Dad had two reasons for shooting squirrels. First and fore-
most, he was protecting his thoroughbreds. Squirrels dig holes
and it would have been easy for a horse to stumble in a hole and
break a leg. Dad's second reason for taking me to shoot squirrels
was to teach me patience. The squirrels would scurry into their
holes and hide there. Dad and I would sit and watch those holes,

just waiting. After five or ten minutes, I'd get impatient and say, "I'm tired of this. Let's go find some other squirrels."

"Shhh," my father would whisper. "Wait. Get ready."

So we'd sit in the shade and wait. Neither of us said a word. Fifteen minutes would go by. Thirty minutes. An hour. Eventually a furry little head would pop up out of the hole. Sometimes Dad would take the shot; sometimes I would. In time, I got to be very good with that .22. Dad was teaching me patience because he knew that was my greatest need. To this day, I get anxious waiting in line at the theater or the grocery store. Though Dad tried to teach me, I never learned patience.

In the fall of 1958, a new Western premiered on ABC, *The Rifleman* starring Chuck Connors. The hero used a lever-action Winchester rifle, which I thought was great—so Dad bought me a lever-action .22. I soon found I was a much better shot with my single-shot rifle than with a lever action. Why? Because the single shot required patience. I had to take careful aim, control my breathing, and apply steady force to the trigger. I only had one shot, and I had to make it count. With the lever-action rifle, I had more bullets. If I missed my first shot, I could pump the lever until I emptied the gun—a sloppy way to shoot. I thought it was cool to shoot Rifleman style—but I was a better marksman with the single-shot rifle.

To give you an idea what kind of marksman Dad was, on more than one occasion, I saw him shoot a running ground squirrel from a moving Jeep. But most of the time, we'd drive out to one of the places where the squirrels proliferated—and we'd wait. And wait. We wouldn't say a word; we'd just listen to the silence. In the process, I learned patience. I learned to enjoy the silence. I learned to enjoy just sitting beside my father, waiting for the next squirrel to appear, waiting for the deafening crack of Dad's gun.

He set down some strict rules about shooting and especially about what I was allowed to shoot. Targets, ground squirrels, and nest-robbing scrub jays—that's it. If Dad ever caught me shooting at blackbirds or sparrows, or if he caught me being careless with my gun in any way, he'd confiscate it for a few weeks. Dad also taught me how to clean, oil, and care for a gun. I treasured not only the time I spent shooting with him, but also the time we spent cleaning and maintaining our firearms.

When I left home for Judson School in Arizona, Dad bought me a .243 hunting rifle and a 12-gauge shotgun. I still have that rifle. In 1963, I used it to hunt javelina on the San Carlos Apache Indian Reservation, and I brought down a 43½-pound sow—the largest javelina sow killed that year. I had it mounted and displayed in my apartment until someone stole it. I still go dove hunting every year with a 12-gauge shotgun. Everything Dad taught me about gun safety I have since taught to my son Cameron—a Reagan family tradition.

I listened carefully to my father and watched everything he did. I wanted to have a confident, optimistic personality like his. I wanted to have his rugged charm. Most important of all, I wanted him to be proud of me. I never wanted to disappoint him.

When people want to listen to you and follow your example, that's called *influence*. My father, Ronald Reagan, had an incalculable influence on the lives of millions of people around the world. But long before he became a man of influence on the world stage, he had a deep and lasting impact on the lives of his children.

And especially on the life of one Michael Edward Reagan.

A Boy and His Horse

My father famously said, "There's nothing better for the inside of a man than the outside of a horse." And he instinctively knew that what is true for a man is true for a boy.

I'll never forget one special Saturday when I was nine years old. As we arrived at the Malibu ranch in Dad's red station wagon, I saw a new horse in the corral. He was a beautiful golden palomino quarter horse with a white stripe down his face.

"Dad!" I shouted. "A new horse!"

I jumped out of the car and ran to the corral for a closer look. I had learned to ride on Dad's big thoroughbred, Baby, but this palomino was more my size.

Dad came up behind me. "Well, what do you think? Would you like to ride him?"

"You bet!"

So Dad saddled the palomino and helped me into the saddle. Then he took the lanyard and led the horse around the corral. The question burning inside me as we loped around the corral was a question I didn't dare ask out loud: Whose horse is he?

Dad said, "Michael, would you ever want to have a horse of your own?"

Would I? I wanted that horse more than anything I had ever wanted in my life.

"Wow, Dad! Yes! Can I have this horse?"

"Whoa, there, Michael. I meant, would you like to have a horse of your own—someday. But this horse belongs to another man. The man's son is about your size, so we'll get this horse used to being ridden by a boy your size and weight, so the man can give it to his son for Christmas. As long as we're training him, you can ride him."

"Oh."

"I hope you're not too disappointed, son. The horse doesn't have a name. Would you like to name him?"

I thought for a moment. "Can we call him Rebel?"

Dad nodded. "Rebel it is."

I always looked forward to Saturdays when I could ride that palomino horse. One December day in 1954, I rode to the ranch with Dad. During the last mile of our drive, Dad said, "Michael, there's something I need to tell you about Rebel."

My heart froze.

"Remember, I told you that Rebel has another owner—a man and his boy. Well, that boy is going to get Rebel as a Christmas present."

"Did they take Rebel away?"

"No, not yet. He's still in his stall."

"Can I say good-bye to him?"

"Of course you can, Michael."

Dad pulled the station wagon up near the stable. I got out of the car and raced to the stall—Rebel's stall. I opened the top door, and Rebel poked his head out. He was freshly washed and beautiful. His coat shimmered like molten gold.

Then I saw a big red bow someone had tied around his neck, along with a card that read, "Merry Christmas, Michael. Love, Dad and Nancy."

Dad followed me into the stable, grinning ear to ear.

"Is it true, Dad? Rebel's really mine?"

"He's all yours, Michael. Merry Christmas, son."

I whooped and jumped up and down. I spent most of that day riding, feeding, and grooming my Christmas present. It was one of the happiest days of my life.

That night, I went back to Mom's house and told her all about Rebel. I went to bed that night and couldn't sleep. Finally, I crawled out of bed. Often, when I had trouble sleeping, I would sneak into my sister's room to see if she was still awake. Many times throughout my childhood, Maureen and I had stayed up, talking to each other in whispers. She was my best friend, and she knew me better than anyone else. When I was scared or worried or just too excited to sleep, she could calm me down.

I slipped out of my room and started down the hallway toward Maureen's room—then I froze in my tracks. Mom was just walking out of her bedroom. In her arms were a brand-new saddle and bridle. She turned and saw me—and her eyes went wide.

"Well, I had planned to surprise you with this." She dropped the tack on the floor with a heavy thud. "Here's my Christmas present for you, Michael. You can go down and put it under the tree yourself."

So I picked up the saddle and bridle and carried them downstairs. I set them carefully next to the tree, beside the other gifts. There was a card attached to the stirrup. In Mom's flowing handwriting, it read, "These are for Rebel. Ride him well. All my love, Mom."

Dad saw Rebel as much more than a Christmas present for his son. Yes, he enjoyed watching how happy it made me—but that horse was part of Dad's plan to influence my life, to teach me important lessons, and to help me grow in my character, my life skills, and my physical and emotional maturity.

Few people were more keenly aware of the benefits of riding than Dad. Owning a horse involves much more than riding, just as owning a gun involves much more than shooting. A horse owner must work hard and be responsible to look after the horse's health and grooming. Dad instructed me in caring for Rebel. He told me I needed to be responsible and disciplined.

I didn't realize it at the time, but Dad was using Rebel to teach me character qualities of patience, self-discipline, accountability, and kindness to animals. He wanted me to learn the skills needed to safely and responsibly control a thousand pounds of horseflesh. He also knew that riding a horse is good for one's health. A rider works a lot of muscles while riding, which is why horseback riding often leaves people feeling tired and sore. And of course, a horse owner gets a great upper body workout while grooming the horse and cleaning out the stalls.

It was character-building for me to not only ride Rebel, but to care for him and to clean up after him. At the time, all I knew was that Dad was giving me the best gift anyone could want. Looking back, I realize that Rebel was part of Dad's plan to help me grow into responsible manhood. I truly loved that horse. In the process of caring for Rebel, I gained strength and confidence that helped me endure the wounds of my childhood.

I miss that horse, and today my yellow Labrador is named Rebel.

A Manipulative Ploy

As I moved into adolescence, I became increasingly rebellious. I loved Mom, but there was a huge obstacle in our relationship that she knew nothing about. On a number of occasions, beginning when I was in the third grade, I was molested by a day camp counselor. This evil man controlled me with guilt and fear, threatening to show my parents some pictures he'd taken of me. I kept the secret and didn't tell a soul until I was in my early forties. (I've written about these incidents, including my redemption and recovery, in two books, *On the Outside Looking In* and *Twice Adopted*.)

Because of the molestation, I was afraid of being in an all-boys Catholic school. I didn't want to be in an all-male environment, which only reminded me of what I had gone through. There was so much fear in my life, and I couldn't tell Mom why I was afraid and why I didn't want to go to school. Some Sunday nights when Mom was working, she'd send a cab to pick me up and take me to school. When the cab arrived, I'd be hiding on the roof. My sister Maureen and Carrie, our housekeeper, would find me and talk me down from the roof.

Mom was at her wits end trying to understand my rage, much of which was rooted in guilt and fear because of the molestation. I was scared to death that Mom would find out what the day camp counselor had done to me, and she would hate me for it. Paradoxically, I actually provoked conflict with Mom out of my love for her. I wanted her to send me away so that she would never find out about the molestation. So I battled her and rebelled against her in an attempt to protect her from the awful truth I carried inside.

She sent me to a priest for counseling, but I steadfastly refused to cooperate with the priest or discuss with him why I was so rebellious. "Talk to me, Michael," he said. "Let me help you."

"Father John," I said, "if I want to tell God something, do I have to go through you? Can't I just talk to God?"

"Certainly, you can always tell God anything."

"Then I'm not going to tell you."

At the end of the session, Father John told Mom, "I can't do anything for your son. He refuses to talk to me."

Mom's next step was to send me to a Beverly Hills child psychiatrist. The prospect of going to a psychiatrist terrified me. I was about fourteen years old and I thought that only crazy people went to psychiatrists. The whole field of psychiatry seemed shrouded in mystery, and I was afraid that this doctor might uncover my darkest secrets.

Over the course of four or five sessions, the psychiatrist gave me all sorts of tests and asked me countless questions, which I answered guardedly. He told me that everything I said to him would be kept strictly confidential—but I didn't believe him. I suspected that the psychiatrist was a friend of Mom's and I was sure he'd report to her anything I said. I decided to test my theory—and use the psychiatrist to my own advantage.

In one of our final sessions, I told the psychiatrist, "Do you want to know why I don't get along with Mom? She won't let me spend time with Dad. I only get to see my father every other weekend. I want to go live in his house. It's that simple."

It was a manipulative ploy—and it worked. The psychiatrist must have relayed my words to Mom because the next time Dad came to pick me up and take me to the ranch, he said, "Michael, how would you like to come live with Nancy and me?"

Mom had probably told Dad to make it seem it was his idea— but I was sure my ploy with the psychiatrist had worked. From my immature perspective, I was convinced I had won. I didn't think about how much I had hurt my mother by choosing Dad's home over hers. All I thought about was that I would finally get to be with Dad.

So in 1959, I moved in with Dad and Nancy at their General Electric showcase home on the bluff in Pacific Palisades. Dad was at the height of his eight-year tenure as host of *General Electric Theater* on CBS. By that time, Dad and Nancy had two children—Patti, age seven, and Ron, a newborn. I was looking forward to being their big brother.

I had assumed that by moving in with Dad, I wouldn't have to go to boarding school anymore. But Mom had made arrangements for me to attend Loyola High School in the fall. Though I lived in Dad's home, I could only be with the family on weekends.

A Lesson in Ethics

In 1960, when I was fifteen years old, Dad—who had been a lifelong Democrat—became involved in the "Democrats for Nixon" movement. (He would become a Republican two years later.) Through his involvement with the Nixon campaign, Dad became acquainted with leaders of the Republican National Committee.

One night, Dad, Nancy, Maureen, and I were gathered at the dinner table. "A friend of mine at the RNC (Republican National Convention) told me about some photographs today," Dad said. "The photos apparently show Senator John F. Kennedy entering and leaving hotel rooms with different women." It appeared that Senator Kennedy was cheating on his wife, Jacqueline.

After President Kennedy's death, it became widely known that he had a number of affairs, both before and during his White House years. But at the time, as he was running for president, his infidelities were kept out of the national press. The outcome of the Nixon–Kennedy race was incredibly close. If Kennedy's trysts with women had become a scandal during the election, he would certainly have lost.

I said, "Dad, are the Republicans going to give those pictures to the newspapers?"

"No," my father replied. "We shouldn't use those photos."

"Why not? Wouldn't those pictures help Nixon win?"

"Maybe they would, but it would be wrong to attack his personal life. Senator Kennedy isn't running for husband of the year. He's running for president of the United States, and we need to base the campaign on issues and a candidate's leadership ability. There are bad husbands who are good leaders, and good husbands who are bad leaders. What he was doing in those hotels with those women is a matter between Senator Kennedy and his wife. It's not part of the political discussion."

I didn't understand at the time, but my father was trying to teach me a lesson in ethics. He wanted me to understand that people of good character set ethical boundaries that they will not cross. They want to win—but they don't want to win at any cost. Dad wanted me to learn to guard my character, my values, and my moral principles.

This is the same lesson my father tried to teach the American media and the American people during his first press conference on January 29, 1981. He took a question from Sam Donaldson of ABC News: "Mr. President, what do you see as the long-range intentions of the Soviet Union? Do you think, for instance, that the Kremlin is bent on world domination that might lead to continuation of the Cold War?"

Dad replied that the Soviet leaders had "openly and publicly declared that the only morality they recognize is what will further their cause, meaning they reserve unto themselves the right to commit any crime—to lie, to cheat—in order to attain that. . . . We operate on a different set of standards."[1]

Whether he was speaking to his fifteen-year-old son or holding a White House press conference, Dad was influencing, teaching, and yes, preaching ethics and morality. Issues come and go, but principles are truly timeless. My father lived by his principles, and he taught those principles to me—and to the nation. That was the key to his enduring influence.

Influence through Storytelling

The world remembers Ronald Reagan as a storyteller. But before Dad told his stories to the world, he was telling them to his kids, including yours truly. At the time, I didn't always appreciate and understand his stories. It took me years to realize that he used stories as a way of influencing people.

Everybody loves a good story, but few of us have the ability to tell stories well. Dad learned the art of storytelling from his father, Jack. Dad also taught a boy's Sunday school class in the church basement when he was fifteen years old. To keep things lively, he would mix Bible parables with sports stories.

Dad's most famous story is one that I heard him tell when I was a boy. It seems there were two brothers—an incurable pessimist and an incurable optimist. The boys' father took them to a doctor in hopes of curing the one boy of his extreme pessimism and curing the other boy of his extreme optimism.

The doctor took the young pessimist into a room filled with shiny new toys and said, "These toys are all yours to play with." The young pessimist burst into tears. The doctor said, "What's wrong?"

"I just know that when I play with these toys, they'll break and be ruined."

Next, the doctor took the young optimist into a stable filled with horse manure. "See that pile of manure?" the doctor asked. "You cannot leave this stable until you've cleaned out all this manure."

"Oh boy!" the young optimist shouted. Then he climbed to the top of the pile and began digging with his bare hands. The doctor shouted, "Young man! What are you doing?"

The boy replied, "With all this manure, there's *got* to be a pony in here somewhere!"

Why am I retelling a story you've probably heard many times before? Because after hearing the story numerous times, you may have forgotten the point my father was making—and it's the same point he tried to get across to me when I was a boy: *attitude is everything.* Optimists dig in, get things done, and succeed while pessimists never get started. Dad wanted me to grow up to be the optimist in the stable, not the pessimist in a roomful of toys.

When you tie a lesson to a story, you make the lesson memorable. You increase the odds that both the story and the lesson will be remembered in years to come.

Another story Dad often told was about a teacher who called a mother in for a parent–teacher conference. The teacher said, "I'm afraid I'm going to have to discipline your boy, Irving."

"Oh, please don't be too hard on Irving," the mother said. "He's a sensitive boy. All you have to do is slap the boy next to him, and Irving will behave."

Again, it's a story with a point. The point might apply to parents being too lenient and permissive with their children—or to liberal, paternalistic government being too lenient and permissive toward criminals or terrorists. The point of the story is that when you coddle people who behave badly, you end up punishing the innocent.

The overindulgent mother didn't care that the boy next to Irving would be unfairly punished—just don't lay a hand on her precious little snowflake. In the same way, when liberals make excuses for bad people—when they blame terrorism on global warming or when they blame the Tea Party for mass shootings— they excuse the perpetrator and blame the innocent.

Isn't it amazing how much insight Dad could squeeze into one of his little stories?

Judge William P. Clark Jr. was one of Dad's most trusted friends and advisors. Bill Clark was a rancher like Dad, and he served as my father's national security advisor. I once talked to Bill about Dad's unique gift for storytelling. He pointed out something I should have known but had never noticed before: "Michael," he said, "your father was not just a storyteller. He spoke in parables."

The moment Bill told me that, everything snapped into focus. Instantly, I understood why my father told so many stories. Parables are stories that teach a lesson. During his early religious instruction, Dad had learned how to teach moral lessons through parables. Yes, his stories were entertaining—but if you really *listened* to what he was saying, you'd discover a deeper truth. Dad would never spell it out for you. He'd tell you a story and hope you'd get the point.

Dinesh D'Souza describes an encounter my father had with Richard Nixon in early 1981. Nixon wanted to advise the newly elected president on strategy for dealing with the Soviet Union. Well, Dad already knew what his strategy would be—and he was not interested in pursuing the Nixonian policy of détente (meaning "a relaxation of tension"). So when Nixon came to the White House, Dad regaled him with jokes about how farmers in the Soviet Union weren't producing crops under the Communist system.

As Nixon listened to my father's stories, he was horrified. He thought Dad was being flippant, that he wasn't taking the U.S.–Soviet relationship seriously. Over the next few years, Nixon wrote several books in which he criticized my father's lack of "realism" about the Soviets. Nixon vehemently disagreed with Dad's prediction that the Soviet Union would collapse—and he urged a return to détente.

Two and a half years after my father left office, the Berlin wall came down. Soviet Communism collapsed. My father was vindicated—and Richard Nixon finally admitted that he had been wrong and Dad was right: "Ronald Reagan has been justified by what has happened. History has justified his leadership."[2]

Richard Nixon didn't understand that my father spoke in parables. He didn't realize that when Dad was telling jokes about farmers in the Soviet Union, he was actually making a serious point about life under the flawed Soviet system. An economic and political system that forces farmers to be unproductive is doomed to failure. My father knew that, and that's why he could confidently predict the fall of the Iron Curtain. That was the lesson in Dad's parable.

Dad spoke in parables, while today's politicians speak in sound bites. My father influenced people through stories because stories help us see the essential truth of a problem. If Richard Nixon had understood what Dad was saying to him through parables, he wouldn't have had to eat his words. And if I had truly understood Dad's parables, my early years might have gone a lot more smoothly.

Influencing the Next Generation

In March 1984, my father went to speak at Congress Heights Elementary School in Washington, D.C. At the end of his talk, he announced the winner of the school's "Writing to Read" contest—an African American boy named Rudolph Lee-Hines. The prize? A pen-pal friendship with the president of the United States. Rudolph was selected on the basis of his excellent reading skills (though he was only six years old) and his ability to write letters with very little help from grown-ups.

For years afterward, Dad and Rudolph maintained a correspondence. The boy asked the president about the acting profession, how to maintain friendships, advice about schoolwork, and how to ride a horse. Dad gave the boy advice, much of it based on his own boyhood experiences. Dad and Nancy visited the school a number of times and on one occasion even had dinner with Rudy and his mother at their apartment.[3]

Dad and Rudy exchanged many letters. Here's an excerpt from Dad's letter to Rudy shortly after the space shuttle *Challenger* disaster:

Dear Rudolph,

It was good to get your letter and to hear about those grades, keep it up. You know we have something in common—I didn't do well in science either but like you I kept trying. We have to do that. . . .

I shared your feelings about the shuttle tragedy. I think most everyone in the country was saddened. Your folks are right about the debt we owe to those who have pioneered in our country. Each of the families of those who lost their lives told me we must keep the space program growing, that their loved ones would want it that way.

Well I'm off to Grenada for a meeting down there. I'll be back the same day which means a lot of hours in the air.

Give my regards to your folks.

Sincerely,

Ronald Reagan[4]

Dad was continually aware of his influence on people and his responsibility to be a good influence on the next generation. My friend Dana Rohrabacher, Republican congressman from the Forty-Eighth District of California, used to be a speechwriter for my father. Dana once told me about an incident he witnessed when Dad was running in the 1976 GOP primaries.

Dad was speaking at a rally in North Carolina. During the speech, a woman came up to Dana and said, "I've brought a group of blind children to the rally. It would mean a lot to the children if they could meet Governor Reagan and shake hands with him after his speech. Would that be possible?"

Dana conveyed the woman's request to Dad, and he was happy to meet with the children. But he warned his staff, "Not a word to the press. I don't want anyone to think I'm trying to exploit these kids."

So Dana Rohrabacher brought five kids, ten to twelve years old, over to the candidate's bus, and he introduced them to my father. Dad talked with them for a few minutes, then he had an idea. "Would you children like to touch my face?" he asked.

As Dana concluded the story, he said, "I'll never forget that moment. It wouldn't have occurred to me to make that offer to those kids. But your dad understood that blind kids wouldn't be able to 'see' him unless they could touch his face. As I watched those kids gather around him and place their hands on his face, I thought, *Any politician in the country would pay millions to have his picture on the cover of* Time *with all those hands outstretched to touch him—yet that's the last thing Ronald Reagan wants.*"

Dad refused to exploit kids for political gain. He genuinely cared about influencing the next generation. That's the way he raised me, that's the way he lived his life, that's the way he conducted his presidency.

Ronald Reagan, Teacher and Influencer

The reality of my father was that he was the same man as an actor and a father as he was when he was governor of California and president of the United States. What was that reality? Simply this, Ronald Reagan loved America. He'd get a lump in his throat as he sang the National Anthem. He'd get tears in his eyes as he recited the Pledge of Allegiance. Maureen and I used to say that the presidency was Dad's eagle badge, because he was truly a boy scout at heart. Love of God and love of country were woven into his being. More than anyone else I've ever known, my father absolutely loved America.

When we'd drive out to the ranch, Dad would sing every military and patriotic song in the book. And he knew them all— "The Marines' Hymn" ("From the Halls of Montezuma to the shores of Tripoli"), "The Air Force Song" ("Off we go into the wild blue yonder"), "The Army Goes Rolling Along" ("Over hill, over dale, we will hit the dusty trail"), and on and on. He was a commissioned officer in the reserve corps of the U.S. Cavalry and was ordered to active duty from 1942 to 1945 (poor eyesight kept him stateside, working with the First Motion Picture Unit of the Army). That's why the official flag of the aircraft carrier USS *Ronald Reagan* is my father's Cavalry flag.

When I was growing up, I didn't fully appreciate my Dad's immense love for America. And I think it's tragic that many people today don't have that same love of country that Dad had—it hasn't been passed down from generation to generation.

A few years ago, I played golf with a young man in his twenties, a restaurant manager. As we played golf together, I mentioned that I had been asked to go to France the next day and raise the flag at the American cemetery at Normandy. This young man looked at me with a puzzled expression and said, "Why is there an American cemetery at Normandy?"

Here was a guy who was bright, successful, and well-educated—yet he knew nothing about D-Day, the invasion of Normandy, or the liberation of Europe. He didn't know why there is an American cemetery at Normandy. And because he didn't know about the sacrifices Americans had made for the cause of liberty around the world, he didn't have the kind of love of country that I learned from my father.

Dad taught me to love America, just as he taught me so many other important values and truths. Dad was a teacher— and that's why he had such a profound influence on me and on everyone he met. Whether you grasped his message or not, he was always teaching, always influencing, always telling his stories and sharing his parables.

Dad wanted to teach the Soviet leaders about the greatness of America. During his time in office, the Communist Party of the Soviet Union had four different leaders—Leonid Brezhnev, Yuri Andropov, Konstantin Chernenko, and Mikhail Gorbachev. Dad was eager to meet with the Soviet leaders and school them in the blessings of American liberty—but, he said, "They keep dying on me." In his autobiography, *An American Life*, he wrote:

> One of my regrets as president is that I was never able to take Mikhail Gorbachev on a trip across our country: I wanted to take him up in a helicopter and show him how Americans lived. . . . We'd fly over a residential neighborhood and I'd tell him that's where those workers lived—in homes with lawns and backyards, perhaps with a second car or a boat in the driveway. . . . [I'd say,] "They not only lived there, they *own* that property."
>
> I even dreamed of landing the helicopter in one of those neighborhoods and inviting Gorbachev to walk down the street with me, and I'd say, "Pick any home you want; we'll knock on the door and you can ask the people how they live and what they think of our system."[5]

Dad's autobiography was published in 1990. In May 1992, Mikhail Gorbachev—who had resigned as the leader of the collapsing Soviet Union in August 1991—arrived at the Santa Barbara Municipal Airport aboard a Boeing 727 jetliner, "The Capitalist Tool," which had been loaned to Gorbachev by Forbes, Inc. Dad and Nancy went to the airport to meet Mr. Gorbachev, his wife Raisa, and their daughter Irina, and they rode with the Gorbachevs in a limousine to Rancho del Cielo.

Colleen and I were at the ranch during Mr. Gorbachev's stay. (In fact, I was the only person who dared to point out to Mr. Gorbachev that he was wearing his Stetson cowboy hat— a gift from my father—backward.) Though Dad never got to give Mr. Gorbachev the helicopter tour he envisioned in his autobiography, Dad did teach the former Communist leader about the advantages of living in the Land of the Free.

During Mr. Gorbachev's flight from the East Coast, he had noticed the checkerboard pattern of America's farmlands. He asked my father who owned all of those fields. Dad said, "On each square of farmland there's a farmhouse, and the family in the farmhouse owns the house and the land—just as I own this ranch and house."

When Dad gave Mr. Gorbachev a tour of the ranch, Gorbachev noticed that Dad had his own gasoline pump on the property. Dad used that pump to fuel his vehicles on the 688-acre ranch— including the blue Jeep Scrambler that Dad used to chauffeur Mr. Gorbachev around Rancho del Cielo. (That Jeep, with the personalized "GIPPER" license plate, is displayed at the Young America's Foundation Reagan Ranch Center in Santa Barbara.) Mrs. Gorbachev noted that there were severe fuel shortages and gas lines in Russia at the time. She marveled that the former American president had his own gasoline pump. Dad told Mr. and Mrs. Gorbachev that it was not uncommon for American ranchers to buy their fuel in bulk and to own their own pump. It was a benefit, he added, of living in a free country.

Dad even talked to Mr. Gorbachev about the "unalienable rights" that are set forth in our Declaration of Independence— life, liberty, and the pursuit of happiness, which encompasses the right to the ownership of property. You see? Dad was always the same man as an actor, governor, president, father, and genial host to his former Cold War adversary. He was always influencing, always teaching, always talking about his great love for America. And even though America sometimes took my father away from his family, Dad never hesitated to make the sacrifice for the country he loved.

How to Become a Person of Influence

My father was the most influential man I've ever known. It's humbling to realize that he first influenced the course of my life, then he influenced the course of human history. When I was growing up in his home, I didn't realize how much he devoted himself to being a man of influence. I was too close to him to see all the ways he was influencing me, influencing my sisters and my brother, and influencing the world around him.

Influence is something that you understand and appreciate better after you gain life experience, wisdom, and perspective. Over the years that I have been studying my father's life, I have discovered some of the key principles of his influence. Here are some of the lessons in influence my father taught me:

Influence is an investment of time. My father invested time in teaching me to shoot and ride a horse. He wasn't just teaching me how to hit a target or sit in a saddle. He was teaching character. Dad taught me that shooting wasn't a matter of killing animals for fun, and he taught me to respect the deadly power of a gun. Dad knew that shooting and riding are character-building, confidence-building activities and that an afternoon spent hunting or horseback riding can do more for a young person's heart than a thousand parental lectures.

If you want to influence the next generation, you must invest your time. The activity you choose doesn't have to be shooting or horseback riding. Pick an activity that you love to do and share it with a young person. Invest your time, invest your life. Talk is cheap, but time well spent with young people is an investment that will pay dividends for decades to come.

To influence others, be direct—and indirect. There are two forms of influence. One form is when you talk, lecture, teach, give speeches, and otherwise communicate a message to others. That's direct influence, and it's an important way of influencing our children and the people around us. Ronald Reagan, the Great Communicator, was a master of the art of direct influence.

But over the years, I have learned to appreciate my father's gift for indirect influence. He had a great (and underappreciated) gift for teaching and influencing people without letting them know they were being influenced. When Dad and I were out shooting or riding, I thought we were just having fun. And we *were* having fun—lots of it.

But looking back, I realize now how much thought Dad put into using those fun times as teaching opportunities. I didn't realize back then that I was learning responsibility and self-discipline while I was feeding and grooming Rebel. In many ways, his indirect lessons had a much more profound impact on my life than the words he spoke.

Know your audience. If you want to impact and influence others, you've got to know your audience. And sometimes your most important audience isn't sitting in front of you. Sometimes your real audience is on the other side of the world.

On March 8, 1983, my father addressed the annual convention of the National Association of Evangelicals in Orlando, Florida. That speech has become famous among conservatives and infamous among liberals because of a little two-word phrase that occurs only once in the entire speech: "evil empire." In fact, that speech has become known as the "Evil Empire Speech" even though less than one percent of the speech deals with what my father called "the aggressive impulses of an evil empire," the Soviet Union.

Why did a speech that is 99.9 percent about something *other* than the "evil empire" come to be known as the "Evil Empire

Speech"? The original speech, written by speechwriter Tony Dolan, made no reference to the Soviet "evil empire." My father added those paragraphs to the speech shortly before he delivered it. With those additional sentences, he changed a fairly routine speech into a historic and controversial foreign policy manifesto—and he completely changed the audience of the speech.

Reaction to the speech was blistering. Presidential historian Henry Steele Commager, in *The Washington Post*, called it "the worst presidential speech in American history." *New York Times* columnist Anthony Lewis asked, "What must Soviet leaders think?" The Soviet news agency TASS said the speech proved that President Reagan could only think "in terms of confrontation and bellicose, lunatic anti-Communism."[6]

What had my father done in that speech? He had simply spoken the obvious, undeniable truth that the Soviet Union was an evil empire. He didn't care if the truth made the Soviets upset. He was going to say it anyway, boldly and without compromise. The Soviet state had violated every right our founding documents held sacred: freedom of the press, free speech, freedom of conscience and religion, freedom to own property, and the freedom to travel and emigrate. The Soviet state had slaughtered tens of millions of its own citizens, many by starvation. If such a government was not an evil empire, what was it?

At the time Dad delivered the Evil Empire Speech, Jewish–Russian dissident Natan Sharansky was serving time in a Soviet gulag. One day, a prison guard read a Soviet news account of Dad's speech to Sharansky. The guard thought that Ronald Reagan's words would discourage Sharansky. Instead, the news report filled Sharansky with joy. "It was the brightest, most glorious day," he later recalled, adding, "The lie had been exposed and could never, ever be untold now. This was the end of Lenin's 'Great October Bolshevik Revolution' and the beginning of a new revolution, a freedom revolution—Reagan's Revolution."[7]

Sharansky spread the news to his fellow prisoners, using a secret code that he tapped on the pipes of his cell. He and his fellow prisoners knew that the evil empire could not withstand the white-hot glare of truth. Three years later, in February 1986, Sharansky and many other prisoners were freed as a result of a deal between my father and Mikhail Gorbachev. In May of that year, Sharansky came to the United States and was awarded the Congressional Gold Medal. Sharansky also met with my father at the White House.

"The first time I met President Reagan," Sharansky recalled in a 2004 interview, "I told him of the brilliant day when we learned about his Evil Empire speech. . . . When I said that our whole block burst out into a kind of loud celebration, . . . the president, this great tall man, just lit up like a schoolboy. His face lit up and beamed. He jumped out of his seat like a shot and started waving his arms wildly and calling for everyone to come in" and hear Sharansky's story. Only then did Natan Sharansky realize how my father had been bitterly attacked in the American press because of the Evil Empire Speech. Sharansky concluded, "Our moment of joy was the moment of his own vindication."[8]

When Dad gave that speech, his real audience was on the other side of the world—men without conscience in the Soviet Kremlin and men without hope in the Soviet gulags. My father was always conscious of the wider audience for his speeches.

He knew that the audience for his "Tear Down This Wall" speech at the Brandenburg Gate in Berlin was not the audience in front of him, but the people behind him—the oppressed people of East Berlin; the ruthless Communist oppressors of East Germany; and yes, the Soviet leader, Mikhail Gorbachev. My father let the people of East Germany know that the American president seriously intended to tear down that wall. My father's example reminds us that the impact of our words may be felt far beyond the walls of our auditorium, our classroom, our church, or our home.

Dad's example also reminds us that we should not be too quick to defend ourselves against the accusations of our opponents. All too often, when someone attacks us, we want to find a microphone or get on social media and defend ourselves. Dad didn't do that. Instead of responding to criticism, he shrugged it off.

For example, when Dad ran for president in 1980, his critics in the media and the Democratic Party called him a "cowboy," a reckless gunslinger, a man so dangerous and unpredictable that you never knew when he might start a war. CBS television journalist Leslie Stahl recalls how President Jimmy Carter's attacks actually helped my father's campaign:

> By the fall of 1980 . . . the only thing holding the Carter candidacy together was whatever fear of Reagan he could drum up. Carter warned that it was too risky to leave the serious business of leadership in the hands of a cowboy actor. Confrontation in the nuclear age, he said, "is not just another shoot-out at the O.K. Corral." . . .
>
> His portrayal of Reagan as a "mad bomber" and a racist produced the "meanness issue." . . . Within a few months Carter's image had flipped from that of an ineffectual but decent religious man to a vindictive villain.[9]

One of the best things my father said in the campaign was what he *never* said. He never refuted the charge of being a "cowboy"—he embraced it. He had his campaign print up posters in which he wore a cowboy hat and smiled at the camera. The posters read, "America—Reagan Country." That poster became enormously popular, and helped turn the smears of the Left into a political asset—and a foreign policy triumph.

Dad knew the leaders of Iran were closely watching the American election. He wanted the Iranian radicals, who were holding more the sixty Americans hostage, to see him as a dangerous and unpredictable "cowboy." Let the Iranians worry that Reagan was just crazy enough to turn their country into a sea of molten glass. No matter how extreme and ridiculous the accusations of the Democrats, Dad never denied them. He understood his audience. He knew the Iranians were listening—and quaking in their sandals.

As Dad took the oath of office as president of the United States, what did the Iranians do? They set the hostages free. If Dad had tried to refute the "cowboy" charge, those Americans might have spent the rest of their lives as hostages.

Dad knew his American audience, his audience in the Kremlin, his audience in the gulags, and his audience in Tehran. He was aware of the impact of his influence, and he wielded his influence with the precision of a surgeon wielding a scalpel.

Know what you believe and why you believe it. Most political consultants today believe only in the greenback dollar. They play an endless game of musical chairs, working for candidate after candidate, campaign after campaign. It amazes me that so many consultants keep getting hired even though they've never won an election.

When my father ran for president, he had two close aides who believed in him. Their names were Michael Deaver and Lynn Nofziger. They knew my father well and they believed in his message and his values. If my father had dropped out of the campaign, they would not have surfaced with the campaign of George H. W. Bush or Bob Dole. They believed in my father because they knew that Dad's message didn't come from a focus group—it came from the core of his being. They trusted my father because he knew what he believed and why he believed it.

If you want to be a person of influence, you have to know who you are, what you believe, and why you believe it. When my father ran for governor in 1966, his opponents were eager to brand him as an extremist—a tactic that had destroyed

Barry Goldwater's presidential hopes in 1964. The Democrats and their allies in the press repeatedly suggested a sinister link between Ronald Reagan and the far-right John Birch Society.

My father refused to step into the trap of either aligning himself with the Birchers or renouncing them and their support. His standard reply whenever he was asked about the John Birch society was, "Anyone who chooses to support me has bought my philosophy. I'm not buying theirs."[10] If you know yourself and you know what you believe, your critics and opponents won't be able to throw you off message. You'll be able to turn bad news into good news, weaknesses into strengths, and problems into opportunities.

Use the events of the day as object lessons. I'm not sure why Dad told us about the photographs of Senator Kennedy, but I do know two things: First, he trusted us to keep the matter confidential, and we did. Second, he used that situation as an object lesson to teach us important ethical principles. He used the current event of the election, along with some insider knowledge he had gained, and he taught Maureen and me the importance of separating issues that were public from issues that were personal and private.

Become a storyteller. Practice the art of storytelling, and become a collector of stories that you can use in your personal interactions and even in public speaking. Dad loved to collect stories. He would write them down on index cards and try them out in his speeches. He kept the best stories, the ones that always got a reaction from the audience—and if a story fell flat, he'd toss the index card into the trash.

Stories are among the most powerful and persuasive tools you have as a communicator and influencer. Stories rivet the attention. Stories are memorable and make your ideas and lessons unforgettable. Stories are the ideal vehicle for smuggling truth into the minds of your children or your audiences. Most of Dad's stories had a kernel of truth in them. Sometimes the "moral of the story" was so obvious you couldn't miss it. Sometimes it was almost subliminal in its subtlety. But most of the stories Dad told had a point to make. He used them as instruments of influence.

During the 1976 campaign, I did a lot of speaking on Dad's behalf—and I was terrible. So I asked him, "What's the best lesson you can teach me about speaking?"

"Michael," he said, "it's pretty simple. Remember that while you may be giving that speech for the fifteenth time that day, it's the first time your audience has heard it. So deliver it like it's the first time you've said it."

"Anything else I should know?"

"Always start with a story with a great punchline. Here's a story that always works at political gatherings. There was a cattle rustler in Texas who stole a bunch of cattle. The sheriff assembled a posse to track him. After a few days, they caught up to him. There being no need for a fair trial, they threw a rope over a hanging tree, set the cattle rustler on a horse, and put the noose around his neck. The sheriff said, 'Before you die, you have five minutes to make your peace with the Lord.'

"The thief said, 'I don't need five minutes.'

"A politician in the posse raised his hand and said, 'May I have those five minutes?'"

I've used that story many times, and Dad was right—it never fails, especially in a roomful of politicians.

"The next story," Dad said, "works well at religious gatherings. There was a man who wanted to be a preacher. He practiced and practiced his sermon, and on Sunday, he stepped up into the pulpit, looked out over the pews—but there was only one parishioner in the church.

"The pastor stepped out of the pulpit and said to the man, 'I've been working on this sermon for a long time. Do you want to hear it?'

"The man said, 'Pastor, I'm a rancher. When I get up to feed my cows in the morning, if only one cow shows up, I feed it.'

"So the preacher went back to the pulpit and preached his sermon for the next hour and a half. When he was finished, he said, 'What did you think of my first sermon?'

"The rancher said, 'Pastor, I told you that if only one cow shows up, I feed it. But Pastor, I don't feed it the whole load.'"

I've used that story many times as well. Take it from the Great Communicator—if you start with a story, you'll never go wrong. Stories get attention, stories put your audience at ease, and stories can become parables that teach important lessons. To be a person of influence, become a storyteller.

Look for opportunities to influence the next generation. Dad wrote countless letters to young fans when he was a Hollywood star, and he continued that practice when he was governor of California and president of the United States. He wasn't thinking about what the public could do for him, but what he could do for his public. The story of the blind children who touched my father's face is just one example among many of how he was always influencing the next generation—and he preferred to do so without any reporters or photographers around.

Good people have great influence. If you want to have great influence, be a person who blesses the next generation with good words and a good example. Invest your life in influencing others.

5

Make Your Marriage Work

IN JUNE 1971, when I was twenty-six, I married a young woman of eighteen. I had known her and her family for years. She came from an intact family, and I wanted to be part of that, so I really went into the marriage for the wrong reasons. The wedding took place on Maui. Maureen and Mom helped with the arrangements. Though Dad and Nancy couldn't come, he sent a letter to me a few days before the wedding, and I got misty-eyed as I read it:

Dear Mike,

You've heard all the jokes that have been rousted around by all the "unhappy marrieds" and cynics. Now, in case no one has suggested it, there is another viewpoint. You have entered into the most meaningful relationship there is in all human life. It can be whatever you decide to make it.

Some men feel their masculinity can only be proven if they play out in their own life all the locker-room stories, smugly confident that what a wife doesn't know won't hurt her. The truth is, somehow, way down inside, without her ever finding lipstick on the collar or catching a man in the flimsy excuse of where he was till three a.m., a wife does know, and with that knowing, some of the magic of this relationship disappears.

There are more men griping about marriage who kicked the whole thing away themselves than there can ever be wives deserving of blame. There is an old law of physics that you can only get out of a thing as much as you put in it. The man who puts into the marriage only half of what he owns will get that out.

Sure, there will be moments when you will see someone or think back on an earlier time and you will be challenged to see if you can still make the grade, but let me tell you how really great is the challenge of proving your masculinity and charm with one woman for the rest of your life. Any man can find a twerp here and there who will go along with cheating, and it doesn't take all that much manhood. It does take quite a man to remain attractive and to be loved by a woman who has heard him snore, seen him unshaven, tended him while he was sick and washed his dirty underwear. Do that and keep her still feeling a warm glow and you will know some very beautiful music.

If you truly love a girl, you shouldn't ever want her to feel, when she sees you greet a secretary or a girl you both know, that humiliation of wondering if she was someone who caused you to be late coming home, nor should you want any other woman to be able to meet your wife and know she was smiling behind her eyes as she looked at her, the woman you love, remembering this was the woman you rejected even momentarily for her favors.

Mike, you know better than many what an unhappy home is and what it can do to others. Now you have a chance to make it come out the way it should. There is no greater happiness for a man than approaching a door at the end of a day knowing someone on the other side of that door is waiting for the sound of his footsteps.

Love, Dad

PS: You'll never get in trouble if you say "I love you" at least once a day.

Notice Dad's apologetic tone when he mentioned "an unhappy home." I know he felt that the divorce had shortchanged Maureen and me. With this letter of advice, he was hoping to spare me some of the heartbreak he'd gone through—and he was hoping that any future children I might have would be spared that heartbreak as well.

I wish I could say that Dad's advice enabled my bride and me to live happily ever after, but that was not to be. Breaking up wasn't my idea, but in the end, my first marriage—like Dad's first marriage—ended in divorce.

My first wife and I had been living in another state, so after the divorce, I returned to California feeling defeated, humiliated, and lonely. It truly felt like the end of everything. I called Maureen and she said that I should talk to Dad, and he would help me gain some perspective. If anyone understood what I was going through, he did.

So I went to Pacific Palisades and sat down with Dad and Nancy in their living room. Nancy sat quietly, and Dad did most of the talking.

"Michael," he said, "I think I have a pretty good idea what you must be going through right now. I was raised to believe that divorce is unthinkable. So when your mother divorced me, I couldn't imagine a worse fate. I didn't think I'd ever get out of the doldrums—until Nancy came into my life. Something wonderful will happen to you one day. I know you may not believe it now, but I promise you, it will. Meanwhile, all you can do is pull yourself up by your bootstraps and get on with your life."

I was so mired in hurt and self-pity that I couldn't believe what Dad was telling me. I couldn't believe that real love and a great marriage were in my future. But in this, as in most things, Dad turned out to be right.

God's Angel of Healing in My Life

On December 7, 1973, a boat-racing buddy and his wife invited me to dinner to meet a young lady named Colleen Sterns. She was everything Dad said I would find—and more (blind dates do work!). Her best quality was one I didn't appreciate at the time: Colleen was a Christian.

And what was I? I'd been raised Catholic, baptized with Mom and Maureen on the Feast of the Immaculate Conception, December 8, 1954—but I had never internalized the faith. I was tormented by guilt over the molestation, and wounded by taunts of "bastard" from kids who knew I was adopted. (To this day, some on Twitter and Facebook call me "illegitimate" and not a true Reagan; they call Dad my "stepfather." Cruel children never grow up.)

God chose Colleen to be His angel of healing in my soul. She was patient with my anger and she gently confronted the sin in my life. She, too, believed that God had brought us together for a purpose. I couldn't understand how she could be so sure, but she was right.

In 1975, after Colleen and I had been dating for two years, Nancy began calling us, urging us to set the date. Nancy knew that Dad was preparing to run for president. He had missed my first wedding because of a prior commitment to attend the wedding of Richard Nixon's daughter, Tricia. Nancy said, "You'd better get married soon if you want your father to attend."

So Colleen and I planned the wedding for November 7, 1975, in a chapel across from Disneyland. Most of Colleen's family from Nebraska flew in. My sister Maureen couldn't attend, but my mother, Jane Wyman, arrived in a limousine wearing a gold lamé gown.

Dad and Nancy arrived late, and Nancy wore an elegant green outfit with a mink collar. They sat across the center aisle from Mom.

After the ceremony, Colleen and I stood by the altar for wedding pictures. When the photographer asked for the father and mother of the groom to come up, we realized there was one detail we had forgotten to settle: Who would be in those pictures as "mother of the groom"? If Dad and Nancy were in the picture, that would upset Mom. But how would Nancy feel if Mom was in the picture?

Mom looked around in hesitation. Nancy looked at Dad— and he stared straight ahead. I feared the worst.

Then Mom stood up, looked straight at Nancy, and said, "Don't worry, Nancy. Ron and I have had our picture taken together, and if you'd like to join us, please do. Now Ron, come on, the photographer's waiting."

Instantly, the tension broke.

Dad and Nancy came up and we had our picture taken. Afterward, we went to the reception. There, Dad took me aside and said, "Michael, remember that letter I sent you a few years ago about marriage? Everything I wrote in that letter still stands."

I still live by the advice that Dad gave me in that letter. I especially make a point of staying true to the advice Dad gave me in the PS—I tell Colleen I love her every day, and I haven't missed a day since we've been married.

A Hundred-Hundred Proposition

Twelve days after our wedding, Dad announced he was running for president of the United States. He campaigned hard in the primary against incumbent President Gerald Ford and came up just a few delegates short.

Four years later, Dad ran again—and this time he clinched the nomination and went on to defeat Jimmy Carter to become president. Upon entering the White House, Dad did something he had never done before: he started keeping a diary. His White House diaries were edited by historian Douglas Brinkley and published by HarperCollins in 2007. In Dad's entry for March 4, 1981, he wrote: "Our wedding anniversary. 29 years of more happiness than any man could rightly deserve."[1]

Near the end of that month, on March 30, a mentally disturbed loner shot my father and three others outside the Washington Hilton Hotel. Dad nearly died. He later wrote a detailed account of that day, including his thoughts upon coming out of the anesthesia after surgery: "I opened my eyes once to find Nancy there. I pray I'll never face a day when she isn't there. Of all the ways God has blessed me, giving her to me is the greatest and beyond anything I can ever hope to deserve."[2]

(I didn't understand that magnitude of love until November 2015, when I awoke after quadruple bypass surgery and the first vision I saw was the face of my wife Colleen.)

My father believed in old-fashioned, Bible-based morality— not because he was a prude, but because he believed that the Bible offered sensible guidelines for living a happy life. Sure, he sowed a few wild oats in his early Hollywood days—but deep inside, he was still Nelle Reagan's son, the good Christian boy who taught Sunday school in the church basement in Dixon, Illinois. And he wanted his children to grow up with the same moral values he had.

So Dad found it troubling when he learned in 1974 that my sister Patti had moved in with guitarist Bernie Leadon of the rock group The Eagles. Dad was rarely confrontational with his children, but on this occasion, he told Patti that living together with this young man was immoral, and the young man would not be welcome in their home. When Patti demanded to know what was wrong with a man and woman living together without the benefit of clergy, Dad told her, "It's a sin in the eyes of God. It's in the Bible."

What Dad didn't know was that Patti wasn't the only sinner in the Reagan family—and that was fine with me. As long as Patti was on the hot-seat, the heat would be off the rest of us.

Dad believed that God's plan for strong, healthy families is found in the Bible. And that plan is for a man and a woman to marry for life. Dad knew the suffering divorce causes. Yes, there can be redemption and a new beginning after a divorce. But there would be fewer broken lives and fewer damaged children if parents would follow the biblical prescription for a happy, healthy family.

My sister Maureen told me that Dad once sat her down and had a long talk with her about the importance of saving herself for the right man. He wanted Maureen to have an elevated view of marriage and of her own worth as a young woman. Dad told her, "Out there, somewhere, is your future husband. Don't waste your body on someone who isn't your lifelong mate." Years later, Maureen said, Dad had the same conversation with Patti.

If you are a dad, the best thing you can do for your children is to love your wife. If you are a mom, the best thing you can do for your children is to love your husband. As Colleen has often told me, "Divorce is not an option." We recently celebrated our fortieth wedding anniversary by getting married in the Catholic Church.

Maintaining a healthy marriage is hard work—but it's also a joy. I enjoy spending time with Colleen. When I come home from work, I pour two glasses of wine, sit down with Colleen, and we talk. We share. We enjoy each other's company.

Many people enter marriage through the front door, but they keep an eye on the back door for a possible escape. They think that love is a feeling, an emotional high. Then when the emotions subside, and they discover that a big part of marriage is paying the bills, doing laundry, washing the dishes, and taking out the garbage, they ask, "Where did the love go? I don't feel all fluttery and tingly. I guess we're not in love anymore. Time to call it quits."

But the kind of love that makes marriage work isn't a feeling. It's a decision. True love is a decision to put your marriage partner ahead of yourself, to serve instead of being served, to give instead of taking, to swallow pride instead of insisting on rights. To build a stronger marriage, you'll do whatever it takes—go to counseling or marriage seminars, stay up until two in the morning to talk, apologize even when you think you're right, and more.

Why do you sacrifice your own wants and needs in order to make the marriage work? You do it for the sake of your husband or wife. You do it for the sake of your kids. And yes, you even do it for your own sake because divorce is one of the worst things you could possibly inflict on yourself and your family.

I've heard people say, "Marriage is a fifty-fifty proposition." Wrong. Marriage is a hundred-hundred proposition. If you go into marriage thinking it's a fifty-fifty partnership, then you'll always be trying to draw a line down the middle—and you'll be arguing about who's keeping up his or her half.

I give Colleen most of the credit for keeping our family together through the tough times in our marriage. She had the character I lacked, she had the faith I needed, and I thank God every day that I married above me.

In a healthy marriage, both sides accept full responsibility for the entire relationship. When you are 100 percent committed to making the entire relationship work, not just to your half of the rights and your half of the responsibilities, you'll go farther and work harder to make the relationship succeed.

Lessons in Building a Healthy, Happy Marriage

The letter my father wrote meant a lot to me when I first read it— but it meant even more when I was entering my second marriage.

The older I was, the more I realized that Dad was not just sharing his favorite platitudes with me. He was speaking from his heart, from his own experience, and from everything he had learned over the years.

Here are some of the lessons I learned from my father about how to make a marriage work:

Understand the power of the past to impact the future. People sometimes question the strong role that Nancy had in my father's life and why Dad allowed Nancy to have so much control. And I think we can find the answer to that question by looking into Dad's past. His father, Jack Reagan, was a good man who worked hard and cared for his family. But Jack was also an alcoholic. His alcoholism weakened and undermined him as a role model for my father.

Nelle, Dad's mother, was a strong woman who absolutely ruled the roost. Nelle and my mother, Jane Wyman, were very good friends, and Mom used to refer to Nelle as "the first Hollywood mother." After Nelle moved to California, she went everywhere with Dad, including his auditions and interviews. My father came from a generation where the father worked outside the home and the mother stayed home and managed the household, and that included being very involved in the lives of children.

After my father and mother divorced, Dad was so devastated that he determined that he would keep his next marriage together, no matter what. He would never go through the agony of divorce again. So he did everything he could to make sure that his marriage to Nancy remained strong, even if that meant deferring to her in order to keep the peace.

Nancy had her own childhood problems to deal with—and her issues were a perfect complement to Dad's issues. Nancy's birth father walked out the day she was born. Nancy's mother, stage actress Edith "Edie" Luckett, placed Nancy with an aunt for several years. Edie resumed her stage career in order to support herself and Nancy. When Nancy was eight years old, Edie married Loyal Davis, a prominent neurosurgeon, who formally adopted Nancy in 1935. Though Nancy had a good relationship with her new father, she never forgot what it felt like to be abandoned by her birth father—and she was determined that no man would ever walk out on her again.

So here were two people, Ronald Reagan and Nancy Reagan, one determined never to have another failed marriage, the other terrified of abandonment. The two of them were so tightly fused together by the experiences of their past that even their own children felt as if they were on the outside looking in.

I spent years being angry over the divorce and being sent away to boarding school. But as I grew older, I began to ask myself, "What was Dad's reason for doing what he did? What was Mom's reason for doing what she did? What was Nancy's reason for doing what she did?" The more I came to terms with Dad's past, Mom's past, and Nancy's past, the more everything seemed to fall into place. Looking at Dad's early family, I see that Nelle ran the household, and that was the only family pattern my father knew. So he married Mom, a very strong woman much like Nelle, and she ran the household, too. Later, when Dad married Nancy, she gave up her Hollywood career and she ran the household, too.

And you know what? I'm no different from my father. My wife Colleen is in charge of our household. I'm in charge of my career decisions, and the choices I make to support my family. I defer to her on household issues. I'm not saying that all marriages should function that way. There's no one-size-fits-all pattern for marriage. But this pattern worked for Dad and Nancy, and it works for Colleen and me.

Focus on winning the relationship, not the argument. Let me share with you the Michael Reagan "Rules for a Good Marriage."

There are only two rules, and both of these rules are directed at the husband:

1. *Never win an argument in her house.*
2. *Never lose an argument in the privacy of your own car.*

First rule: The house you share is not your house, it's hers. If you disagree, try this: Give the family dog a bath, then let that soaking-wet dog run through the house. You'll hear, "Get that dog out of my house!" Not "our house"—"my house." So never win an argument in her home. If you win the argument, you'll lose the relationship. Learn the art of saying, "I'm sorry," and you'll win the relationship.

But don't forget rule number two: Never lose an argument in your car. Do what I do: get in your car and yell at the right front seat.

You're watching football and your wife says, "Honey, would you go to the market for me?" Don't argue, don't complain. Just get in your car and go to the market. While you drive, rant and yell and take out your frustration on the right front seat.

That's what I do, and when I get back from the market, I hand the groceries to the love of my life, give her a kiss, and she's happy. Then I sit down, watch the game, and I'm happy. (Meanwhile, in the garage, the right front seat of my car is cringing.)

Where did I learn this marriage-saving principle? From Dad, of course.

One Christmas, I gave Dad a McCulloch Power Mac 6 chainsaw as a Christmas present. The following year, Nancy called and asked, "Michael, you know that chainsaw you gave your father—do they make bigger ones?"

I connected her with some people at McCulloch, and today there are two chainsaws on display at Rancho Del Cielo—the chainsaw I gave him and the bigger one Nancy gave him. Dad dearly loved Nancy—but we all have frustrations with our spouses. Between you and me, Dad often worked off his frustration with Nancy by mowing down trees with a chainsaw.

Respect your marriage relationship. Dad called marriage "the most meaningful relationship there is in all human life." These days, however, marriage is ridiculed in much of our entertainment media and neglected by many in our culture. Our own government places a "marriage penalty" in the tax code, creating a financial incentive for couples to simply "shack up." These trends spell disaster for the children in these relationships.

In 1960, only 5 percent of babies in America were born to unmarried women. By 1995, 32 percent of babies were born to unmarried women. By 2008, that figure had risen to 41 percent. And those numbers continue to rise.[3] Children born out of wedlock tend to suffer higher rates of poverty, illiteracy, abuse, and other tragic consequences.

We need to restore respect for marriage as a safe place where vows are kept and children are protected. Marriage is not just a "piece of paper," as some people would have you believe. Marriage is a sacred covenant, established in the eyes of God and the community in order to create this safe enclosure we call a "home." Marriage is not intended to be a trap that imprisons people in a relationship. It's a set of boundaries that protect two people who love each other from the corrosive forces of the outside world.

If you maintain an attitude of respect for your marriage, if you view the boundaries of your marriage as a defensive wall around your fortress instead of a prison wall, you and your marriage partner will have a safe enclosure in which your love for each other can flourish. It will also be a safe place in which to raise happy, emotionally healthy children.

What if you're already divorced? Well, do what my mother and father did: make your *divorce* work. Mom and Dad never said a disparaging word about each other—not in public, not in private. They never tried to get back at each other through Maureen and me. They always treated each other with respect, civility, and courtesy. Even though they were no longer married to each other, they respected the marriage they'd once had. They made their divorce work for the benefit of my sister and me.

For most of my life, I assumed that Mom and Dad had almost nothing to do with each other after the divorce. Yes, they had to talk now and then about parenting issues involving Maureen and me—but I figured they only discussed practical matters, such as when to pick us up from school or where we would be for Christmas.

But after my mother passed away, I was going through her effects, and I found a packet of letters. I keep them in a safe deposit box because they are letters my father wrote to my mother, thanking her for donating to his campaigns for governor and president. I was amazed to learn that Mom used to support Dad's political career with substantial donations, and he sent her letters of appreciation. What made those letters all the more amazing to me was that, for all those years, I thought Mom was a Democrat!

Be faithful. Some people say, "What my wife doesn't know won't hurt her." Dad knew better. He said that, way down deep, one partner always suffers when the other cheats. That deceived partner may not know for sure what is wrong—but something has gone out of the relationship. If you think you can cheat and no one will be hurt, you're not just lying to your marriage partner—you're lying to yourself. Keep your marriage vows sacred. Be faithful.

Say the words. And the words I'm talking about, of course, are "I love you." That's the advice Dad gave me in the PS to his letter, "You'll never get in trouble if you say 'I love you' at least once a day."

Of course, along with saying the words every day, we need to make sure that our actions match our words. Often, marriage partners—especially husbands—will say, "You already know I love you. I do this and that for you. I'm always there for you. I wouldn't be here if I didn't love you."

Yes, the actions of love are crucial. But the words of love are powerful, and we tend to underestimate the power of our words.

We need to express our love in words. When one partner in the marriage withholds those words, the other partner wonders why. Instead of asking, "Why do I need to say the words?" We should flip that question around and ask ourselves, "Why am I afraid to say those words? If I truly love this person, why wouldn't I want to say the words that he or she wants to hear?"

When you say "I love you" to someone you truly care about, don't just toss it out there as if you are saying, "What's up?" or "How's it goin'?" Look into your loved one's eyes and say it like you mean it. If it seems like your expression of love is becoming routine or cliché, find unusual ways to say it. Leave love notes on his pillow at night or taped to her steering wheel before work. Email it or text it. Send flowers or chocolates and a note, for any reason or for no reason at all.

Are you going through tough times with your husband or wife? Are you dealing with some anger and resentment? Maybe you just don't feel like saying, "I love you." Well, this is a great time to start saying the words. Maybe the best time ever. Many marriages have been transformed when one partner chose to say "I love you" even when he or she didn't feel particularly romantic. Can you imagine how emotionally powerful it would be if, in the midst of a conflict, you were to say "I love you" and really mean it—even if you don't fully feel it.

One of the most important discoveries I ever made was the realization that authentic love is a *choice*, not a feeling. We can actually *choose* to love another person through our actions, even if we don't have warm, fuzzy feelings for that person. This is the kind of love the Bible talks about, "Love is patient, love is kind. It does not envy, it does not boast, it is not proud. It does not dishonor others, it is not self-seeking, it is not easily angered, it keeps no record of wrongs. Love does not delight in evil but rejoices with the truth. It always protects, always trusts, always hopes, always perseveres. Love never fails. . . . And now these three remain: faith, hope and love. But the greatest of these is love."[4]

You'd be amazed at how often, after saying "I love you" when you didn't feel like it, your feelings change. The moment you say "I love you," your feelings will probably begin to align with your words. By simply saying the words, you've taken your mind off your own grievances, and you've started to focus on your loved one. Those words have the power to make us less self-absorbed and more loving.

Those words are a gift to your husband or wife—and a gift to yourself. Take my father's word for it: you'll never get in trouble if you say "I love you" at least once a day.

6

Turn Defeats into Successes

Ronald Reagan first ran for president in 1968, only two years into his first term as governor of California. Though Dad only carried one state in the 1968 Republican primaries (compared with Richard Nixon's nine states), Dad actually won a greater proportion of the popular vote (37.93 percent) than Nixon (37.54 percent), who went on to win the nomination and the White House.

Dad sat out the 1972 race, and in late 1975, producer and retired brigadier general Frank McCarthy (who produced the 1970 blockbuster *Patton*) asked Dad to consider playing the title role in *MacArthur*. Dad declined because he considered himself retired from acting—and he was already gearing up to challenge GOP incumbent president Gerald Ford for the nomination in 1976. In February 1976, while Dad was campaigning in Iowa, McCarthy announced that Gregory Peck had been cast as General MacArthur.

The 1976 primary campaign was a bruising contest. With no support from the GOP power brokers, Dad waged a grass-roots campaign and nearly wrested the nomination from the sitting president. He carried twenty-three states; Ford won twenty-seven.

At the beginning of the 1976 Republican National Convention in Kansas City, there was still a chance he might capture the nomination in a roll-call vote of the delegates. But during dinner in Dad's hotel suite on the night before the roll-call vote, Dad informed us that the campaign had polled the delegates. He was going to come up short in the vote. My father had been defeated.

A melancholy mood settled over us. It was the first time I had ever seen my father lose at anything—and he handled the defeat in his usual upbeat style. "A man couldn't ask for a finer family," he said. And he thanked us for our support.

Later, Nancy poured champagne, then raised her glass and proposed a toast to Dad. We drank the toast—then Nancy said, "I'm sorry, Ronnie. I really believed you would win. But no matter what, we still have each other."

Dad smiled, took her hand, and said, "I love you. We gave it a good run, and that's all there is to say."

Later that evening, the suite was full of people, and the mood was somber.

I found myself sitting by the fireplace with Dad. I remember noticing that a fire blazed in the fireplace, even though it was August and it was hot outside. "Tell me, Dad," I said, "why do you want to be president?"

"Michael," he said, "for so many years, I've watched American presidents sit down to negotiate with Soviet leaders. And time after time, the Soviets have told us what we will have to give up in order to get along with them. I wanted to win the nomination and win the election so I could sit down at the negotiating table with the Secretary General of the Soviet Union. I would let him choose the place, choose the table, and select the chairs because that's how they do things at that level. And while the Soviet Secretary General was telling me, the American president, what we would have to give up to get along with them, I was going to get up from my chair, walk around to the other side of the table, lean over, and whisper in his ear—'nyet.' I want to be the first president to say 'nyet' to the Soviets."

That was August 1976. And as we sat there that night by the fireplace, Dad didn't know if he was going to run again in 1980. (Nancy hadn't told him yet.) So as far as my father knew, he had just come as close as he would ever be to realizing that dream.

But Dad did run in 1980—and he was inaugurated in 1981. In November 1985, in Geneva, Switzerland, Dad met face-to-face with Soviet General Secretary Mikhail Gorbachev. The Geneva summit was essentially an icebreaker, in which the two leaders would lay a foundation for future talks. The real test came in October 1986, in Reykjavík, Iceland—the summit where Secretary General Gorbachev told the American president what he would have to give up to get along with the Soviets: the Strategic Defense Initiative (SDI).

My father didn't literally stand up, walk around the table, and say "nyet" in Mr. Gorbachev's ear—but Dad did reject the Soviet demands. In fact, Dad demanded concessions from Gorbachev on a number of issues, including the Soviet occupation of Afghanistan and the denial of emigration by Jews and other dissidents. It had taken a little more than a decade, this journey from Kansas City to Reykjavík, from the defeat of August 1976 to the summit of October 1986.

But Dad finally got to tell Gorbachev that a new kind of president was on the job. No longer would America give ground to the Soviets, just to get along. Dad said "nyet," and the world began to change. The Reykjavík summit ended without an agreement— but it did not end in failure. On the flight home, Dad's longtime friend and advisor Charles Wick said, "Cheer up, Mr. President. You've just won the Cold War." And it was true. He had.

Thank God for Dad's steadfast commitment. Though his dream of an impenetrable missile defense shield was never deployed

(President Clinton scaled back SDI to a theater defense system), many SDI technologies have been deployed, including interceptor missiles, laser and particle beam weapons, and advanced sensor systems. Israel's Iron Dome missile shield, which is based on SDI technologies, has successfully intercepted hundreds of rockets and artillery shells, saving an untold number of lives.

As military historian Max Boot wrote in *Commentary* on November 18, 2012, "The latest Gaza war is only a few days old, but already one conclusion can be drawn: missile defense works. This is only the latest vindication for the vision of Ronald Reagan who is emerging as a consensus pick for one of the all-time great U.S. presidents."[1]

One of the most powerful and important lessons Dad taught me was not expressed in words, but in his example. The way he handled defeat with grace and optimism was crucial to his eventual success—and to the success of America in the 1980s and beyond. Dad parlayed his defeat in 1976 into the "Reagan Revolution" of the 1980s. He showed us all how to turn defeats into successes.

Defeat is never final unless we surrender to it. We *can* turn defeat into a launching pad for incredible success.

Breaking through the Clouds

On Sunday, April 27, 2014, Colleen, Ashley, and I had the privilege of being in St. Peter's Square at the Vatican for a double-canonization mass for John Paul II and John XXIII. We were guests of Newsmax president Christopher Ruddy, and our delegation included former president of Poland Lech Wałęsa, former House Speaker Newt Gingrich, and political commentator Dick Morris. The skies were overcast and most people in the crowd of 500,000 carried umbrellas.

A man standing next to me said, "It's too bad the weather is so gloomy."

"If I know God," I replied, "when the canonization takes place, you won't need your umbrella. The sun will shine on Pope John Paul II."

The skies were still cold and gray as the ceremony began. We listened to the homily of Pope Francis and received Holy Communion that he had blessed. When the pope made the canonization announcements, the clouds overhead were still unbroken.

Then as Floribeth Mora, the woman healed by a miracle, presented the relic of John Paul II to Pope Francis, it was as if another miracle took place. The dark sky parted, the sun broke through, and a brilliant light shone upon St. Peter's Square.

The man next to me looked at me in shock and said, "How did you know that was going to happen?"

I said, "Some things you just know."

How did I know? I knew because I had seen it happen before—on January 20, 1981, the day my father took the constitutional oath of office and became the fortieth president of the United States. That day, too, was dark and overcast, and the skies over Washington, D.C., threatened rain.

My father's left hand rested on the well-worn pages of his mother Nelle's Bible, which was opened to Nelle's favorite verse. In that verse, God tells King Solomon, "If my people, who are called by my name, will humble themselves and pray and seek my face and turn from their wicked ways, then I will hear from heaven, and I will forgive their sin and will heal their land."[2] In the margin, Nelle had written, "A most wonderful verse for the healing of nations."

After taking the oath, Dad kissed Nancy. Then he stepped up to the lectern and delivered his first inaugural address. As he spoke, the clouds overhead parted, and rays of golden sunlight shone upon the Capitol building and the vast crowd. It was a miraculous moment, as if God himself smiled down on the nation and its new leader.

That's how I knew the clouds would part again during the canonization mass of Pope John Paul II. Ronald Reagan and John Paul II were two men who were linked together by faith, by a spirit of forgiveness, and by a common destiny. God used these two men to collapse the Soviet empire and spread freedom around the world. It was only fitting that the light of the sun would break through the clouds on each man's special day.

The First Day of the Reagan Revolution

Of all the words Dad spoke during his first inaugural address, these are my favorite:

> We are too great a nation to limit ourselves to small dreams. We are not, as some would have us believe, doomed to an inevitable decline. I do not believe in a fate that will fall on us no matter what we do. I do believe in a fate that will fall on us if we do nothing. So with all the creative energy at our command, let us begin an era of national renewal. Let us renew our determination, our courage, and our strength. And let us renew our faith and our hope. We have every right to dream heroic dreams.

After the inauguration ceremony, we attended a luncheon in Statuary Hall of the Capitol. At the beginning of the luncheon, Dad received some exciting news, which he immediately passed on to the guests in the hall: after 444 days in captivity, more than 60 Americans were on their way home.

"I couldn't ask for a better Inaugural Day gift," Dad said. The hall erupted in cheers and applause. Dad offered former president Jimmy Carter a final trip aboard Air Force One so that he could go to Germany and greet the freed Americans.

The day was full of events, from a parade and a cocktail reception to a family photo session. I noticed that, as my father conducted his ceremonial duties, he was followed everywhere he went by a military attaché who carried a black briefcase—the nuclear launch codes. I remember thinking in amazement that the loving hands that held me when I was a baby now had the power to launch Armageddon.

That evening, Dad and Nancy were to make an appearance at nine inaugural balls in various ballrooms around the city. Colleen and I hosted the ball at the Washington Hilton Hotel (sixty-nine days later, Dad would be shot by a would-be assassin on the sidewalk outside that hotel). The Hilton ball was the first stop for the new president and first lady. Before going out to greet his guests, Dad checked his appearance in a mirror. He looked dashing in a white tie and tails.

Then he turned to us, jumped in the air, and clicked his heels—an astonishing achievement for a man almost seventy years old. "I'm the president of the United States!" he announced with boyish glee.

We all laughed, and I said, "Yes, Dad, you sure are!"

Then we went out and greeted our guests.

The first day of the Reagan Revolution was like something out of a fairy tale. Soon, however, the fairy tale was over and it was time to get to work.

Dad's diary shows that the very first order of business for the Reagan administration was a meeting on terrorism with the heads of the FBI, Secret Service, CIA, State Department, Defense Department, and others. In that meeting, Dad made decisions on rescinding some of Jimmy Carter's policies and executive orders that hindered the counterterrorism abilities of those agencies (then as now, terrorism was one of the first issues a president must deal with). Dad also chaired a cabinet meeting and sessions with congressional leaders on the economy.

At the end of a busy and productive first day in office, Dad remarked, "It's been a very wonderful day. I guess I can go back to California—can't I?"

Joking aside, Dad enjoyed the presidency as few presidents have, before or since. The job suited him, and he dignified and elevated the office of president more than anyone since Lincoln. From the historic Resolute desk in the Oval Office, Ronald Reagan changed the world. He faithfully executed the office of president of the United States. He preserved, protected, and defended the Constitution. And when my father handed the presidency over to his successor, the office was in much better condition than when he'd received it.

He used his defeat and failure in 1976 as a launching pad for his dreams of a better world—a world of economic opportunity for all, a world without the glowering presence of the Soviet "evil empire," a world in which America shone brightly like a city on a hill. My father didn't believe in small dreams.

During the eight years of his leadership, America recovered from the national trauma of Vietnam and Watergate, the disastrous Ford–Carter recession, and the humiliating Iranian hostage crisis. As America recovered, the American people learned that they could dream heroic dreams once more. We learned that, both as individuals and as a nation, we could turn past defeats into future successes.

It's time we relearned that lesson all over again. It's time to dream heroic dreams once more.

Willing to Do Whatever It Took

Dad almost never talked about failure. It was not a subject he liked to dwell on, He often talked about success—not his own successes, but what it takes to be successful in life. He taught me the importance of hard work, of doing my work well, of applying myself to my studies and to sports and to work, of setting goals and staying focused on those goals, and of persevering through obstacles and opposition.

So to learn how Dad responded to failure, I couldn't draw much from his words—but I learned a lot from studying his example.

I know it was hard for my father to talk about emotions, especially his feelings about failure. His father, Jack Reagan, was an alcoholic who would occasionally lose his job because of his drinking. Jack was not a mean drunk, but he often caused embarrassment to his devoutly Christian wife, Nelle, and his boys, Ronald and Neil. Sometimes Jack would simply leave the family for days, and Nelle would explain to the boys that their dad had a "sickness," and they should remember what a good man he was when he was sober.

The children of alcoholics tend to respond to their parents' example in one of two ways: they either adopt their parents' failings and habits, becoming alcoholics themselves, or they go to the opposite extreme. Though Dad admired many of his father's qualities, he chose to become the opposite of his father when it came to drinking. Throughout his life, Dad avoided alcohol except for the occasional glass of wine—or sometimes, after working hard at the ranch, a cold Budweiser with his ranch foreman.

My father had an experience when he was just eleven years old that had a deep and lasting impact on him. One winter night, he was returning home from the YMCA. Nelle, who worked part time as a seamstress, was away from home. As Dad approached the house, he found his father, Jack, lying among the snow drifts on the porch, reeking of whiskey. The young Ronald Reagan knew that the whole neighborhood could see his father passed out on the porch. So he opened the front door and dragged his father inside.

Dad learned at an early age to hide the shame of his father's failures. And if Dad suffered any failures of his own, he didn't talk about them. Failure just wasn't in his vocabulary. When I was a boy, he never let me see him in a moment of weakness. He never seemed to lack confidence and optimism, even during times in which (as I later learned) he was dealing with major crises in his career.

In the early 1950s, Dad's film career foundered. So Dad took a job emceeing a comedy show at The Last Frontier in Las Vegas. A Vegas night club was often the last stop in an entertainer's fading career—but Dad was willing to do anything to provide for his family.

Audiences loved him and the gig paid well. But when the night club offered him a four-week extension, Dad declined. Better screen roles were trickling in, including scripts for *Cattle Queen of Montana* and *Hellcats of the Navy*. Dad was eager to get back in front of the camera.

I remember some advice Dad gave me during one of our rides to the ranch. He said, "If you're an out-of-work actor in Oshkosh, maybe you should move." In other words, do whatever it takes and go wherever the jobs are in order to make a living.

Dad's advice kept me focused and motivated when I got into talk radio. The only station that offered me my own show was in San Diego, more than 120 miles from my home. So I made that long commute every weekday to provide for my wife and two children. One of the most important lessons my father taught me was to go anywhere, do anything—just be the breadwinner.

A few months after turning down the extension in Vegas, Dad won a part that was sought by such top-drawer actors as Walter Pidgeon and Kirk Douglas—hosting television's *General Electric Theater* on CBS. In show business and in politics, timing is everything. *GE Theater* would ultimately steer him into the realm of politics.

After a time of struggle and failure, Dad's time was coming.

Signposts to Success

My father always made the best of bad situations. That was the narrative of his life. When his motion picture career began to fade, he found television. When his television career began to fade, he found politics. Again and again, he used failure as a launching pad for his next big success. What seemed like a fading career in one field always opened up new worlds to conquer.

Dad began hosting *General Electric Theater* in 1954. Under his contract with GE, he toured the country by train, visiting GE plants and meeting workers while giving hundreds of speeches to business and civic groups. GE never told him what to say—or what not to say. *General Electric Theater* aired Sunday nights at nine, and always ranked in the top ten. So it came as a shock when, one day in 1962, Dad called the family together and told us the show was canceled and he had been fired by GE.

Why would CBS cancel a successful show? Answer: CBS didn't. General Electric pulled the plug. While GE was negotiating government contracts, Robert F. Kennedy, the Attorney General of the United States, informed GE that, in order to do business with the government, the company needed to cancel *General Electric Theater* and fire the host, Ronald Reagan. The Kennedy administration had been monitoring Dad's speeches and didn't like what he was saying. So the show was canceled and my father was out of a job.

All too often in America today, people say, "I won't take that job—it's beneath me." My father never saw *any* job as beneath him. What some people would call a "dead-end job," he saw as a stepping stone. A job other people would consider embarrassing, he saw as a doorway to a new opportunity. Being the opening act at The Last Frontier was not his dream job—but it provided a paycheck until General Electric came along. Losing his job with GE was a huge disappointment—but it opened up new possibilities, including his run for governor of California four years later. My father always used the setbacks in his life as bridges to the next plateau.

One memory from my father's boyhood had a huge impact on his view of work. I remember Dad telling the story—and the somber look in his eyes as he told it. One Christmas Eve during the Great Depression, when Dad's mother Nelle worked as a seamstress and his father Jack was a traveling shoe salesman, a letter arrived at their apartment. Jack was happy when he saw that the letter came from his employer, the shoe company. "I'll bet this is my Christmas bonus," he said.

Jack opened the letter, began reading and then swore. "They laid me off."

It took weeks for Jack to find another job—and his new job was in a town 200 miles away. But Jack did what he had to for the sake of his family. The lesson of that bleak Christmas stayed with my father for life. It was a lesson he shared with me, and I often thought of the Christmas letter story during my own tough times. A good provider does whatever it takes to care for his family, even if he has to reinvent himself, take a "lesser" job, or move 200 miles away.

I don't remember Dad ever saying to me, "Michael, notice how I keep reinventing myself. Notice how I keep turning old defeats into new successes." But I listened to his stories and I watched his life. I absorbed the lessons of his failures and triumphs. The way he lived his life spoke volumes to me, and I watched him reinvent himself again and again.

From Dad, I learned that I didn't have to be locked into a single career for life. I could go from the trucking dock to a job at Matrix Science Corporation, a company that produced components for the space shuttle. I could be a boat racer one week and a boat salesman the next. I could be an after-dinner speaker one week and a radio talk show host the next. I recreated and reinvented myself many times to take care of my family and keep my career moving forward.

Here are some of the lessons I have learned from my father's example:

Failure is a great teacher. Failure teaches us unforgettable lessons that lead to success—if we are willing to be taught. Dad was always willing to learn the lessons of failure.

The 1976 primary battle between President Ford and Governor Reagan was brutal. Dad lost the first six contests—Iowa, New Hampshire, Massachusetts, Vermont, Florida, and Illinois. Next stop: North Carolina. Contributions were drying up and the campaign was $2 million in debt. The campaign plane sat on the tarmac—there was no money for fuel. If Dad lost in North Carolina, he'd have to quit the race.

At that point, North Carolina Senator Jesse Helms stepped in and saved Dad's political career. Helms' endorsement and grassroots organization handed Dad an upset victory in North Carolina—Dad's first win of the 1976 primaries. From there, he went on to big wins in Texas, Georgia, California, and other major states.

As the Republican convention neared, Dad saw that President Ford was having success with his "Rose Garden strategy"—swaying uncommitted delegates by inviting them to the White House. Following the advice of consultants, Dad tried to counter Ford's strategy with a surprise move. Hoping to win over moderate Republicans by "balancing the ticket," Dad named moderate Pennsylvania senator Richard Schweiker as his running mate.

Dad's decision didn't sit well with the Senator from North Carolina. Helms launched a "draft Buckley" campaign to nominate James L. Buckley (brother of William F. Buckley), to derail Dad's campaign. Though Helms would become one of Dad's closest political allies in 1980, he road-blocked Dad's quest for the nomination in 1976.

My father learned from his mistake and returned to California, where he continued to speak and write and hone his message about the issues he believed in. He vowed never to water down his conservative credentials with a "ticket-balancing" move before the convention. From then on, he preached a political philosophy of "bold colors," not "pale pastels."

He knew his time would come again. When it came, he was ready.

Learn to look at failure from a different perspective. If you have a tendency to be down on yourself when things go wrong, find a more positive perspective on the experience. Instead of saying, "I screwed up again," say, "I learned a valuable lesson." Both statements may be perfectly accurate appraisals of the situation, but one reinforces defeat, while the other looks forward to success.

Dad was a born optimist. He didn't waste time lamenting his loss in 1976. As soon as he knew that his quest for the nomination was over, he began looking forward to new challenges.

When Dad lost the nomination in 1976, Maureen and I hoped Gerald Ford would ask Dad to be his running mate. Because of Dad's age, we didn't think he'd get another chance to run for national office. So it was a crushing blow to our hopes when Mr. Ford didn't even ask Dad to consider joining the ticket— crushing to Maureen and me, but not to our father.

Dad's first thought after losing the nomination was not a comeback in 1980, but, "How do I pay my bills today?" As it turned out, the answer was to go right back where he started, behind a radio microphone. He began recording weekly syndicated radio commentaries immediately after losing the nomination. Those commentaries not only helped pay his bills, but they also built his reputation as an opinion leader. He also formed a political action committee, headed by Lynn Nofziger, which enabled him to support conservative candidates at every level. Those candidates later supported Dad when he ran again in 1980.

Dad didn't fail at much—but when he did, he failed forward. He didn't stay down, he bounced back—and the bounce came from his optimism. For some, like my father, optimism seems to come naturally. But even if you're not a natural-born optimist, you can acquire optimism as a learned skill. You can nurture close friendships with optimistic people and absorb their positive attitude. Shake off the gloom of failure, and start making plans for your next big success.

Accept mistakes and failures as normal. Everybody makes mistakes. Everybody fails at one time or another. Successful people usually make more mistakes than the rest of us because making mistakes means you're trying. If you never fail at anything, you are probably not risking and not putting out enough effort. Successful people embrace mistakes and failures as necessary stepping-stones to success.

It's said that Thomas Edison tried thousands of substances to use as the filament for his electric lightbulb before he discovered that tungsten provided the perfect combination of electrical resistance, brilliance, and durability. Asked if he considered his earlier experiments to be failures, he replied, "I haven't failed. I've just found ten thousand ways that won't work."

Be prepared to make mistakes and encounter setbacks along the way. Don't be dismayed. They're just signposts on the road to success.

Accept the responsibility for your mistakes and failures. When people try to shift the blame for their failures onto "bad luck" or other people, they short-circuit the learning process. Instead of saying, "What can I learn from this failure?," they say, "Why am I always the victim of other people's incompetence?"

We can't learn from our mistakes if we don't own them. When we admit our failures to ourselves and others, we actually take control of the situation. When we say, "I made this mistake, and I will learn from it and succeed next time," we are actually saying, "I have the power to affect my own destiny." Until we accept responsibility, we reject our ability to control our lives. Accepting blame can be an enormously empowering experience.

Recent scandals, such as the deadly "Fast and Furious" gun-walking operation, the IRS persecution of Tea Party groups, and the 2012 Benghazi attack cover-up, have conditioned us to expect deception, blame-shifting, stonewalling, and obstruction from our leaders. But when a serious foreign-policy scandal threatened my father's administration in 1986, he acted swiftly and decisively—and he took personal responsibility. Many Americans forget that such principled leadership once existed in the Oval Office.

The Iran–Contra scandal grew out of a plan hatched by the CIA and the National Security Council to circumvent the Boland amendment, which forbade U.S. aid to the anti-Communist Contra rebels in Nicaragua. The Iran–Contra affair was first exposed by a Lebanese magazine on November 3, 1986, a month after a CIA cargo plane was shot down over Nicaragua. On November 13, ten days after Iran–Contra became public, my father addressed the nation from the Oval Office, promising an independent investigation of the matter.

On November 25, he announced the creation of an independent review commission consisting of Republican senator John Tower, former Democratic secretary of state Edmund Muskie, and former national security adviser Brent Scowcroft. The Tower Commission began its work on December 1, and the first witness, Ronald Reagan, appeared before them on December 2. The Tower Commission completed its work in less than three months and delivered its report on February 26, 1987. Six days later, on March 4, my father again addressed the nation from the Oval Office, taking responsibility and apologizing to the nation:

> First, let me say I take full responsibility for my own actions and for those of my administration. As angry as I may be about activities undertaken without my knowledge, I am

still accountable for those activities. As disappointed as I may be in some who served me, I'm still the one who must answer to the American people for this behavior. . . .

As the Tower board reported, what began as a strategic opening to Iran deteriorated, in its implementation, into trading arms for hostages. This runs counter to my own beliefs, to administration policy, and to the original strategy we had in mind. . . . But as President, I cannot escape responsibility.[3]

It took my father just four months—from November 3, 1986, to March 4, 1987—to lay the Iran–Contra scandal to rest. That is the benchmark for how to deal with a scandal. You own your mistakes, you tell the truth, you get the facts on the table, and you apologize. Once my father apologized for Iran–Contra, the issue became a nonissue—and the final two years of his administration were hugely successful.

Among the achievements of those final two years were the "Tear Down This Wall" speech at the Brandenburg Gate, the Washington and Moscow summits with Mikhail Gorbachev, and the end of the Cold War. Another, less well-known achievement of the final two years of my father's administration was his veto of a June 1987 attempt by Congress to preempt the Federal Communications Commission and reinstate the unconstitutional Fairness Doctrine. My father's veto defended the First Amendment and made the world safe for conservative radio hosts like Rush Limbaugh, Sean Hannity, and Michael Reagan.

If my father had not acted swiftly and apologized to the American people, those final two years would have been consumed by scandal and marked by failure. The American people are good-hearted and forgiving, and they will accept you if you apologize and own your mistakes. But people don't like being lied to and stonewalled. When my father apologized for Iran–Contra, he made it possible for his administration to finish strong and achieve his goal of winning the Cold War.

The lesson of this story: honestly accept responsibility for your past failures, and you'll open the door to future success.

Remember that failure is temporary—unless you surrender. Perseverance is essential to turning failures into success. The dream only dies when you give up on it.

Many of us in the Reagan family concluded that Dad's loss in 1976 was the end of the dream. We thought that by 1980, when Dad would be pushing seventy, he'd be too old to run. We underestimated him. But Dad never lost faith in the dream. Yes, for a while he became wistful about losing the chance to say "nyet" to the Soviets. But he never thought the dream was over—just deferred.

While flying back to California after the Kansas City convention, one of my father's policy advisors, Marty Anderson, asked Dad to autograph his convention pass as a souvenir. Dad wrote, "We dreamed—we fought, and the dream is still with us. Ronald Reagan." Those are hardly the words of a guy who thinks he's seen his last rodeo. He knew that a bigger opportunity could come again in four years.

Summon all your creative energy, then renew your determination, your courage, and your strength. Above all, renew your faith and your hope. As Dad would say, you have every right to dream heroic dreams.

7

Don't Worry about Who Gets the Credit

THE SOVIET UNION AND East Germany began building the Berlin Wall in August 1961. The Wall stood for nearly three decades, and during that time more than 200 people were killed attempting to escape from East Berlin to the West.

My father hated that wall from the moment he heard about it. He first spoke out publicly, demanding that the Wall come down, in a nationally televised debate with Robert F. Kennedy on May 15, 1967. He repeated that call the following year in a May 21, 1968, speech in Miami. Ten years later, during a speaking and fact-finding tour of Europe, Dad visited the Wall with a number of advisors, including Peter Hannaford and Richard V. Allen. Glaring angrily at the concrete barrier and guard towers beyond the broad "death strip" separating East and West, Dad said to his companions, "We have got to find a way to knock this thing down."[1]

Immediately after his inauguration in 1981, my father went to work on his goal of dismantling the Berlin Wall—and the oppressive Soviet empire that erected it. He pursued what came to be known as the Reagan Doctrine—a rejection of Nixon-Ford-Carter-era détente, an end to the truce with Communism, and a concerted effort to provide material support to people fighting for freedom in places like Angola, Nicaragua, Afghanistan, Poland, and yes, East Germany.

On January 17, 1983, my father signed National Security Decision Directive 75 (NSDD-75), which secretly but formally committed the United States of America to a strategy of confronting Communist aggression and destabilizing the Soviet economy. Norman A. Bailey, president of the Institute for Global Economic Growth and a former member of the National Security Council, called NSDD-75 "the strategic plan that won the Cold War."[2]

My father repeatedly tried to warn Mikhail Gorbachev that the United States would break the Russian economy if the Soviets continued to pursue nuclear superiority. At their first summit in Geneva, in November 1985, Dad warned Gorbachev that the Soviets would be "driven into bankruptcy" by the arms race. Gorbachev wouldn't listen. Instead, according to U.S. officials, Gorbachev spent 80 percent of his time in the arms control discussions trying to talk my father into shutting down the Strategic Defense Initiative.[3]

Martin Anderson, one of Dad's top national security advisers, was directly involved in the Reykjavík summit in October 1986, and he reports that Dad again warned Gorbachev that America would bankrupt the Soviet economy. "I was with Reagan," Anderson recalled, "and let me tell you, it was brutal. Behind closed doors, Reagan stiff-armed Gorbachev."[4] Still, Gorbachev wouldn't listen.

In the early 2000s, I made several appearances with Mikhail Gorbachev at town hall meetings, and we discussed the events of the 1980s. During one meeting, I said to Mr. Gorbachev, "My father told you that America would bankrupt your economy. Just how bad did your economy get?"

"Oh, Michael," he said, "it was so bad that I had to appoint a czar of pantyhose. Women in Russia could not buy pantyhose.

And you cannot believe how angry Russian women become when they cannot get their pantyhose. So I appointed an official whose only job was to import pantyhose into the Soviet Union to calm the women down."

The fall of the Berlin Wall in 1989 and the collapse of Soviet Communism in 1991 were no mere accidents of history. These events were conceived in the mind of Ronald Reagan and engineered from the Oval Office of the White House.

During his administration, my father was relentless in his attacks against the Berlin Wall. The world remembers his speech at the Brandenburg Gate on June 12, 1987: "Mr. Gorbachev, tear down this wall!" Yet he made frequent references to the Wall throughout his administration. In August 1986 alone, he gave three speeches demanding that the Wall be torn down. And in an interview with a West German newspaper, ten days before his Brandenburg Gate speech, he said "We want the Berlin Wall to come down." In his February 1988 "Address to the Citizens of Western Europe," he said, "To the Soviets today I say: I made my Berlin proposals almost nine months ago. The people of Berlin and all of Europe deserve an answer. . . . Make a start. Set a date, a specific date, when you will tear down the wall."[5]

But the most significant effort my father made to dismantle the Berlin Wall came on May 29, 1988, when he met face-to-face with Soviet General Secretary Mikhail Gorbachev on Gorbachev's home turf, St. Catherine Hall in the Kremlin. Leaders of the two great superpowers met to discuss human rights. Gorbachev's translator, Igor Korchilov, later recalled that Ronald Reagan "suggested to Gorbachev that the Berlin Wall be torn down. . . . Gorbachev said he could not agree with the president's view."[6] My father wrote about that conversation in his 1990 autobiography, *An American Life*:

I said Americans were very encouraged by the changes occurring in the Soviet Union. . . . And for all the changes that Gorbachev had made, I said, wouldn't it be a good idea to tear down the Berlin Wall? Nothing in the West symbolized the differences between it and the Soviet Union more than the Wall, I said; its removal would be seen as a gesture symbolizing that the Soviet Union wanted to join the broader community of nations.

Well, Gorbachev listened and seemed to take in my opinions; from his expression I knew he didn't like some of the things I was saying, but he didn't try to say anything harsh in rebuttal. Whether my words had any impact or not I don't know. . . . In time, the Wall came tumbling down.[7]

My father spent years speaking out and working to bring down the Berlin Wall. Mikhail Gorbachev refused to dismantle the Wall when my father confronted him. When the Wall finally did come down in 1989, Gorbachev's entire role in that historic event was to stay out of the way of the East German dissidents who tore it down. He never wanted the Wall to fall and he never wanted the Soviet Union to collapse. That was all Ronald Reagan's idea.

In 1990, the year after the fall of the Berlin Wall, Mikhail Gorbachev was awarded the Nobel Peace Prize and given credit for the end of the Berlin Wall and the Cold War. Ronald Reagan, who planned and engineered it all from the beginning, received no credit, no award, no thanks.

And he never complained. My father wasn't hungry for praise and applause. He just wanted to achieve the goal. One reason my father was willing to let Mikhail Gorbachev take all the credit was that he knew that Gorbachev needed to look like a hero and a leader to his own people, or he would be undermined in his own country. So Dad was willing to give Gorbachev the credit if it would enable Gorbachev to relax the restrictions on the people of East Germany.

Throughout his eight years as president, my father kept a brass plaque on the Resolute desk in the Oval Office that read:

"There is no limit to what a man can do or where he can go if he doesn't mind who gets the credit." That was not a mere platitude. That was *literally* how he lived his life.

Another example of my father's humility was his approach to strategic arms control. When he came into office, he didn't support the old SALT (Strategic Arms Limitation Talks) doctrines of the Nixon, Ford, and Carter administrations. Every SALT agreement permitted both sides to build *more* weapons in order to limit them. He wanted to replace SALT with START—the STrategic Arms Reduction Treaty, a treaty that would actually *reduce* nuclear stockpiles on both sides of the equation.

In 1982, as my father prepared to meet with European leaders in Geneva, he needed to deliver a major policy speech outlining his arms reduction agenda. As his advisers argued over the right venue for such an important speech, Dad said, "I'm delivering the commencement address at Eureka College." And his advisers said, "That's fine, Mr. President. Now about your arms reduction speech—" Dad interrupted and said, "You don't understand. *I'm delivering the commencement address at Eureka College.* That's where I'll announce my arms reduction agenda."

So on May 9, 1982, on the campus of Eureka College, a private liberal arts college in Illinois with an enrollment of fewer than 800 students, my father delivered one of the most important policy speeches of his presidency. Soon afterward, he went to Europe and began the process of negotiating a *real* reduction in the nuclear arsenals on both sides of the Atlantic. American negotiators met with Soviet negotiators for START talks four times. The first three times, the Soviets walked away. The fourth time, the Soviet negotiators put a proposal on the table—and the proposal was amazingly similar to the proposal my father had outlined in his original speech at Eureka College.

Why did the Soviet negotiators offer a proposal that mirrored Dad's original plan? I think they expected Dad to say, "That's *my* plan! Those are *my* ideas!" Then the Soviets would say, "Well, if that's your proposal, we reject it!" And they'd walk away again. They didn't understand that Dad truly didn't care who got the credit, as long as the job got done. So the Soviets ultimately signed the START agreement—and took credit for it.

And that was just fine with Dad. There was absolutely no limit to what he could accomplish—including nuclear arms reduction—because he truly didn't mind who got the credit.

Fame Didn't Change Him

My father was always aware of his place in history, yet he remained humble and self-effacing throughout his life. My sister Maureen told me the story of visiting Dad at the White House. They were in the family residence on the second floor, and Dad brought out an armload of books. "I'm giving these books away," he said, "and I thought you might want to go through them and see if there are any you want." While Maureen was going through the books, Dad brought out a briefcase and said, "Here's something to take the books home in."

"Is there some significance to this briefcase?"

"No, not really. I'm getting a new one, so you can have this one."

But when Maureen looked more closely at the briefcase, she realized it was the same one Dad had used both as governor of California and throughout his first term as president. My father was a humble man, and he wouldn't come out and say, "Here's a piece of history." Instead, he was passing it along as if it had no value at all, though he was aware that Maureen would recognize its worth. He was giving her a priceless piece of his legacy—yet in his humble way, he said it was just an old briefcase.

Dad never used his fame or his position to impress people, intimidate people, or get his way. Unlike many Hollywood stars, he would never try to get out of a speeding ticket by saying,

"Don't you know who I am?" He understood his place in history, yet he would never take advantage of it.

Visitors to Rancho del Cielo were often amazed at how simple and modest the ranch house is. The Spanish-style house is cozy and tastefully decorated but hardly a mansion. Yet my father didn't hesitate to receive world leaders—including Margaret Thatcher, Queen Elizabeth and Prince Philip, and Mikhail Gorbachev—at the ranch. The pictures on the walls were not photos of Dad with famous people. They were pictures of beautiful scenery around the ranch. My father was a humble man who didn't feel any need to impress other leaders with ostentatious surroundings.

If you go to Illinois, you can travel the Ronald Reagan Trail— a network of highways connecting places that were important in the early life of my father—places like his birthplace at Tampico, his boyhood home in Dixon, the town of Monmouth where he lived from 1918 to 1919, Galesburg where he attended first grade, and Eureka where he went to college. All the houses where he was raised, and even the college he attended, were modest and unassuming. Ronald Reagan was a humble man who came from humble beginnings, and he never lost his genuine humility, even in the throes of Alzheimer's disease.

In January 1996, seven years after my father left office, I visited him at his home in Bel Air. At the time, he was less than two years into his battle with Alzheimer's. He had some trouble remembering details, but his wit and personality were still sharp. We talked about his political career, and I reminded him that it had been thirty years, almost to the day, since he announced he was running for governor of California.

"Back then," I said, "you had no idea of all that lay ahead of you."

He winked at me and said, "How did I do?"

I laughed. "Pretty good, Dad. You did all right."

Typical Reagan humility. That's the example Dad set for me, and the role model I have set for myself. I want to be a man like Ronald Reagan, a man of humility who maintains a sense of proportion and who can accomplish great things by not seeking glory and not taking himself too seriously.

Of all the leadership qualities my father possessed, perhaps the most important was his humility. It was one of the traits everyone noticed about him, whether observing him from afar or from up close. As his longtime speechwriter Peggy Noonan observed, Ronald Reagan "was probably the sweetest, most innocent man ever to serve in the Oval Office. . . . 'No great men are good men,' said Lord Acton, who was right, until Reagan."[8]

Dad's sense of humor was always humble and self-deprecating, never mean-spirited. For example, when he heard that Alan Cranston (who was a few years younger than Dad) was running in the Democratic primary, Dad's response was, "Imagine running for president at his age!" Who was the butt of that joke? Senator Cranston? Of course not. Dad's age-related joke was actually on himself.

A few days after he was shot in 1981, Vice President Bush visited him at the hospital, along with several White House aides. Entering the room, they found Dad's hospital bed empty. They called for him—and heard a voice from the bathroom. "I'm in here, fellas," he said. They found the leader of the free world on his hands and knees on the cold tile floor, mopping up a puddle of water under the sink. "I was giving myself a sponge bath," he explained. "I guess I sort of made a mess of things."

"You should let the nurse clean that up," Mr. Bush said.

"No," Dad said, "this is my mess. I'd hate for the nurse to have to clean it up."

The virtue of humility isn't respected very much in our society today, but my father possessed it, and it was the foundation of his leadership ability and his greatness on the world stage. To Dad, humility wasn't an act or a performance. It's just who he was. I can state that as a fact because I have seen the private

Ronald Reagan and the public Ronald Reagan, and he's one and the same man.

As president, Dad put the "serve" in public service. He didn't run for president to inflate his ego or complete his résumé. He genuinely wanted to make the world a better place by eradicating Communism and spreading freedom around the world. He had many political opponents, but few, if any, personal enemies. I believe his genuine humility is the true source of his likability.

Today, there are a lot of people (and I'm chief among them) who are frustrated and angry that Ronald Reagan doesn't get the credit he deserves for bringing down the "evil empire." But I never once heard my father complain about not getting the credit. I really don't think he cared about getting credit for his accomplishments. All he cared about was setting people free.

I have studied Dad's life, character, and actions from very close range. Why? Because I wanted to be like him. He was the standard I measured myself against. And I can tell you that Ronald Reagan was never anyone else but Ronald Reagan. Hollywood fame didn't change him. Political fame didn't change him. Flying around the globe and meeting with world leaders didn't change him. Awards and honors didn't change him.

The humility of Ronald Reagan set him apart as a leader among leaders.

Not "I" but "We"

The flipside of humility is responsibility. Arrogant people hunger for praise and acclaim—and do everything in their power to escape blame. But humble people, who don't care about getting the credit, are quick to accept full responsibility. Early in my father's administration, the White House sent mixed signals regarding tax exemptions for religious schools. As a result, a lot of people on both sides of the issue became frustrated and angry. On January 19, 1982, Dad held a press conference in which a reporter asked if Dad himself had made the mistake— "or did your staff put something over on you?" Dad's humble response was to take full responsibility: "I'm the originator of the whole thing." When was the last time you heard *that* from a politician?

How did my father handle the cheers and adulation of the crowd? With humility. He once wrote, "A member of my staff who's been reviewing some of the videotapes of the campaign asked me the other day if you can feel an audience's adulation. I said that, yes, you could. (In fact, I bet I have a better idea of what it feels like to be a rock star than most twenty-year-olds.) So then he said, 'Well, how do you handle it?' I said, 'I pray that I will be deserving.'"[9]

Dad used to tell a story about humility—I remember him telling this back when I was in my teens. It seems there was a man who lived in Western Pennsylvania, and when he died, he was greeted at the pearly gates by St. Peter. And Peter told this man about a bunch of heavenly old-timers who enjoyed hearing stories about happenings on Planet Earth. The Pennsylvanian said, "Great! Have I got a story to tell them! You see, I'm a survivor of the Great Johnstown Flood."

So Peter led the man over to the group of old-timers and introduced him, saying, "This man is a new arrival with an exciting story to tell." Then Peter whispered in the man's ear, "I hope it's a good story, young man. See that fellow in the front row? His name is Noah."

Funny story. But that was also one of Dad's parables— a story with a lesson tucked inside it. He didn't just want to make you laugh, he wanted to make you *think*. It's a story about perspective—and humility. No matter how great your accomplishments or your sufferings, there's always someone who can top it. You don't want to be bragging about your flood experiences—and find out that the guy in the front row is Noah.

Dad always kept a balanced perspective on his own achievements. In his show business career and his political career, he had plenty of fans and plenty of critics. He let both the cheers of the fans and the jeers of the critics roll off him like water off a duck's back. When he received credit, he tended to reflect that credit onto others—and when he received accolades as president, he turned around and applauded the American people.

In his farewell address to the nation, delivered from the Oval Office on January 11, 1989, Dad reflected on his two terms in office:

> In all of that time I won a nickname, the "Great Communicator." But I never thought it was my style or the words I used that made a difference: it was the content. I wasn't a great communicator, but I communicated great things, and they didn't spring full bloom from my brow, they came from the heart of a great nation—from our experience, our wisdom, and our belief in the principles that have guided us for two centuries. They called it the Reagan Revolution. Well, I'll accept that, but for me it always seemed more like the great rediscovery, a rediscovery of our values and our common sense. . . .
>
> And as I walk off into the city streets, a final word to the men and women of the Reagan Revolution, the men and women across America who for eight years did the work that brought America back. My friends: We did it. We weren't just marking time. We made a difference. We made the city stronger, we made the city freer, and we left her in good hands. All in all, not bad, not bad at all.

Listen to a lot of political speeches these days, and you'll hear a lot of "I" statements—"I did this" and "I did that." But if you listen to my father's speeches, you won't hear him use "I" statements very much, except to deflect credit away from himself and onto others. Dad didn't talk a lot about what *he* did—he almost always talked about what *we* did together. He didn't say "I," but "we." He always saw himself as one of the people—a humble *servant* of the people. And he acknowledged "the men and women of the Reagan Revolution," the grassroots patriots who believed in America and who supported his efforts to bring America back.

These days, there are all too few leaders who have the kind of humility that makes a leader great—the kind of humility that marked the life and words of my father, Ronald Reagan. To be a great leader, you must first be a good human being.

And the first trait of a good human being is humility.

Good News and Bad News

In July 1982, during my speedboat racing days, I set the world speed record on the Mississippi River—a 1,027-mile run from New Orleans to St. Louis to win the Grace Challenge Cup. The event was a fund-raiser for the United States Olympic Team, and we raised half a million dollars. Racing analyst Sam Posey was the announcer for the television coverage by *The American Sportsman* on ABC. We had arranged for my father, who was in his second year as president, to speak at the fund-raising dinner at the end of the event.

I really wanted Dad to be at the finish line of the race—but he would only come to the dinner. I later learned that his reason for not coming to the race was that he didn't want to steal the limelight from me. He thought he was doing me *a favor* by staying away—but I would have loved for him to be there! After all, I was insecure, hungry for approval, and eager for my father's applause. Yet he thought that if he showed up, all eyes would be on him, and it would take away from what I had accomplished.

That night at the dinner, Augie Busch—that is, August A. Busch III, then chairman of Anheuser-Busch—was honored with the Sportsman of the Year award for his work on behalf of the U.S. Olympic Committee. Dad, of course, was the keynote speaker. Before Dad introduced Augie Busch, he said some very touching words about me.

He said:

I hope you'll forgive me if I indulge in a little paternal pride. Mike, my son, you know, broke the record in that boat run, New Orleans to St. Louis. And Mike, I'm proud of you. And not just proud of what you did, but proud because you did it for the cause that brings us together here tonight. I know it wasn't just a boat ride. I don't know how you're still awake, but a lot of effort went into that boat ride, and it was for a great effort, the effort of the Olympic Committee. Whether you'd gotten a record or not, I think all of us here hope that other Americans will emulate you and give of themselves in behalf of our country and our Olympic team.

Those are beautiful words for a father to speak to his son. I only wish I had heard them.

I had spent twenty-five hours racing up the Mississippi River, and I had been up for hours both before and after that race. I was totally spent—and while Dad was talking, I fell asleep. Right after Dad spoke those words about me, Bill Simon—the president of the U.S. Olympic Committee and former treasury secretary under Nixon and Ford—nudged me and said, "That was really nice."

I perked up and said, "What was really nice?"

"What your father just said about you."

"My dad just said something about me?" Here I had been waiting for my dad's words of approval—and I had slept through them! But I knew he had said them, and that's what mattered. Later I was able to read a transcript of his remarks, and that was the next best thing to hearing them

That was quintessential Ronald Reagan: always humble, always deferential, always wanting to make sure that others got the credit for what they did, always making sure that he didn't steal the limelight—even when I would have loved to share it with him.

Another way Dad showed his humility is by admitting he didn't have all the answers. In fact, he would sometimes ask for help from yours truly. Dad didn't ask my advice very often, but one day in 1977, Dad called out of the blue and said, "Your brother Ron has dropped out of Yale after only one semester. He's rebellious, and he won't listen to me or Nancy. He says he wants to become a ballet dancer."

I wasn't sure I heard him right. "Did you say he wants to become—"

"Yes, Michael, a ballet dancer. You understand his generation better than I do. What can I do? What should I say?"

My first impulse was to suggest that Dad buy Ron a tutu—but I could tell that Dad was seriously concerned about Ron's future, and it was no time for jokes. I couldn't think of any profession Ron could choose that would be more at odds with Dad's rugged image than the ballet. I was flattered that Dad wanted my advice—and I was enjoying the fact that Ron was on the hot seat instead of me.

Dad and I met in his office and talked for quite a while, but I don't think I provided much insight. I had grown up around Ron—or "Skipper," as Dad nicknamed him—but I didn't feel I knew him well. I couldn't understand why Ron would be so rebellious. After all, *his* parents weren't divorced, *mine* were. And I certainly couldn't understand what would make a young man join the ballet.

Within a few days, Ron returned to California and publicly announced his career plans. Several media outlets greeted Ron's announcement with snide hints that he was gay. The gossip about Ron was far more upsetting to Nancy than to Dad because

Nancy was worried about Ron's image. She wanted Dad to run for president in 1980, and she was worried about the Christian vote. What would Christian conservatives think if they thought Ron was gay?

Unlike Nancy, Dad didn't spend a lot of time worrying about his image. His main concern about my brother was his rebellious attitude. The ballet dancing didn't bother him, and even the gay rumors didn't bother him. Dad was supportive of Ron's goals. He told me his old friend, dancer Gene Kelly, had recommended a good ballet school. Soon Ron began studying at the Stanley Holden Dance Center in Los Angeles, and he showed real talent.

A few days later, Dad called me again, this time at the boat showroom where I worked. From the sound of his voice, I knew he was upset. "Nancy and I came back from a trip," he said, "and we caught your brother."

"You caught my brother doing what?"

"Well, he brought a young lady, the wife of one of our friends, into our house for the weekend. Nancy and I found them in our bedroom—and he had the cook fixing breakfast for them."

It was hard not to laugh—yet I knew that Dad took this matter seriously. Ron was breaking Dad and Nancy's rules and violating their trust.

"Dad," I said, "I have good news and bad news."

"What do you mean?"

"Well, the bad news is that Ron disobeyed you and broke your rules."

"And the good news?"

"You found out he's not gay."

There was a moment of stunned silence—then Dad brightened and said, "Oh, I must tell Nancy."

I was glad I could point out a silver lining, and I'll always treasure the times my father humbled himself and asked for my advice.

Lessons in Humility

It has taken years of watching my father and studying his life to understand that his leadership greatness is rooted in his innate humility. Where did my father's humility spring from? It was undoubtedly ingrained in him by his mother, Nelle. Humility, after all, is a Christian virtue, and Dad learned all the essential Christian virtues at his mother's knee. It's amazing to think that the lessons his mother taught him so long ago helped shape his life—and through him, those values helped reshape the world.

Here are some of the lessons in humility I have learned from my father, Ronald Reagan:

Don't worry about who gets the credit. Dad didn't originate the quotation on his desk plaque, but it epitomized his life. It bears repeating, "There is no limit to what a man can do or where he can go if he doesn't mind who gets the credit." I'm not sure why Dad kept that plaque on his desk. I doubt that he needed to be reminded every day to remain humble. Maybe he kept that plaque on his desk as a reminder to everyone around him. Maybe that was Dad's way of setting the tone and creating a culture of humility in the White House.

Washington, D.C., is a town that reeks of ego and arrogance. Power has a way of inflating human vanity, and the closer people get to the center of power, the more arrogant they become. I think Dad used that plaque as a silent reminder that a key principle, a core value, of the Reagan administration was humility. Every staffer was to keep his or her ego in check and share the credit. If the chief executive himself was committed to a humble style of leadership, then no one on the team had any right to be arrogant.

The tone of unselfish teamwork that my father set for the Reagan White House undoubtedly contributed to the success of the Reagan Revolution.

You are never too important to be a servant. Even though he was the president of the United States, my father didn't consider himself too important to clean up spilled water on the hospital bathroom floor. He was well acquainted with the story about Jesus and his disciples in Mark 9—a story he had undoubtedly taught to his young pupils when he was a Sunday school teacher in Dixon, Illinois. Jesus overheard his disciples arguing among themselves as to which of them would be the greatest leader in the kingdom that Jesus would establish. So Jesus called them to himself and said, "Anyone who wants to be first must be the very last, and the servant of all."[10]

Leadership could be defined as the art of accomplishing great goals through other people. And great leaders accomplish those goals not by intimidating people and bossing them around, but by equipping them, empowering them, encouraging them, motivating them, and serving them so that they can achieve great things. Dad understood that a truly great leader is not the boss of everybody, but the servant of everybody. He saw himself as a servant to his staff, to his cabinet, and to the American people, and by serving them and empowering them, he was able to achieve his goals of changing the world.

Here's another story about the humble serving attitude of my father. In November 1985, Dad went to Geneva for his first summit meeting with Mikhail Gorbachev. The subject was international diplomatic relations and arms control. During the summit, Dad and Nancy stayed at a lakeside villa in Geneva. When they arrived, they found a note next to a goldfish bowl. The note, written by the young son of the family who owned the villa, asked President Reagan to please feed his goldfish.

So the president of the United States dutifully got up every morning of the summit and fed the goldfish. One morning, he discovered one goldfish floating on the water, dead. So he summoned an aide and said, "We've got to find another goldfish for that boy." So the aide went out and found a replacement. Dad handwrote a note explaining what had happened, and expressing his hope that the boy would find the new goldfish acceptable.[11]

The leader of the free world demonstrated his greatness by serving, by feeding a little boy's goldfish. Great leaders are great servants. Those who want to be first must become the servant of all.

Be humble enough to admit mistakes. Many people think that admitting mistakes causes them to "lose face." In reality, most people actually admire those who are honest enough and humble enough to own their mistakes instead of shifting blame. Nothing builds trust like being accountable.

Leadership isn't about always being right or never making mistakes. Great leaders make decisions, explain those decisions to their followers, and accept responsibility for the results. And when the results are bad, great leaders say, "I made a decision that didn't turn out well. I learned a lesson from that mistake, and I'm now going to make a new decision to correct that mistake."

You tell me, who would you rather trust—the leader who denies his own mistakes, who pretends everything is going fine when it's obviously not, and who blames predecessors or staffers or circumstances for the mistake? Or are you more likely to trust the leader who admits his mistake and offers a plan to correct it?

Yes, admitting mistakes makes a leader vulnerable—but it also makes a leader more human, easier to relate to, and easier to trust. If you are a parent, a church leader, an educator, a business leader, or any kind of leader at all, take a lesson from Ronald Reagan. Be humble enough to admit your mistakes.

If you are in leadership, practice saying "we" instead of "I." Instead of hogging credit for the team's success, acknowledge and thank everyone who made that success possible. In your speeches, in your written communication, in your one-on-one conversations, practice getting "I" out of your vocabulary. Learn to speak in all-inclusive terms of "us" and "we."

Be humble enough to learn. My father had a rare combination of leadership qualities—strong self-confidence combined with selfless humility. He absolutely believed in the rightness of his values, principles, and positions—but if you showed him where he was wrong, he would immediately adapt to the new information, discover new ideas, and adopt a new viewpoint. You can't teach an arrogant person anything, but a humble person is always learning. That's why confident people with humble attitudes make great leaders.

You might think that humility is an old-fashioned virtue that no longer applies in today's fast-changing world. Not true. The same humble willingness to learn that marked my father's life is one of the key ingredients for success in the Internet age.

Laszlo Bock is in charge of "People Operations" (hiring and personnel) at Google, one of the most successful companies in the world. He says that Google long ago learned that grade point averages and test scores are worthless in determining who should be hired. Those criteria he said, "don't predict anything." Instead, Bock says he looks for a quality that he calls "intellectual humility," the willingness to patiently acquire new skills and knowledge. "Without humility," he said, "you are unable to learn."[12]

It was Dad's intellectual humility that enabled him to conceive of possibilities that many of his closest advisers couldn't imagine—such as the Strategic Defense Initiative (SDI), also known as the "Star Wars" missile defense shield. The idea for SDI did not come from one of Dad's aides or advisors. It was an idea that my father had been nurturing and thinking about ever since 1967. That's when Dad, as the newly elected governor of California, visited the Lawrence Livermore National Laboratory and met physicist Edward Teller. One of the topics Teller spoke about involved ways to defend the nation against nuclear attack. My father took everything he learned at that briefing and distilled it into his SDI proposal.

People who are always learning have a way of coming up with visionary new ideas. That's why my father, who was known for his old-fashioned conservatism, was also known for his visionary ability to foresee the future. A humble attitude is essential to learning, and a willingness to learn is essential to great leadership.

My father didn't mind who got the credit. That's how he achieved so much and went so far. That's how he changed the world.

How far might your humility take you? How will you humbly change the world?

8

Put Others First

M Y FATHER WAS SIXTEEN years old when he began working as a lifeguard on the Rock River at Lowell Park in Dixon, Illinois. Every summer for seven years, from 1927 to 1933, he worked twelve hours a day, seven days a week, all summer long. Over the course of those seven years, he was credited with saving seventy-seven lives—and he never lost a swimmer.

In fact, the very first time Dad was on the front page of a newspaper was when he saved a young man named James Raider on August 2, 1928. The next day, the *Dixon Evening Telegraph* carried an above-the-fold headline: "James Raider Pulled from the Jaws of Death." Beneath the headline, the story told how "lifeguard Ronald 'Dutch' Reagan," age seventeen, had just rescued his twenty-fifth swimmer from death-by-drowning. From that point on, the *Telegraph* kept a running tally of "Dutch" Reagan's saves.

If you asked my father what his favorite job was, you might expect him to talk about the presidency or being governor of California or being a Hollywood actor or a radio broadcaster—but that's not what he would say. He would always answer, "My beloved lifeguarding may be the best job I ever had."

One time, after he told me some stories from his lifeguarding days, I said, "Dad, you're really proud of those seventy-seven lives you saved." He leaned closed to me and said, confidentially, "Some of those seventy-seven lives were young ladies who just wanted to meet the lifeguard."

Even after my father left the banks of the Rock River and pursued less heroic lines of work, he continued to save lives. As a radio broadcaster at WHO Radio in Des Moines, he saved two people from drowning in a public swimming pool, though details of the incident are sketchy.

Another incident occurred during his time in Des Moines: One autumn night in 1933, Dad heard a commotion on the street below his second-floor apartment. He picked up his .45 caliber revolver, leaned out the window, and saw a mugger attempting to rob Melba King, a twenty-two-year-old nursing student. Dad pointed the gun at the mugger and shouted, "Leave her alone or I'll shoot you right between the shoulders!" The mugger fled, and Dad walked the young lady home. Decades later, when Dad was in Iowa during his reelection campaign, Dad and Melba King were reunited onstage at a campaign event. Dad told her—and the crowd—"This is the first time I've had a chance to tell you the gun was empty. I didn't have any cartridges. If he hadn't run when I told him to, I was going to have to throw the gun at him."

And there was yet another incident in the late 1960s, when Dad was governor of California. He saw a girl fall into a swimming pool at a political reception—and when she didn't come back to the surface, he dove into the pool with his clothes on and saved the child's life.

If I had to name the two greatest concentrations of narcissistic, self-important, self-centered people in the country, I would say Hollywood and Washington, D.C. Yet my father was able to easily navigate his way in Hollywood and D.C. as a man selflessly devoted to others. When he went to Washington, determined to restore the economy, topple Communism, and advance the cause of freedom around the world, he was just doing what he had already done seventy-seven times in the swirling waters of the Rock River outside Dixon, Illinois, on a much grander scale.

Putting others first—that has been one of the themes of my father's life for as long as I can remember. Where did his devotion to serving others come from? Again, I think we have to give a lot of credit to his mother, Nelle. She raised my father and his brother in the Christian faith and taught them to put others first. She wrote plays that were performed in church, many of which dealt with values of compassion and serving others—and she often wrote acting parts for young "Dutch" Reagan. Nelle also exemplified a devotion to helping others and often invited homeless men and ex-convicts into their home for a hot meal and a Gospel sermon.

Dad was always putting others first, always saving lives, always confronting the muggers and helping the innocent feel safe. From the age of sixteen till the end of his days, Dad was a lifeguard and a hero. To him, saving and serving others was all in a day's work.

The Unforgivable Sin

My father said that when he was growing up, there was no more grievous sin than uttering a racial or religious slur. Dad's father, Jack Reagan, told him how Irish immigrants were looked down upon, and some stores had signs that read "No Dogs or Irishmen Allowed." Nelle taught my dad and his brother the Golden Rule. Though segregation was widely practiced in Dixon in those days (e.g., whites sat in the floor seats of the theater, blacks in the balcony), Nelle encouraged her sons to invite their black school friends into their home.

When Dad played on the Eureka College football team, the team once traveled by bus to dad's hometown of Dixon. The bus

pulled up to a hotel and Dad went into the hotel with the football coach to help check the team into their rooms. The hotel
manager said, "I can take everybody but your two colored boys."

Angered, the coach said, "Then we'll go someplace else."

When the manager said that no hotel in Dixon would take
black people, the coach was ready to have the entire team sleep
on the bus. Dad offered another solution: let the rest of the team
stay in the hotel. He and the two black players would stay at his
parents' house nearby. Dad didn't even have to call ahead and
ask if it was OK. He knew that Nelle and Jack would welcome
his teammates.

Dad was raised not merely to be "color-blind," but to go out
of his way to show acceptance, fairness, and compassion to others. Yet because of dad's conservative values, he has often been
unfairly smeared as a bigot. It's untrue, but as a political tactic,
it's often effective.

In 1966, when my father entered the primary campaign for
governor of California, his fiercest opponent was George Christopher, the liberal Republican ex-mayor of San Francisco. Christopher's strategy was to brand my father an extremist. The two
men debated each other in several public forums, including a
convention of African American Republicans. At this event, Dad
spoke first, followed by Christopher, who repeatedly implied to
this mostly black audience that my father was a racist.

Dad fumed as he listened to these assaults on his character.
Finally, he'd had enough. He got up in front of the audience
and demanded that Christopher stop defaming him. Then he
stormed off the stage, leaving the audience in stunned silence.

At that time, Dad was no seasoned politician. He was unac-
customed to the rough-and-tumble of hardball politics. In his
mind, Christopher's false accusations were so outrageous that
he couldn't stay in the same room with the man.

Two of Dad's campaign aides followed him and convinced
him to return to the hall. Dad cooled down and agreed to

go back inside. He got up on the stage before the crowd and explained his outburst. He said that he had been raised by Jack and Nelle Reagan to treat everyone as an equal. He described the Christian home where he was raised—a home in which bigotry was the unforgivable sin. And when he had finished, the audience gave him a huge round of applause, along with their support—but the phony charges didn't stop.

When my father ran in the general election, his opponent—incumbent Democratic governor Edmund G. "Pat" Brown—leveled over-the-top accusations at him. Brown called Dad's supporters "shock troops of bigotry, echoes of Nazi Germany, echoes of another hate binge that began more than thirty years ago in a Munich beer hall." Dad calmly, reasonably replied, "Extreme phraseology from one who professes to deplore extremism."[1]

Next, Brown went to an elementary school classroom and filmed a commercial in which he told two African American girls, "I'm running against an actor. You know who shot Abraham Lincoln, don'tcha?"[2]

My father trailed in the polls until the commercial appeared. But when voters and pundits saw the outrageous ad, with its message that an actor equals an assassin, Dad vaulted over Brown in the polls and he never looked back. On election day, my father beat Brown by a 58 to 42 percent margin.[3]

The Brown ad violated common decency, and decent people rejected it. Today, however, half the country would find nothing wrong with such a dishonest ad and such blatant character assassination. The political climate in America has changed—and not for the better. Accusing one's opponent of racism or comparing one's opponent to John Wilkes Booth would hardly raise any eyebrows today. It would be considered politics as usual.

The character assassination of my father continues even after his death. The 2013 motion picture *The Butler*, produced and directed by Lee Daniels, is based on the life of longtime White

House butler Eugene Allen, an African American who served under eight presidents, from Truman to Reagan. Inexplicably, the filmmakers changed Allen's name to "Cecil Gaines."

After Eugene Allen retired, Dad and Nancy invited him and his wife back to the White House as guests for a state dinner in honor of German Chancellor Helmut Kohl. In interviews, Eugene Allen always spoke of his fondness for Dad and Nancy. Yet Lee Daniels defamed my father as racially insensitive and portrayed "Cecil" as resentful toward the Reagans.

My father was raised to see all people as equals. His mother, Nelle, taught him to love everyone, regardless of race. His father Jack refused to let him see the movie *Birth of a Nation* because it glorified the Ku Klux Klan.

At Eureka College—a school founded by abolitionists—Dad was friends with an African American coed, Willie Sue Smith. In fact, Willie Sue sometimes passed notes between "Dutch" Reagan and his girlfriend, Margaret Cleaver. Dad and Willie Sue kept in touch throughout his Hollywood years and on into his political career. She died in 2011 at age 101, the last remaining member of the Eureka College class of 1932.

In 1952, as president of the Screen Actors Guild (SAG), my father made news by calling upon Hollywood studios to provide more opportunities for African Americans in the film industry. I could go on and on. When it comes to my father's attitudes on race, the truth is far more interesting than any left-wing propaganda film.

And it's not just the left that has misrepresented Ronald Reagan's character. Many candidates and commentators on the right have tried to co-opt my father for their own purposes. Some have claimed that Ronald Reagan would be quick to deport the children of illegal immigrants. Though Ronald Reagan tried to solve to the problem of illegal immigration when he was president, he would not hold children accountable for the sins of their parents. Anyone who believes my father would do so doesn't know him and doesn't know what he stood for.

Dad once wrote about his frustration that he was unable to convince more people of color of his concern for their problems. It hurt him deeply that he was often falsely portrayed as racially insensitive. "Of all things that were said about me during my presidency," he wrote, "this charge bothers me the most personally. I abhor racism."[4]

I know that politics is a blood sport, but I've never gotten used to the notion that it's acceptable to lie about your opponent's character and portray a decent, honest, fair-minded Christian man as a bigot. Of course, my father was bigger than all the false accusations leveled against him. He survived character assassination just as he survived an assassin's bullet. He lived and he forgave, but he was wounded nonetheless.

My Father's Compassion

My father had one of the most compassionate hearts of anyone I've ever met. His compassion extended not only to people in need, but to suffering animals. Ray Jackin, the foreman of Dad's Malibu ranch, once told me a story about Dad's love for animals. One of the thoroughbreds, a mare named Bracing, was dying of cancer and had to be put down. She had birthed Ronnie's Baby—the only one of Dad's horses to actually win at Santa Anita. The thought of her death absolutely devastated my father.

Ray offered to handle the chore of putting the horse out of her misery, but Dad felt he owed it to her to do it himself. So Dad loaded a .30-30 rifle, and he and Ray went out to the corral. Ray took a piece of chalk and drew an X on Bracing's forehead, just above the eyes.

"Just put a bullet right at the center of the X, Mr. Reagan. She'll never feel a thing."

Holding the rifle at his side, Dad looked into the trusting eyes of that horse. Finally, he raised the gun and took aim at the X. The mare didn't flinch. Dad tried to squeeze the trigger, but couldn't.

Finally, Ray walked over, took the rifle from Dad's hands, aimed and fired. The horse dropped to the ground, dead.

"That's how you do it," Ray said.

Ray Jackin told me he would never forget the sight of my father's shoulders shaking, tears in his eyes, as he looked down at that horse.

Barney Barnett, Dad's driver when he was governor of California, told me another story of my father's compassion. Dad got a letter from a young soldier in Vietnam. "My wife and I will soon celebrate our first anniversary," the soldier wrote. "I can't be there, so could you call her and wish her a happy anniversary for me?"

Dad had a better idea. He had Barney buy a dozen roses, then they drove to the lady's home. Dad knocked on the door. When the lady opened the door, the Governor of California presented her with a dozen roses and an anniversary message from her husband. The story never appeared in the newspapers because Ronald Reagan did acts of kindness for people, not for publicity.

As president, Dad once hosted members of the U.S. Senate Youth Program in the White House Rose Garden. He encouraged the students to tour Washington, D.C. "Have you been to the Lincoln Memorial yet?" he said. "If you stand on one side of the statue and look at Lincoln's profile, you see his compassion. Stand on the other side and you see the strength of the man. You get a different view of Lincoln's character, depending on which side you view."

Those two qualities—strength and compassion—characterized the presidency of Abraham Lincoln. The official biographer of President Lincoln, Carl Sandburg, describes Lincoln this way: "Not often in the story of mankind does a man arrive on earth who is both steel and velvet, who is hard as a rock and soft as a drifting fog, who holds in his heart and mind the paradox of ter-rible storm and peace unspeakable and perfect."[5]

Those words also describe my father, Ronald Reagan. Dad was a great student and admirer of Lincoln, and the insight he shared with those young people was the guiding principle of his personal and public life: strength and compassion working together. Under my father's leadership, America became both stronger and more compassionate. As he restored and rebuilt our long-neglected American military—America's strength—he also lifted millions out of the pit of dependency and set them on the road to self-reliance.

Strength and compassion go together. My father exemplified both qualities, and our society needs to rediscover these quali-ties in order to thrive.

As president, my father believed that part of his job was to maintain direct contact with the people. Though he could not personally answer the mountain of mail he received, his director of correspondence, Anne Higgins, would bring him a representative selection of letters. He answered many of them with handwritten notes. On more than one occasion, he actually took out his checkbook and sent money to people in need.

On one occasion, a mother wrote to Dad, telling him how hard it was for her young son to keep up his grades in school. She worried that she would not be able to afford to send him to college. Dad was so touched by her letter that he sent her a check for a hundred dollars so that she could start a college fund for the boy. When the woman received the check, she was thrilled and took it to the bank. The bank manager, however, told her not to cash the check, advising her that it would one day be worth far more as a collector's item. The woman wrote to Dad and told him she was keeping the check and would not be cashing it. Dad replied, "Deposit the check. I'll have my accoun-tant send the canceled check for you to keep."

My father always told aides and staffers not to publicize his good deeds. He followed the biblical advice, "Don't do your good deeds publicly, to be admired by others, for you will lose the reward from your Father in heaven."[6] Most of his kind acts will never be known, but here's an example I saw with my own eyes:

During Dad's presidency, the Reagan family always had Thanksgiving at the ranch. Thanksgiving was our big family holiday; for Christmas, Dad and Nancy remained at the White House. Why? Because Dad believed his Secret Service agents should be with their families on Christmas Day.

You may recall the controversy surrounding a trip that Dad and Nancy made to Japan in October 1989, after he left office. A Japanese media company paid Dad $2 million for an eight-day visit that included several speeches, a TV interview, and lunch with Emperor Akihito. Media pundits were aghast that an American president would reap such a rewards after leaving office. (Those same pundits said nothing when the Clintons reaped *hundreds of millions* of dollars for themselves and their foundation after Bill left office.)

One aspect of Ronald Reagan's journey to Japan went largely unreported. In Dad's chartered 747, he brought 229 spouses and children of American military personnel stationed in Japan. These military dependents traveled round-trip as his guests. Even when Dad was criticized in the media, he never said a word about his good deed for those military families.

Dad's kindness defined him even during his long battle with Alzheimer's disease. I remember one visit with Dad at his home in Bel Air, when the disease was in its late stages. I saw a Secret Service agent standing beside Dad, spoon-feeding him. That wasn't part of the agent's job description, but the man didn't mind. He loved and respected my father.

As I moved closer, the agent took a step back so that I could greet my father. But as the man stepped back, Dad reached out, took the agent's arm, and kissed his hand.

I'll never forget the look of gratitude in my father's eyes—even though there were tears in mine.

A Role Model of Selflessness

Dad loved lifeguarding. He thought working twelve hours a day, seven days a week, rescuing people was the best job he ever had. Why? Because he was helping others. Dad was never happier than when he was putting others first.

My father's selfless devotion to serving others seemed as natural to him as his smile and the Irish gleam in his eye. And a spirit of selflessness was part of his spiritual heritage from his mother, Nelle. I knew and loved Nelle when I was young because she took my sister Maureen and me to Sunday school. That same quality of selflessness and compassion that I observed in my Dad, I also saw in Nelle.

The ability to put others first is a wonderful quality—and I hope I've learned it from Dad and Nelle. I want other people to see in me that same quality they saw in my father. Here are some of the lessons my father taught me in how to put others first:

Treat all people as equals. There's no room in this world for bigotry or racism. We need to learn how to truly love one another and understand one another in our society—or our nation will rattle apart. Go out of your way to meet and befriend people of other races, other cultures, other religions, and other political beliefs.

If you are liberal, stop stereotyping conservatives and start talking to them, listening to them and understanding them. And if you are conservative, stop stereotyping liberals. Everybody is an individual, and there is something we can learn even from people we disagree with. In fact, we almost never learn anything from people who think the same way we do. We learn by listening to people who are different.

My father didn't believe that race, color, and culture should be barriers to friendship between people. Neither should we.

Live compassionately. Take an interest in the people around you. Go out of your way to meet people, listen to people, and help people. Find tangible ways to encourage and thank the people who help you—the servers at the restaurant, the clerk at the store, the people who tend your yard, the teachers who educate your children. Don't take them for granted—put others first.

Live generously. Dad sometimes sent generous checks to strangers who wrote to him about a problem or need. You may not be able to afford that kind of generosity—but you can still live generously.

You can be generous with your time. Volunteer to read stories to kindergartners or tutor students in math or language skills. Mow a neighbor's lawn or wash a neighbor's windows. Visit shut-ins in the nursing home. Volunteer to serve food at a rescue mission or soup kitchen. Even if you don't have much money, you can be generous with your time.

Be generous with compliments and encouragement. When Dad flew on Air Force One, he always exchanged greetings with the flight crew before takeoff. After the flight, he'd lean into the cockpit and say, "Great flight. Thanks, fellas!" It meant a lot to the crew.

We tend to treat those who serve us—waiters, baristas, delivery people, barbers—as nonpersons. We don't think of them as people with hopes, dreams, sorrows, and needs. What if we started treating each one as a real human being? What if we looked them in the eye and thanked them, encouraged them, empathized with them, prayed for them, and got to know them as people? What if we began treating the people around us the way my father treated people? What kind of impact would that make on the world?

Every day, we have opportunities to live generously and compassionately. Let's make the most of those opportunities, and let's put others first.

9

Forgive and
Be Forgiven

THE MARCH 30, 1981, ASSASSINATION attempt nearly
ended my father's life. It also left three other people severely
wounded. A few days after that attempt, Dad recorded his
thoughts of that day in his diary. It wasn't until his diaries were
published in 2007 that I read this entry:

> Getting shot hurts. Still my fear was growing because no
> matter how hard I tried to breathe it seemed I was getting
> less & less air. I focused on that tiled ceiling and prayed.
> But I realized I couldn't ask for God's help while at the
> same time I felt hatred for the mixed up young man who
> had shot me. Isn't that the meaning of the lost sheep? We
> are all God's children & therefore equally beloved by him.
> I began to pray for his soul and that he would find his way
> back to the fold.[1]

When those thoughts were going through his mind, Dad had
a bullet lodged about a quarter of an inch from his heart. For
all he knew, that gurney could have been his deathbed. Yet his

chief concern was forgiveness for the young gunman who had shot him.

I visited my father in the hospital after the surgery, and he told me he believed God had spared him for a purpose. "Michael," he said, "I'm committing the rest of my presidency to God."

In June 1982, Dad visited the Vatican and met with Pope John Paul II. What did these two men have to talk about? What did they have in common? They shared a special bond—both had recently survived assassination attempts. The pope had been shot by a Turkish gunman six weeks after the attack on my father. Both the pope and the president had had come within inches of death—and both freely forgave their attackers. Because they both exemplified forgiveness, their leadership was blessed. Freedom ultimately came to Poland, the land of the pope's birth. And the Berlin Wall that Ronald Reagan had hated for years ultimately came down. Neither man demanded credit. Both acted in humility and forgiveness—and the world became freer as a result.

Many of us can recite The Lord's Prayer—"And forgive us our debts, as we also have forgiven our debtors."[2] Ronald Reagan and Pope John Paul II *lived* The Lord's Prayer. Both men expressed forgiveness for their attackers even before they left the hospital. I believe that's why God used them to change the world.

In 1983, my father reached out to Dr. Roger Peele, head of psychiatry at St. Elizabeth's Hospital, where Dad's attacker was confined after being found "not guilty by reason of insanity." Dad wanted to meet privately with the young man and express his forgiveness in person, but he didn't want to do anything that might interfere with the young man's treatment. Dr. Peele recommended against a meeting, fearing it might diminish his patient's sense of responsibility. So the meeting never took place. But I was impressed that my father wanted to take that extra step and express his forgiveness man-to-man. Dad's ability to forgive the troubled young gunman made a huge impression on me.

Forgiveness wasn't just a one-time event in my father's life. Like his traits of compassion, humility, and generosity, the trait of forgiveness was an ongoing theme of his life.

It's no secret that the Reagan family experienced its share of dysfunctional behavior. For example, my sister Patti was involved in the nuclear freeze movement and she organized protests against Dad's strategic policies. She also wrote a scathing tell-all book in 1992 that she later disavowed (she has since written two loving tributes to my father, *The Long Goodbye* and *Angels Don't Die*). Dad was frustrated by her political activities and hurt by her first book, but he never held a grudge. At Thanksgiving dinner, we all sat at the same table, we ate from the same turkey, and we were a family. A few years after Dad passed away, Patti wrote:

> My father, for his part, was not a man to begrudge anyone a divergent opinion; he'd have been fine if I had written some articles disagreeing with his policies, or even given interviews, as long as I was respectful and civil. But I chose stridency instead. . . . I was a child railing against a parent, nothing more. . . .
>
> Decades later I would look into my father's eyes and try to reach past the murkiness of Alzheimer's with my words, my apology, hoping that in his heart he heard me and understood.[3]

And let's face it, there were some things in *my* first book, *On the Outside Looking In*, that must have been difficult for Dad to read—yet he wrote a very gracious and loving foreword for the paperback edition of that book.

Conservative journalist Patrick B. McGuigan once wrote a book about the Reagan administration's failed attempt to confirm Judge Robert Bork to the Supreme Court—and that book included a number of harsh criticisms of my father. Dad read the book, then wrote a public letter urging conservatives to study

McGuigan's book and learn the lessons so that the next conservative nominee would be confirmed.

McGuigan was amazed that my father forgave him for what he wrote in the book, and observed, "That was classic Reagan. He never held a grudge. It served him well in a profession where grudge-holding has defined too many. . . . He was the gentlest of souls after political conflicts."[4]

It's true. Dad regularly forgave his many political opponents. He forgave George H. W. Bush, who attacked Dad's economic policies as "voodoo economics," and he brought Bush aboard as his running mate. He even forgave the vicious attacks from Ted Kennedy and Tip O'Neill and managed to win their support for many of his most important policy initiatives.

I studied the way my father responded to his would-be assassin; his political rivals and enemies; and yes, his often ungrateful and ungracious children, and I learned lessons in forgiveness that have impacted my life in a powerful way. Why was my father always so positive and optimistic despite all the obstacles and opposition he faced? Without any doubt, it's because he had learned the secret of forgiveness.

A Huge Temptation

For most of my life, I had hated myself for being molested. I carried around an enormous load of rage, guilt, and fear. My wife Colleen knew I was struggling with a terrible inner conflict, but she didn't know what it was. I had never told her about the molestation. I was scared to death that she would hate me and leave me if she ever found out. So Colleen could only pray for me and ask God to heal me. Thank God, he honored and answered my wife's prayers.

One day, with Colleen at my side, I went down on my knees beside my bed and prayed, "God, forgive me, make me clean, take over my life." And in the days that followed, a change took place in my life. I felt forgiven and accepted at last—and my anger began to melt away. On Father's Day 1985, Colleen and I were baptized together at Faith Church in the San Fernando Valley. Colleen had been baptized years earlier, and I had been baptized as a child into the Catholic Church, but we wanted to be baptized together.

That was the turning point of my life. God has been reshaping and rebuilding my life ever since. But even though I had turned a spiritual corner, I still had a lot of residue from the old life inside me. I saw my past through the eyes of a child—and I blamed God and Mom and Dad for the problems in my life.

I hadn't told anyone, not even Colleen, about the molestation. And I intended to take that secret to my grave.

But God had other plans.

In early 1987, a publisher offered a huge sum of money for me to write a book about my life in the Reagan family. There was one huge condition: it had to be a revealing tell-all book—one of those scandal books in which Hollywood children tell the world what miserable parents they had. In 1978, Christina Crawford, daughter of actress Joan Crawford, had shredded her late mother's reputation in *Mommie Dearest,* a runaway bestseller that was made into a movie. In 1983, Gary Crosby had published a similar tell-all, *Going My Own Way,* about his late father, Bing Crosby.

Here I was, with the offer of a huge advance on the table— and all I had to do to claim that money was to blow up the reputation of Dad, Nancy, and my mother, Jane Wyman. It was a tremendous temptation. I was working hard, struggling to make ends meet—but I could cure all my financial woes with one book.

But what about the truth?

Dad had taught me to speak the truth and live the truth. Could I write a book about my life and leave out the truth about the molestation? If I didn't mention what the pedophile had done to me, the book would be a big lie.

Yet I didn't dare mention the molestation. I had kept that secret from a psychiatrist, a priest, and even my own wife. I sure wasn't about to tell the whole world in a book!

I decided to take the easy way out. I would tell my story, but leave out the molestation. I would blame all my problems on my parents, on the divorce, on boarding school. And after selling out my parents for cold hard cash, I would put that money in the bank and never have to work again.

After all, I had been blaming God and Mom and Dad for my problems throughout my life. Why not blame them in a book and get paid for it?

Looking back, I'm amazed that I was ready to betray my parents. I'd had a life-changing encounter with God—yet, like Judas, I was willing to sell out Mom and Dad for cash.

How could I do that?

I remember my mind-set at the time. I wanted to follow God, but I also wanted that money, and above all else, I had to keep my darkest secret hidden.

The publisher put me together with writer Joe Hyams, a syndicated Hollywood columnist who had interviewed such celebrities as Humphrey Bogart, Lauren Bacall, Frank Sinatra, Spencer Tracy, and Katharine Hepburn. Before the publisher would pay out such a large advance, the editors wanted to see a thirty-page treatment so they'd know what they were getting for their money. So Joe and I met together to hammer out the treatment.

We met at Joe's house, and he spent a lot of hours asking questions and recording my conversation. I knew I would have to give him material that would make Dad and other family members look bad. That's the essence of a tell-all book. I wasn't planning to tell an outright lie or make anything up. But I was prepared to make the facts seem as scandalous as possible.

As Joe interviewed me, I felt uneasy. Maybe it was an attack of conscience. Maybe it was God trying to get through to me. It was as if a voice inside me said, "Michael, what are you doing? The story you're telling isn't true—and you know it. By leaving out the key truth—the molestation—you're turning this book into a pack of lies. Stop lying. Tell the truth."

I couldn't go on. I broke down and began to cry uncontrollably. Poor Joe! He had no idea what I was going through, so my emotional breakdown seemed to come right out of the blue. He leaned away from me and said, "What's wrong with you?"

"I can't do it, Joe. I just can't do it."

As my writing partner, Joe Hyams was to receive half the advance and royalties from the book—so when I said, "I can't do it," he was thinking, *There goes a ton of money, right out the window.* He said, "What do you mean, you can't do it?"

"I can't do this to my parents," I said. "I can't write a book that blames them for all my problems. It's not their fault. They never knew what happened to me."

"What happened to you?"

I took a deep breath—then I told him the story of how a day camp counselor repeatedly molested me when I was in the third grade. I didn't go into all the details, but I told him how the memories, the fear, and the guilt had affected my relationships with everybody in my life.

"Joe," I said, "if I write a book blaming Mom and Dad for all my problems, it'll be a lie. I can't do that."

"Who else have you told about this?"

"No one. You're the first person I've told. Even my wife doesn't know."

"You need to tell her. Let's sleep on this and talk tomorrow."

I left Joe's house and drove home, determined to finally tell Colleen about my past. We had been married for twelve years, and I owed her the truth. If I didn't tell her that night, I might never work up the nerve again. I arrived home and found Colleen in the kitchen. "Honey," I said, "we've got to talk."

We went into the living room and sat together on the couch. I took her hand and said, "I've got to tell you something about my life—something I've never told you before. And I'm going to write a book about it."

Then I told her the story of how the man molested me, took pictures of me, controlled me, and blackmailed me. I had told Joe Hyams a sketchy version of the story, but Colleen was the first to hear the details. I was scared to death. She held my life in her hands, and everything depended on what she would say after hearing me out.

For all I knew, she'd be disgusted—and she'd want to end the marriage. I wouldn't have blamed her one bit. I blamed myself for what happened to me—and hated myself for it.

I finished and I waited for her reaction. She put her arms around me, cradled my head, and told me over and over in a soothing voice, "I love you, Michael. You didn't do anything wrong."

For the first time in my life, someone knew my secret—and still loved me. For the first time, I truly felt loved.

I knew that Mom, Dad, Colleen, and the kids all loved me. But they didn't know my secret. I always felt that, if they knew, they could never love me. At last, it wasn't a secret anymore—and Colleen still loved me.

Now the healing could begin.

The Secret Comes Out

On Sunday, April 12, 1987, Colleen and I took the kids to Dad's Santa Barbara ranch to celebrate our daughter Ashley's fourth birthday. And I had another reason for visiting Dad and Nancy. While Colleen took Cameron and Ashley to the corral to see the horses, I walked with Dad and Nancy to the edge of Lake Lucky—the pond where Dad took Nancy for canoe rides.

When the three of us reached the water's edge, Nancy broke the silence. "Michael," she said, "we know you're writing a book. What's in the book that we should know about?"

I tried to look them in the eye, but I couldn't. All I could do was look at Dad's belt buckle and his boots. I took a deep breath—then I began telling them the story. They needed to know exactly what that child molester did to me, so I explained it in blunt terms.

As the story came out of me, *everything* came out of me. I was crying and I was throwing up, and it was all landing on my dad's boots. I thought, *Dad, don't look down at your boots or you'll be really mad at me. Because I'm really ruining your boots.* It's funny the things you think about such times.

I kept talking, and I didn't dare stop or I might never get it all out. I didn't know how Dad and Nancy would take it. I fully expected my father to hate me and turn away from me. Finally, I got it all said, and I fell silent.

Dad was angry. "Where is the guy? I'll kick his butt!"

"Honey," Nancy said, "he probably doesn't have a butt anymore." I think Nancy thought that, after so many years, the molester was probably dead.

To my amazement, Dad and Nancy were as understanding as Colleen had been.

"Why didn't you tell me before?" Dad said. "If you had told me back then, I would've done something."

"I was afraid you wouldn't like me anymore."

"Oh, Michael," Dad said gently. "You should have known better."

Yes, I should have known. My father had always been understanding, forgiving, and protective. If I had told Dad at the time, he would have made sure that the man would never hurt me—or any other boy—again.

But I had been tricked by the abuser's lies. He knew how to keep me under his control—and how to put a wall of fear and guilt between my parents and me. He had used fear and guilt to keep me silent all these years.

For much of my life, Dad had wondered why I was so angry all the time. He had been baffled by my rebellion and rage. He had wondered if he'd failed me somehow. For the first time, the secret was out, and our relationship as father and son finally made sense.

I had kept that secret inside me until I was forty-two years old. And it wasn't until I let go of that secret that I was finally able to see all the good things my father and my mother tried to do in my life. And I thank God that I was finally able to unburden myself and see how God had used Dad and Mom to bless my life.

A Work in Progress

I still struggle with what it means to live out the kind of forgiveness my father showed to the man who shot him. I still struggle daily to live out The Lord's Prayer—"forgive us our debts, as we also have forgiven our debtors." Does that mean I have to forgive the man who molested me when I was a child? Yes, it does. But what does forgiveness mean when we're talking about a monster who destroys the lives of children?

Forgiveness doesn't mean excusing what he did. It doesn't mean pretending it never happened. It doesn't mean he shouldn't be arrested, prosecuted, and punished as harshly as the law allows. Forgiveness simply means that I let go of the right to resentment and revenge. It means I leave him to God's judgment. My decision to forgive benefits me and liberates me, not the child molester.

The man who molested me died in February 2008. For decades, I had lived in fear that the pictures he took of me would become public. After his death, his sister-in-law wrote to me and told me he was dead. She said, "He was as evil the day he died as he was when he molested you. But rest assured, all the pictures he possessed have been destroyed." When I read the letter, I was glad to know that the pictures were gone and glad that he could never hurt any more children. But I didn't feel vindictive. I had moved on.

According to The Lord's Prayer, I can forgive—I *must* forgive—those who do harm to *me*. But I don't have the right or the power to forgive what a child molester does to other children. It's simply not my place to forgive what one person does to another person. It's not my place to forgive what Hitler did to the Jews, or what ISIS is doing to people across the Middle East. Only God has the right to judge sin or forgive sin in that broad sense. All I can do—all God expects me to do—is to let go of bitterness toward those who hurt me.

Forgiveness is not something you do once and for all. When people have hurt us deeply, the hurt keeps coming back, and we have to forgive them again and again. We have to let go of resentment again and again. We may think, "I forgave that person. It's over, it's all in the past." But then some reminder of the old hurt will resurface—and we'll have to forgive all over again.

People often think that when you come out publicly and tell your story, you're over it. But I'm not really over it. Whenever I feel that someone is attacking me or trying to corner me in some way, I'm a child again, being blackmailed by that pedophile. When people attacked me on my radio show or spewed hate on my Twitter feed or my Facebook page, I would take it personally. When I was involved in a tough contract negotiation, I unconsciously saw the person across the table as my molester, my attacker. I could really fly into a rage in my attorney's office.

I'm still learning forgiveness from my father. People have said the most outrageous things about Ronald Reagan. They've lied about him, smeared him, assassinated his character, and attacked his reputation—yet I never saw my father lose his temper (unless you count the "I am *paying* for this microphone, Mr. Green" incident in 1980). Some of the things Sam Donaldson or *The Washington Post* said about Dad would keep Nancy up all night long—but he'd sleep like a baby. No matter what anyone said about him, he never took it personally.

And that's what I'm still trying to learn from my father. He showed me how to forgive, but I haven't mastered it. I haven't figured it all out. I'm a work in progress.

Meanwhile, child molesters continue to prey on children. The average pedophile will victimize 260 children over a lifetime. And more than 90 percent of convicted child molesters will victimize more children after they are released from prison.[5]

If I had the power to write the laws affecting child molesters in America today, I would lift the statute of limitations off the crime of child molestation. I would not protect convicted child molesters from the natural consequences of their actions but would incarcerate them in the general population. And I would like to see the Catholic Church show leadership on this issue, demand harsh punishment of all offenders (including offenders who happen to be clergy), and make strides in protecting the innocence of children, as Jesus taught us to do.[6]

We have to do a better job of protecting children from these monsters. We have a lot of work to do.

Able to Move Forward

When Joe Hyams informed the publisher about our planned content for the book, the huge advance offer came off the table. That was fine with me. Now that I was no longer hiding that secret, I just wanted to tell my story honestly.

So Joe and I hammered out a book about my adoption, my life in the Reagan family, and the molestation and the impact it had on my life. I called the book *On the Outside Looking In*, and it was published in early 1988, during the final year of my father's presidency. The book quickly became a *New York Times* best-seller. The moment it was published, the news media combed it for juicy tidbits to use against Dad. I got to go on the *Today Show* and *Larry King Live* to talk about the stories in the book. Media attention subsided when reporters discovered it wasn't another *Mommie Dearest*.

It was a liberating experience to tell my story. Secrets imprison us; the truth sets us free. For thirty-five years, I was in a prison of silence and fear. Once I let go of my secret, it lost its power over me.

Years ago, when I had my radio talk show, I talked on the air about the molestation. I said:

> People sometimes tell me that, after all these years, those childhood hurts shouldn't affect me anymore. And they really don't, at least not very often. But when you have been keeping a secret for years, with no way of dealing with it and no one to talk to about it, something builds up inside you. I could compartmentalize it, but I couldn't make it go away.
>
> Sometimes I still get angry. I'll be going along for a while and everything will be just fine—and then the moment I feel somebody pressuring me, those old feelings will come right back. Something that happened decades ago will affect me as if it happened just this morning.

After I shared those thoughts, I received a call on the air from a man who was probably in his fifties. He said, "Michael, the same thing that happened to you, happened to me. I was molested when I was a boy, but I never told anyone. That memory has been with me all my life. Tonight, I'm sitting in this chair and all I have is my dog." At that point, he started to cry.

"I understand," I said. "Believe me, I do."

He composed himself and continued, "I lost my wife, I lost my kids, I lost everyone I ever cared about. You're right, Michael. When you've been molested, it affects all your relationships. I've never told anyone about this, and I was never able to let it go. I let this secret destroy my whole life. When you told your story tonight, you gave me the courage to pick up the phone and finally tell someone what happened to me. I knew you would understand."

I pray that this man will learn to forgive himself and receive God's forgiveness, the way I have. I pray that he will continue to let go of his secret so that healing can come into his life.

I have learned from my father and from Colleen how to love and forgive others and how to forgive myself. Once I was able to unlock that secret, I began to move past the trauma of the molestation and toward a new relationship with my father.

To my amazement, I even found that God was able to bring something good out of that awful experience. While that doesn't excuse what the molester did, it does show that God is able to bring his redemptive benefits into my life despite all that I suffered.

I discovered that I owe my personality—and possibly my success in radio and public speaking—to the hurt the molester inflicted on me. As a boy, I developed a gregarious, class-clown personality to hide the fear and rage inside me. Originally, my outgoing personality was a disguise. Today, it's simply who I am. By the grace of God, I've found a pony buried in the manure pile of childhood abuse.

Forgiveness—The Theme of His Life

When my father lay on that hospital gurney, bleeding internally and struggling for breath, there was an excellent chance that he would die in the next few minutes or hours. What was at the forefront of his mind? *Forgiveness*.

Dad was well acquainted with The Lord's Prayer. "Forgive us our sins as we forgive those who sin against us"—he took that prescription literally. If he was about to enter eternity, he wanted to go with his hands clean, his conscience clear, and his soul washed free of sin. So he began by forgiving the young man who shot him.

What if he had not forgiven his attacker? And what if Pope John Paul II hadn't forgiven his? These two men, along with Prime Minister Margaret Thatcher, Czech dissident Václav Havel, Poland's Lech Wałęsa, and others, helped change the world and bring down the Soviet Empire. Would Dad and the pope have succeeded if they had not been men of forgiveness? I don't know.

But I do believe God honored their prayers of forgiveness when their lives were on the line. I believe God crowned them with success because they made themselves available as instruments of forgiveness. Here are some of the lessons I've learned from observing my father—lessons in how to forgive and how to be forgiven:

Don't wait for an apology before you forgive. Dad prayed for his attacker within the same hour that he was shot. If he had waited for an apology, he would still be waiting. In all the years since that day, the man who shot my father has never expressed remorse for the attack.

If the person who hurt you apologizes, that's great. That will make reconciliation much easier. But if that person never apologizes, you can still forgive. In fact, you owe it to yourself to forgive that person and get on with your life.

Try to understand. As a young man, I used every excuse to avoid recognizing how my father really felt about me. But a few years ago, I was going through some of Dad's possessions, and I came across a war bond. During World War II, the government issued war bonds to finance the defense effort. These bonds were sold in banks and even in movie theaters. Many Hollywood personalities, including my mother and father, actively promoted the sale of war bonds to support the defense effort.

I saw that my father had purchased this bond in my name on March 18, 1945, the day I was born. Even before I was officially adopted, he bought this war bond as a "welcome to the family" gift. That piece of paper spoke volumes to me about how my father really felt about me when I was born.

My birth mother was an aspiring actress named Irene Flaugher, and my birth father was an Army corporal named John Bourgholtzer. When Irene became pregnant, John was stationed in Arizona. He gave four hundred dollars to Irene and told her, "Go to California and have the baby." So I was born at the Queen of Angels Hospital in Los Angeles. Irene wanted me to have a good home, so she insisted on meeting my adoptive parents, Ronald Reagan and Jane Wyman. Mom and Dad adopted me three days after my birth.

When I searched for my birth mother in 1987, I learned that she had kept a scrapbook of my life with clippings from movie magazines and newspapers, right up until her death on December 24, 1985. She never got to hear me say, "Thank you, Irene, for giving me life," but I am very grateful and I honor her.

(By the way, both Flaugher and Bourgholtzer are German names. So I was born German, but three days later, I became Irish.)

I used to wonder why my birth mother gave me up for adoption. I wondered why she didn't love me enough to keep me. I used to wonder if Mom and Dad loved me. Today, knowing what I know, I realize I was surrounded by love—but I didn't know it. My birth mother sacrificed her happiness so that I could grow up in a two-parent family. And Mom and Dad showered me with love, but I wasn't able to recognize it.

Only after I let go of my secret did I begin to understand all that my father did out of love for me. It has taken me decades to realize that he was *continually* trying to show me how much he loved me. I think a lot of people grow up angry with their parents because they are dealing with the same issues I was. If they could gain some adult perspective on their childhood, they might understand—and forgive.

In many ways, the art of forgiveness is really the art of understanding—of children understanding parents and of parents understanding children. My father was a master in the art of forgiveness. We, his children, dropped out of college, violated his rules, spoke out against him, and embarrassed him in many ways. And he always welcomed us, embraced us, and forgave us.

When I speak to pro-life groups, I often say, "Do you realize that 80 percent of abortions are performed on young women who profess to believe in God? We have to ask ourselves, 'Why are our daughters having abortions?' Maybe the answer is that we have told them, 'Don't you dare do anything to embarrass our family. Don't you dare get pregnant outside of marriage. If you do, you won't be welcome in this family.'"

Shouldn't we be willing to get on the cross for our children's sins, just as Christ died on the cross for ours? Shouldn't we be willing to accept some embarrassment, some humiliation, in order to show our children we love them, accept them, and forgive them? How many of our daughters have we chased to an abortion clinic through our pride and lack of forgiveness?

If we parents would try to understand our children, if we children would try to understand our parents, I think we would find it easier to forgive.

Understand what forgiveness is—and what it isn't. Forgiveness is a choice, not a feeling or an emotion. Forgiveness is a decision to give up the right to hurt the person who hurt me. When we forgive, we surrender the right to get even.

Another way of looking at forgiveness is that we are canceling a debt. That's why Jesus, when he taught his disciples to pray, said, "Forgive us our debts, as we also have forgiven our debtors." When we forgive, we wipe the slate clean.

Forgiveness doesn't mean condoning evil. When we forgive, we honestly and objectively say that sin is sin, evil is evil, wrong is wrong—but we choose not to hold onto our anger and resentment. The point of forgiveness is not to shield wrongdoers from the consequences of their sin, but to liberate ourselves from bitterness, so that we can get on with our lives.

When my father forgave the man who shot him, he let go of his own personal resentment toward the gunmen, his own right to get even. Dad canceled any debt the gunman owed him. Of course, the gunman had also wounded three other people and committed a crime. So the gunman owed a debt to those victims and to society. In forgiving that man, Dad didn't cancel the gunman's debt to anyone else or to society. The shooter was still accountable for his crime.

Once you understand what forgiveness is—and what it isn't—you may find it easier to forgive.

Forgiving does not equal forgetting. There's an old cliché—forgive and forget. Well, it's not always possible to forget. But we can still forgive even when we can't forget. The memory of the wrong someone did to you may always be there, but you can let go of the right to get even for it. If you don't, you'll remain stuck in bitterness and resentment—and you'll always be an emotional hostage of the person who hurt you.

Don't expect to forgive once and for all. If someone has hurt you deeply, the pain will surface again and again, and you will probably have to make the decision to forgive again and again as well. That's normal and understandable.

Holding a grudge is easy. Forgiveness is hard. It takes a great deal of strength and toughness to forgive.

Being wronged is no excuse for doing wrong. The man who molested me is morally responsible for what he did to me. But I am morally responsible for what I do to others.

I recently talked to Boz Tchividjian, a former child abuse prosecutor who currently teaches Child Abuse and the Law at Liberty University School of Law. Boz is also the founder of GRACE (Godly Response to Abuse in the Christian Environment), which educates the faith community in responding to sexual abuse—and he is a grandson of the Rev. Billy Graham.

I'm on the board of GRACE, and Boz and I were talking about the abuse I suffered as a child. I said, "Here's what most adults don't understand about child abuse. We look at abuse through the eyes of an adult, not the eyes of a child. And what do we always tell the child who is abused? We say, 'You were a child. It wasn't your fault.' And that's true as far as it goes. The guy who molested me was an adult, and what he did wasn't my fault, it was his fault.

"But tell me this: Whose fault was it the way I treated my mother after that? Whose fault was it the way I treated my father? Whose fault was it that I acted out and was disruptive in school? Whose fault was it that I stole money from Dad's wallet to pay for prostitutes on Saturday nights so I could prove to myself I wasn't homosexual? You see, Boz, the first sin—the molestation—belongs to the perpetrator. But everything I did after that, I'm responsible for."

Boz said, "I've never heard anybody put it that way."

I think we are often so eager to comfort the child who has been abused that we are too quick to say, "Everything is the molester's fault. Nothing is your fault." And that's simply not true. The fact that I was molested doesn't excuse the sins I committed against Mom and Dad and others.

I think it is actually a healing and empowering experience for an abuse victim to say, "I am responsible for my own actions. Just because I've been hurt doesn't mean I have to hurt others.

Just because I was exploited doesn't mean I have to hate others. The cycle of abuse ends with me. I am personally responsible for my own actions."

Forgiveness does not equal reconciliation. Forgiving doesn't mean that we condone what other people do. It doesn't mean that there are no consequences for the other person. And it doesn't mean we have to reconcile with, or become friends with, the person who wronged us. It just means we give up the right to retaliate.

Sometimes people are so troubled or mentally ill or obnoxious or just plain evil that it is impossible for us to be friends with them. But we can still forgive them. We can keep them at a distance so they won't hurt us again, but we can give up our right to hate them and hold a grudge against them.

My father wanted a chance to tell the man who shot him that he forgave him, face-to-face. But the young man's doctors said it would not be in his best interests. So it's not always best to say to a person, "I forgive you." But it's always possible to make the choice to forgive that person within your own heart.

If you can express forgiveness to the other person, fine. If you can't, that doesn't take anything away from the forgiveness that you have experienced inside.

Forgive yourself. And let others forgive you. If you're holding a secret you think no one could ever forgive, go to someone— a pastor, a priest, a counselor—and let that secret go. Forgiving yourself may be one of the hardest things you'll ever do. I know it wasn't easy for my father to forgive himself for something that happened during his first term as president.

It took place at dawn on Sunday, October 23, 1983. A truck loaded with the equivalent of 21,000 pounds of TNT, driven by a suicide bomber, plowed into a U.S. Marine compound outside of Beirut, Lebanon. The bomb detonated, producing the largest nonnuclear blast since World War II. The explosion lifted the building off its foundation and collapsed it to a pile of smoking rubble. The attack killed 220 Marines and 21 other U.S. servicemen. It was the heaviest one-day death toll suffered by the Marines since the battle of Iwo Jima. My father called it the saddest day of his presidency, and perhaps of his life. I'll never forget the expression on his face as he and Nancy passed by the rows of flag-draped coffins at Dover Air Force Base.

My father had sent those Marines, sailors, and soldiers to Beirut, and they had died there. And I know that one of the hardest things my father ever had to do was to forgive himself for those 241 deaths. I think many of us find it much easier to forgive others than to forgive ourselves. I know that Dad internalized the blame for that loss of life.

That's why, from that point on, my father was much more forceful in dealing with the Gaddafis and Gorbachevs of the world. He never wanted to see such wholesale slaughter on his watch. It wasn't in my father's makeup to avoid responsibility. If anything, he tended to accept more blame than he deserved. But I believe he ultimately did forgive himself for sending those servicemen to Beirut—and that's why he was able to move forward.

We all have regrets, but we can't change the past. We have to learn the lessons of the past, seek God's forgiveness, and move on. That's the example my father set. That's the lesson he left for me—and for all of us.

Dad's example played a big role in my life. I saw that he was able to forgive himself, and from his example, I learned to forgive myself for being molested, and for all my other sins and regrets.

The next time you struggle to forgive someone who has hurt you, remember my father, lying on that gurney, with a bullet lodged next to his heart. His first impulse was forgiveness.

So forgive and be forgiven. Set yourself free and live.

10

Never Underestimate the Power of One

TODAY, THE SOVIET UNION is on the ash heap of history. But on Inauguration Day 1981, it looked as if the Soviets were on the rise, and America was headed for the ash heap.

The United States was in a full retreat, while the Soviets were on the march. Soviet power was projected around the globe: Cuba, Nicaragua, Asia, the Middle East, Iraq, Ethiopia, Angola, North and South Yemen, and Afghanistan. For years, America had stood by, impotently wringing its hands.

Then came Reagan.

It took a man of rare vision to believe that we could "begin the world over again" (as Thomas Paine once put it). It took a man of rare conviction to decide that the time had come to end the stalemate between the superpowers and to liberate half of the globe from oppression.

Upon his inauguration in 1981, Ronald Reagan made it his top priority to collapse the Soviet Empire. He gave his "evil empire" speech—and his critics went ballistic. He worked with his allies, including Margaret Thatcher and Pope John Paul II, to break the Soviet stranglehold on Eastern Europe. He used overt and covert means to bankrupt the Soviet economy. And in 1987, in defiance of all his advisers, he went to the Brandenburg Gate and demanded, "Mr. Gorbachev, tear down this wall!"

The pundits declared that Reagan was asking the impossible. Today, a slab of the Berlin wall, decorated with butterflies and flowers, is proudly displayed at the Reagan Presidential Library in Simi Valley, California.

I firmly believe—and history shows—that if my father, Ronald Reagan, had never been born, the Soviet Union would still be alive and well today. In fact, when you realize that America in the late 1970s was in steep decline, militarily and economically, it seems likely that, if not for Ronald Reagan, the Soviets might well have won the Cold War, and America would be on the ash heap.

Can one person make such a profound difference in history?

Absolutely. I know one person can. Because I know the person who did.

One Man Alone against Communism

For Dad, the Cold War was not an abstract concept. It was his own personal battle, and he was on the front lines. His enemy was Communism, and the enemy repeatedly tried to destroy him.

Dad's battle began almost soon as World War II ended in the summer of 1945. At that time, the Reagan family—Dad, my mother Jane Wyman, my sister Maureen, and I—lived in Beverly Hills, and Dad had just signed a long-term million dollar contract with Warner Bros. That contract enabled him to achieve his dream of owning a ranch. Life was good, and the future seemed rosy.

But on Friday, October 5, 1945, something happened that upset the apple cart of Dad's life. That was the day "the Battle of Hollywood" erupted on the street in front of the Warner

Brothers studio in Burbank. The "battle" was actually a riot between three hundred strikers from the Conference of Studio Unions (CSU) and the hundreds of nonstriking studio employees who were trying to get to work. The CSU was headed by union organizer Herbert "Herb" Sorrell, an avowed Communist who had organized the cartoonists' strike that nearly shut down the Walt Disney Studio in 1941. The strikers overturned cars and attacked the nonstriking employees with chains, hammers, and metal pipes, injuring more than forty people.

In his autobiography, Dad recalled the scene: "The gates of the studios soon became a bloody battleground.... Homes and cars were bombed and many people were seriously injured on the picket lines; workers trying to drive into a studio would be surrounded by pickets who'd pull open their car door or roll down a window and yank the worker's arm until they broke it, then say, 'Go on, go to work, see how much you get done today.'"[1]

The Battle of Hollywood raged for weeks. Herb Sorrell's thugs blocked the Warner Brothers main entrance, so studio head Jack Warner sneaked actors and production crew into the studio via the storm drain which led to the Los Angeles River. While Dad's colleagues sneaked in via the storm drain, he and some other hearty souls insisted on taking the studio bus straight through the main gate. Though the studio's security chief told everyone to lie flat on the floor, Dad insisted on sitting upright next to the window—making himself a visible target as the bus ran the gantlet of bottle-throwing strikers.

The Communist-inspired violence in front of the Warner Brothers studio continued throughout 1946. Dad, Katharine Hepburn, and Gene Kelly represented the Screen Actors Guild in a series of marathon meetings with Herb Sorrell and other CSU officials. They met on a near-daily basis, week after week, seeking an end to the strike—and every time they seemed close to an agreement, Sorrell would come in with new demands,

When the CSU refused to accept anything but capitulation, Dad pulled the plug on the talks.

Soon after Dad broke off negotiations with Sorrell, he began receiving anonymous threats. He was shooting a motion picture, Don Siegel's production of *Night unto Night* with Viveca Lindfors, at a beach house near Malibu. During a break in shooting, a man from the service station on the highway said there was a phone call for Ronald Reagan. Dad went to the station and took the call. The anonymous caller warned him to meet the union demands or "your face will never be in pictures again." Dad later learned that union thugs planned to throw acid in his face.

Dad told Siegel about the threat, and Siegel shut down the set for the day. Hours later, the police gave my father a .32 Smith & Wesson and shoulder holster, and he wore it for protection for the next seven months. At night, he kept the gun on his nightstand. My mother would sometimes wake up to find Dad sitting up in bed, gun in hand, listening for noises outside the window. When Dad had to be away, he would hire private bodyguards to protect his family (I was eighteen months old at the time, and Maureen was five).

In the end, Dad and the Screen Actors Guild defeated the union. The strike collapsed in February 1947. Because of Dad's dedicated work on behalf of SAG, Gene Kelly nominated him as president of the union. Dad was elected to his first term in March 1947. That was Dad's first experience fighting Communism— and it took real physical courage to stand firm against the threats. That experience prepared him well to take on the global Communist threat in the 1980s—and win again.

It was a costly victory. Dad's long hours spent working on negotiations and union issues, along with the threatening calls and the gun on the nightstand—all of this took its toll on my mother. When baby Christine died and Dad was in the hospital, that was the final straw. Mom filed for divorce soon after that.

The Soviet Communists tried to take over Hollywood and threatened Dad's life, along with his family and his livelihood—and their threats prompted him to action. The Communists made a big mistake when they took on Ronald Reagan. Decades later, he was still standing tall, and Soviet Communism lay in ruins.

Dad's anti-Communist activism continued into the 1950s and beyond. He lent his name and energies to such groups as the Crusade for Freedom, founded by General Lucius Clay, and the Christian Anti-Communism Crusade. In the fall of 1956, after Soviet tanks crushed the Hungarian Revolution, killing thousands of Hungarian patriots, Dad closed one of his *General Electric Theater* telecasts with a call for donations to help Hungarian refugees.

My father's primary motivation for becoming president was so that he could fight and defeat Soviet Communism. In January 1977, he met with Richard V. Allen. They had a long talk about foreign policy, especially the failure of détente during the Nixon–Ford era. At one point, Dad made a statement that epitomized his no-nonsense approach: "My idea of American policy toward the Soviet Union is simple and some would say simplistic. It is this: we win and they lose. What do you think of that?"

Allen was so impressed by my father's confidence and commitment to winning the Cold War that he was one of the first to sign on as an aide to Dad's 1980 presidential campaign. Allen later became Dad's first National Security Advisor.

Only one man on the political scene in the era of détente dared to say, "We win and they lose." All the experts wanted to get along with the Soviets. Dad wasn't interested in getting along with the evil empire. He wanted to become president so he could *defeat* the evil empire. He had the faith and confidence to believe that one person could make a big difference in the world.

Fear of Flying

If you visit the Ronald Reagan Presidential Library in Simi Valley, California, there is one exhibit that is guaranteed to knock your socks off—Air Force One, the customized Boeing 707 that served every president from Richard Nixon to George W. Bush. Dad logged more than 675,000 air miles aboard that plane—more than any other president before or since. He last flew on that plane on January 20, 1989—the day he and Nancy returned to California to resume private life.

Now I'll let you in on a little secret: Dad was afraid of flying.

I'm absolutely serious. Fact is, he was so fearful of flying airplanes that he nearly passed up a career in politics. It may well be that one of the real unsung heroes of the Reagan era was the man who cured Dad of his aerophobia—his brother, Neil "Moon" Reagan.

Dad's fear of flying is all the more ironic because, in every other way, he was the most courageous man I've ever known. It took courage and confidence to save seventy-seven lives in the Rock River in Illinois. It took courage for him to stand strong against the threats against his life during the Battle of Hollywood. Why, then, was he afraid of flying?

In 1937, while working as a radio broadcaster for the Chicago Cubs, Dad flew to Catalina Island to cover the Cubs spring training camp. It was an exceptionally choppy flight—a flight so harrowing he thought he wouldn't survive. (During this visit to Southern California, Dad also made a screen test with Warner Bros., which launched his Hollywood career.)

Dad was required to fly when he was with the First Motion Picture Unit of the Army Air Corps (his nearsightedness prevented him from being shipped overseas). As soon as the war ended, however, he vowed never to fly again. Dad told me the reason he made that vow: "God only gives you so many air miles. I believed I used all of mine during the Second World War."

In the late 1950s, while hosting *General Electric Theater*, he traveled ten weeks out of the year, giving a dozen or more speeches per day—but he never traveled by air. He went entirely by train or car.

After my father delivered a highly acclaimed speech on behalf of Barry Goldwater in 1964, Republican power brokers urged him to run for governor of California. It was an appealing invitation, but there was one problem: his fear of flying. How could he campaign in such a large state by train and car? How would he carry out his duties without flying?

This is where Dad's brother Neil comes in. John Neil Reagan was a senior vice president of the advertising firm McCann Erickson. Neil was also a senior producer for the CBS television network. Many of the wealthy donors and kingmakers who supported Dad's political career—his "kitchen cabinet"—were clients of McCann Erickson, introduced to Dad by Neil.

"Moon" and "Dutch" were always very close as brothers. Dad had helped put Neil through college, so Neil felt he owed his younger brother a debt. From his office at McCann Erickson, Neil was able to help Dad in many important ways.

One day in 1965, Dad spoke at an event in San Francisco. That evening, Neil phoned Dad in his hotel room and said, "Ron, you want to be governor of California, don't you?"

"Well, yes I do."

"If you really mean that, then be at the Hillcrest Country Club in Los Angeles tomorrow morning at nine. I'll introduce you to the people who will fund your campaign."

"But Moon, in order to get there by nine, I'll have to fly."

"Yes, you will. Good-bye." Neil ended the call not knowing if his brother would show up.

At nine the next morning, Dad arrived at Hillcrest Country Club, fresh from his first airplane ride in twenty years. Soon Dad was electioneering around California in an aging DC-3.

He bounced and white-knuckled his way right into the governor's mansion.

The Untapped Greatness within Each of Us

My father never saw himself as a politician. He was an average citizen who saw that something was very wrong with his government, very wrong with the world—and he stepped forward to help set it right. He was just one man—but he believed in the power of one.

The founding fathers envisioned a government consisting of citizen legislators and citizen leaders—not professional politicians. The political class that rules America today was never part of the original plan for America. Instead, the founders envisioned a nation in which grassroots Americans served a term or two in Congress or the White House, then returned home to their farms, shops, and offices to live under the laws they had created.

My father once remarked as governor of California, "I'm just a citizen temporarily in public service." And during his first presidential race in 1976, he said, "I'm not a politician by profession. I am a citizen who decided I had to be personally involved in order to stand up for my own values and beliefs." He saw a job that needed doing, and he got it done—then he went back home and picked up the life he had temporarily set aside when he first ran for governor—the life of Ronald Reagan, citizen.

He was just one person who believed in the power of one. Here are some of the lessons I've learned by studying my father's example:

Do the thing that scares you. There is untapped greatness within each of us. The only thing holding us back is our fear. For my father, the obstacle was fear of flying. For you, it might be a very different fear. But my father would want you to know that one person can accomplish amazing things—if that person has the courage to try. You'll never know what you can achieve until you stop listening to your fears and start following your courage.

Perhaps you—like my Uncle "Moon"—know someone who needs a little boost, a little kick in the courage, in order to fly. Be the encourager, the older brother or older sister, the mentor, the friend, the one who will give that person the courage to soar.

The Bible tells us, "For God has not given us a spirit of fear, but of power and of love and of a sound mind."[2] You have the power, the love, and the sound mind you need to make a difference in the world. Ask God to take away the fear. Then see where your courage takes you.

When you take on the challenge, think big. Dad easily could have enjoyed more years in television, making investments and saving his money, then retiring to raise horses at the ranch. But he felt called to make a difference—and he began to think *big*.

He had fought Communism in Hollywood in the 1940s and 1950s. In his mind, it was only logical that he should take the fight all the way to Moscow. So the next natural step, of course, was to run for president.

Now you and I don't need to be president of the United States in order to make a difference. You can make a big difference wherever you are. But whatever you do, think big. Start a business, start a charity, start a movement, run for office, build a hospital, shoot for the moon. Once you have a dream, step back and imagine how you could make that dream even bigger. Keep imagining, keep growing that dream, until it's so big it scares you.

Then go make that dream come true.

Set goals that are big, yet easy to understand. Dad was a professional communicator, and he understood the need to communicate big ideas in simple terms. So when he sat down with

Richard V. Allen and laid out his vision for dealing with the Soviet Union, he told Allen, "We win and they lose." The idea was so simple and so powerful that Dick Allen couldn't wait to join my father's campaign team—and his administration.

Big goals, simply stated, are attractive, and they draw supporters to your cause. When you communicate your dreams to others, make them big and keep them simple.

Practice being a visionary. My father once said, "To grasp and hold a vision—that is the very essence of successful leadership, not only on the movie set where I learned it, but everywhere." He was a true visionary. When everyone around him saw a world held hostage by a doctrine of mutually assured destruction, he saw a world in which a missile defense shield made nuclear weapons obsolete. When everyone around him saw only détente with the Soviet Union, he saw a future in which we win, they lose.

We can all train ourselves to become visionaries. Vision, as Dad said, is truly the essence of successful leadership. Many people mistakenly think that vision is the ability to foretell the future. But my father showed us by his example that vision is the ability to foresee a possible future—and the commitment to turn that vision into a reality. Visionaries don't just see the future—they create it. When you have a vision for the future and you commit yourself to making it come true, that vision energizes you in several important ways:

First, your vision draws you forward toward your goals. When you have a vision of the future always in front of you, you can see exactly where you're going. Your vision gives you a sense of focus and direction, and it keeps you from getting distracted and drawn off course.

Second, your vision energizes you. It helps you maintain your excitement and enthusiasm for the goal. It motivates you to push through obstacles and opposition.

Third, your vision fires up your imagination. The world needs leaders who can envision a world beyond terrorism, beyond political division and strife, beyond AIDS and Alzheimer's, beyond pollution and energy shortages. What bold, imaginative, "impossible" dream can you envision? How will you make it come true?

Fourth, your vision enables you to persevere and finish strong. My father had his first inkling of the Strategic Defense Initiative missile shield in 1967. He persevered into the 1980s against opponents and scoffers to get the SDI program up and running. Visionaries always face opposition. You can't be a visionary if you are easily discouraged. The power of your vision enables you to keep going through tough times.

Let me suggest some ways you can sharpen your vision skills and practice thinking like a visionary:

First, discard all limits on your imagination. Overturn all your assumptions. Question every restriction others try to impose on you. When people told Dad that the Soviet Empire would last for centuries and could not be toppled, he said, "Well, we'll just see about that." He rejected the limitations on the future that others simply accepted.

Second, don't listen to your inner critic. There's a voice inside you that says, "It can't be done. It will never work. Let's not go overboard." That inner critic makes us worry about what other people will think, about whether we will make a mistake and look foolish. Dad never seemed to be troubled by that voice. He didn't worry about whether his ideas would be popular. If he was convinced he was right, he didn't care what anyone else thought.

The inner critic makes us afraid to take risks or make ourselves conspicuous. The inner critic tells us to play it safe, to follow the rules, to not make waves. My father was never afraid to take risks, and he was constantly making waves. The boldness of his vision attracted people to his side, and turned Dad's ideas into a revolution—the Reagan Revolution.

Third, consider all possibilities. Dad was never content with just one solution to a problem. He liked having dozens of options and solutions to choose from. He would gather his economic team or his national security team, and they would brainstorm creative solutions to difficult problems.

Case in point, in keeping with my father's doctrine of "We win, they lose," one of his first orders of business was to stop the flow of American technology into the Soviet Union, which propped up the Soviet economy. This was the first order of business at a National Security Council (NSC) meeting Dad chaired about five months after taking office. The subject of discussion: the trans-Siberian oil and gas pipeline, which was then under construction. Once completed, the pipeline would produce huge profits for the Soviet economy—and the Soviets were stealing American technology to build it. At the NSC meeting, Dad called for creative solutions.

A few days later, he attended an economic summit in Ottawa, Canada. There, French president François Mitterrand told Dad about a KGB officer, Colonel Vetrov, who was working for the French. Vetrov, whose codename was "Farewell," provided information on the Soviet theft of Western technology, from machinery to computer software. Dad returned to Washington and assigned NSC staffer Gus Weiss to study the "Farewell" documents—and Weiss came up with an idea: Instead of shutting down the technology thefts, why not let the Soviets steal what we want them to steal?

That was the kind of thinking Ronald Reagan loved. He ordered the CIA to have a specially prepared pipeline control system sent to Canada, where it would be stolen by the KGB. The plan worked and the Soviets stole the device and installed it to regulate pipeline pressure. Instead (as the CIA planned), it caused a pressure buildup and a massive explosion—the equivalent of a three kiloton bomb. The blast dealt a crippling blow to the pipeline project—and the Soviet economy. It was a key factor in the ultimate collapse of the Soviet Union.

Finally, consider this: What if there had been no Ronald Reagan? What would the world be like today if this man had never been born?

In June 2004, we laid my father to rest on the grounds of his presidential library in Simi Valley, California. That night, our family stayed at the Bel Air Hotel, where many of the dignitaries who had attended my father's funeral were staying. When we went downstairs for breakfast, I saw one of my father's dearest friends and closest allies, Lady Margaret Thatcher. I went to her and said hello, and she smiled and greeted me warmly.

We talked about the close relationship she and my father had enjoyed. "Michael," she said, "I've often thought of how close your father came to winning the nomination in 1976, and how much we could have accomplished if he had become president four years earlier. The Cold War might have ended four years sooner, and the world would have been spared so much suffering."

"I think Ronald Reagan arrived in the White House at exactly the right time," I replied. "Had he been elected in 1976, I don't think he would have accomplished all that he did. In fact, if he'd been elected in 1976, the Cold War might still be going on today."

She looked surprised. "Why do you say that?"

"Ronald Reagan needed allies in order to bring down the Iron Curtain, and none of his allies were in place in 1976. You, Lady Thatcher, were my father's strongest ally, and you didn't become prime minister until 1979. Pope John Paul II came on the scene in 1978—and his visit to Poland in 1979 gave rise to Lech Walesa and the Solidarity movement. Vaclav Havel rose to prominence in Czechoslovakia in 1977. Helmut Kohl wasn't chancellor of Germany until 1982. And Mikhail Gorbachev didn't come to power until 1985—a year after Ronald Reagan would have left office if he'd been elected in 1976.

"None of Dad's allies were in place in 1976—but almost all of you were in place when he was inaugurated in 1981. It took all of you, working together, to end the Cold War. I think God's providence put you and Dad and every other player in position at just the right moment in history."

"Thank you, Michael," she said. "I had never thought of that."

The same God who put Ronald Reagan and Margaret Thatcher and all the other players in position in the 1980s is still at work in your life and mine. So I ask you: What if *you* had never lived? How would the world be different if *you* had never been born? What kind of difference have *you* made in the lives of the people around you—in your neighborhood, your school, your community, your world?

And what kind of difference *could* you make? What kind of difference *will* you make?

The sky's the limit. Never underestimate the power of one.

11

Be a Leader

In October 1979, Nancy called a family meeting at the house in Pacific Palisades. My sister Maureen rode with Colleen and me. Even though Nancy hadn't told us what was on the agenda, we were pretty sure we knew: Dad had decided to run for president.

When we arrived, Dad walked out of the bedroom and seemed surprised to see everybody. Apparently, Nancy had called the meeting without telling Dad. We gathered in the living room— Patti, Ron, Maureen, Colleen, and I, facing Dad and Nancy.

"Your father has something to tell you," Nancy said.

Dad said, "I just returned from a speaking engagement in Atlanta. The same thing happened there that's been happening in Pennsylvania and Florida and everywhere I go. When I check into a hotel, the bellmen who carry my bags ask me why I don't run for president. They say, 'Governor Reagan, we need you.' When I go to my room, I find a note on my pillow from the chambermaid: 'Mr. Reagan, please run for president. We need you.' Based on what I'm hearing around the country, I think I have a good chance to be elected president of the United States. So I've decided to run."

There was a moment of awkward silence—no one said anything.

Then Patti began to sob quietly. She was studying acting at the University of Southern California, was politically liberal, and had tried to distance herself from her famously conservative father while he was governor of California. Now Dad was going to run for president—and Patti would still be in his shadow.

Ron, the youngest, stared at the floor unhappily. Also liberal and at a rebellious stage, he had felt oppressed by his parents' expectations of him while Dad was governor. If Dad became president, Ron knew that the glare of the spotlight would become a thousand times hotter.

Maureen, Colleen, and I stood up, went to Dad's side, and told him we would support him all the way.

I'm sure Nancy was distressed by the unenthusiastic reaction of her two biological children. But this meeting was the first step in her campaign to get all four of Dad's children solidly lined up behind his candidacy.

After the meeting, Maureen, Colleen, and I went out for a glass of wine. We raised our glasses and Maureen made a toast: "Here's to our father. If he doesn't win the White House, we'll run him for president of the Chambermaids and Bellhops Union!"

Dad's rationale for running was vintage Reagan. He didn't say that some GOP bigwigs or a group of conservative million-aires had urged him to run. He said, "The chambermaids and bellhops tell me I've got to run." These were Ronald Reagan's people. He was a grassroots American, and he never forgot that it was grassroots Americans who built this country.

Well, Dad ran and captured the nomination, then he went on to win a resounding victory in the general election. Taking office in January 1981, he proceeded to engineer the most astonishing turnaround in American history. He cut taxes and revived the dying economy. He restored American influence on the world stage. He confronted and dismantled Soviet Communism.

Unfortunately, many leaders today claim that Ronald Reagan's ideas are no longer relevant to America in the twenty-first century. Even many Republicans no longer study my father as a leadership model. But principles don't change, and Ronald Reagan's leadership principles are more urgently needed today than ever before.

As the leader of the free world, my father proved that leadership is not about being "the boss." Leadership is about inspiring people and unleashing their enthusiasm and creativity. We have far too many self-important, self-promoting leaders today who have confidence only in themselves. My father had confidence in the American people, and that was the secret of his greatness.

Dad relied on firm principles to guide his decisions. When he strode into the Oval Office in 1981, he put a new policy in place: "We win, they lose." One of his aides, Herb Meyer, recalled, "Ronald Reagan was the first Western leader whose objective was to win. Now I suggest to you that there is a gigantic difference between playing not to lose and playing to win. It's different emotionally, it's different psychologically, and, of course, it's different practically."[1]

In 1980, my father ran on three simple promises: revive the economy, rebuild the military, and defeat Communism. He remained focused on those three promises throughout his presidency. He cut taxes and brought the dying economy roaring back to life. He restored the military and negotiated with the Soviets from a position of strength. He ended the Cold War without firing a shot—and soon after he left office, the USSR collapsed. Mission accomplished.

In my lifetime, there has never been a leader like my father. He is a role model of leadership like no other. What can we learn from his example? The lessons are endless. Let me share with you some of the insights I've discovered by studying the leadership career of my father.

Not a Vote–A Decision

In August 1981, seven months into my father's first term, 13,000 members of the Professional Air Traffic Controllers Organization (PATCO) defied federal law and walked off the job. The union had already signed an agreement giving the workers a $40 million increase in salary and benefits—then the union came back and demanded *more* concessions totaling $681 million. PATCO had endorsed Dad in the 1980 election, so the union probably expected him to support the PATCO strike. Instead, Dad ordered them back to work within forty-eight hours or they would be fired and replaced. The union called his bluff.

The PATCO leaders should have asked me. I would have told them from personal experience: the Gipper doesn't bluff.

When Dad announced his decision, a reporter asked, "Mr. President, why have you taken such strong action . . . ? Why not some lesser action at this point?"

Dad replied, "What lesser action can there be? The law is very explicit. They are violating the law. . . . You can't sit and negotiate with a union that's in violation of the law."[2]

When the strikers continued to stay out on strike, Dad carried out his promise, firing them all and banning them from federal service for life.

Dad's handling of the PATCO strike had far-reaching implications. From then on, everyone who sat across the negotiating table from my father—including Democratic lawmakers and the Soviets—knew he wasn't bluffing. He was a man of his word.

In 1986, Dad gave an interview to *Fortune* magazine about his leadership style. He explained that a large part of his leadership philosophy was "dictated to me by a little plaque on my desk that says there's no limit to what you can do if you don't mind who gets the credit." He added:

Beyond that, I believe that you surround yourself with the best people you can find, delegate authority, and don't interfere as long as the overall policy that you've decided upon is being carried out.

In the Cabinet meetings—and some members of the Cabinet who have been members of other Cabinets told me there have never been such meetings—I use a system in which I want to hear what everybody wants to say honestly. I want the decisions made on what is right or wrong, what is good or bad for the people of this country. I encourage all the input I can get. . . . I want to know.

And when I've heard all that I need to make a decision, I don't take a vote. I make the decision. Then I expect every one of them, whether their views have carried the day or not, to go forward together in carrying out the policy.[3]

My father didn't ask for a show of hands. He decided. His decisions often went against the advice he received. His advisers told him not to give the Evil Empire speech, but he did. They told him not to go to the Berlin Wall and say, "Mr. Gorbachev, tear down this wall," but he did. They told him not to go into Grenada, but he did. And then there was Reykjavík.

My father and Mikhail Gorbachev met in October 1986 for the Reykjavík arms limitation summit. They made excellent progress until they got to the Strategic Defense Initiative. Gorbachev insisted that the U.S. limit SDI to laboratory tests for ten years. My father knew that only field testing could determine whether SDI was feasible.

Dad's advisers pressed him to give in on SDI. Not one adviser agreed with the president. Yet my father stuck to his decision despite all voices to the contrary. As Dad told *Fortune,* "I don't take a vote. I make the decision." And history proved that Dad's decision at Reykjavík was the right one. A year later, at the

Washington Summit, Gorbachev accepted Dad's conditions on SDI, and together they signed the Intermediate-Range Nuclear Forces Treaty.

The Reagan Rules of Engagement

Dad understood that leadership involves communicating big ideas in simple terms so that people can understand and embrace those ideas. Yet he also had a deep and detailed grasp of all the major issues of the day. Go to YouTube and watch video of his televised press conferences, his appearances on *Meet the Press*, or his part in the presidential debates. You'll be impressed with the breadth and depth of his knowledge on a wide range of policy issues. He could discuss any issue with other leaders, with reporters, or with the man in the street, knowledgeably and persuasively.

A president must understand all the problems and challenges we face as a nation. When you sit behind the Oval Office desk, you cannot simply be "the immigration president" or "the education president" or "the wartime president." You have to be the president of *all* the issues and *all* the people. My father was that kind of president.

At the same time Dad was facing down the Soviet Union, rebuilding our military, and restoring our economy, he also had to deal with various brushfires in different parts of the world. One of those brushfires was whipped up by a tinhorn dictator in Libya by the name of Gaddafi.

Years before my father came into office, Colonel Muammar al-Gaddafi had drawn an imaginary line in the sea that he called "The Line of Death." In violation of maritime law, he claimed the entire Gulf of Sidra as Libya's territorial waters and he warned that any foreign warships or planes that crossed the line would be destroyed.

President Carter obeyed Gaddafi's warnings, and he ordered the U.S. Navy to steer clear of the Gulf of Sidra. Nevertheless, Gaddafi's warplanes continually harassed American ships and fighters over the international waters of the Mediterranean Sea. Libyan planes frequently fired on American planes, and the American pilots had to radio for permission before returning fire. By the time the pilot received permission, the Libyan attacker had turned tail and headed for home. So American planes over international waters would get shot at but could not shoot back.

When my father became president in 1981, he immediately canceled the Carter rules of engagement. He told our forces, "U.S. pilots and sailors have orders not to fire at anything but practice targets—unless fired upon." No longer would an American pilot have to wait for permission to return fire. American airmen cheered the new rules and dubbed them "Reagan ROE" (Reagan Rules of Engagement).

Next, my father sent the a naval force, led by the carriers USS *Forrestal* and USS *Nimitz*, steaming across The Line of Death. The ships conducted Freedom of Navigation (FON) operations in the Gulf of Sidra. Again and again, American reconnaissance patrols made contact with Libyan Mirages, Sukhois, and MiG-23s, but the Libyans held their fire.

It was against a backdrop of tension in the Gulf of Sidra that my wife Colleen and I became witnesses to history. On the evening of Tuesday, August 18, Colleen and I had dinner with Dad and Nancy in the Presidential Suite at the Century Plaza Hotel in Los Angeles. We enjoyed a relaxed evening meal and pleasant conversation. Colleen and I were getting ready to leave when the phone rang. Dad took the call. It was Ed Meese, counselor to the president for policy, calling from the White House.

"Mr. President," Meese said, "Libyan aircraft are locking onto our planes over the Gulf of Sidra. What should our pilots do if fired upon?"

Dad said, "They are to shoot back."

"And if the Libyans turn and run?"

"They are to chase them—if necessary, back to their hangers. But they will shoot them down."

"If that happens, Mr. President, should I wake you?"

"No, Ed. Only call me if our boys are shot down."

Dad made each decision without hesitation. Afterward, Colleen and I went home, and Dad and Nancy went to bed. My father didn't call the United Nations and ask permission to be president of the United States. He made the decisions.

Later that night over the Gulf of Sidra, a pair of Libyan Sukhoi Su-22 fighters fired on two American F-14 Tomcats from the carrier *Nimitz.* The American planes gave chase, and both Libyan fighters were destroyed.

My father had served notice on Colonel Gaddafi: the Reagan Rules of Engagement were now in effect.

A Leader of Common Sense and Optimism

Dad was a man of common sense. Unfortunately, common sense is an uncommon quality in today's leaders. How else do you explain the fact that our leaders are systematically bankrupting the country and that legislators in both parties annually vote for bigger and bigger deficits? I guarantee my father, were he president today, would wage all-out war against this fiscal madness.

My father was a fiscal conservative from Day One of his political career. In 1967, when he became governor of California, he discovered that the outgoing administration of Governor Edmund G. "Pat" Brown had left behind reams and reams of official stationery with Brown's name on it. Dad hated to see all that paper go to waste, so he asked his secretary, "Couldn't we just X out his name?"

Dad was the epitome of common sense government. In a speech to Republicans in Atlanta on December 7, 1973, he said, "I've always believed that government could and should be run with the same common sense rules that apply to business or even budgeting a household. But when you start talking about common sense in connection with government, you cause some traumatic shocks."

He maintained that common-sense philosophy of government throughout his political career—and he attributed his successes as president to common-sense leadership. In his farewell address from the Oval Office at the end of his presidency, Dad said, "Common sense told us that when you put a big tax on something, the people will produce less of it. So we cut the people's tax rates, and the people produced more than ever before."

Another trait that has served my father well as a leader is his optimism. In fact, I think *optimism* is too weak a word to describe Dad's outlook on life. *Enthusiasm* might be a better word. He always approached every day with a great enthusiasm for living, for learning, for engaging with people, and for making a positive difference in the world. The word enthusiasm comes from two Greek words, *en* (meaning "in") and *theos* (meaning God). To have *enthusiasm* is to be divinely inspired and possessed by God. That's the kind of enthusiasm Dad always exhibited— a godly joy, an inspired expectation of a brighter tomorrow.

When Dad gave the dedication speech at the Ronald Reagan Presidential Library in Simi Valley, California, November 4, 1991, he talked about the enthusiastic optimism that had characterized his life and his leadership career:

I, too, have been described as an undying optimist, always seeing a glass half full when some see it as half empty. And, yes, it's true, I always see the sunny side of life. And that's not just because I've been blessed by achieving so many of my dreams. My optimism comes not just from my strong faith in God, but from my strong and enduring faith in man.

In my eighty years (I prefer to call that the forty-first anniversary of my thirty-ninth birthday), I've seen what men can do *for* each other and do *to* each other. I've seen war and peace, feast and famine, depression and prosperity, sickness and health. I've seen the depth of suffering and the peaks of triumph.

I know in my heart that man is good, that what is right will always eventually triumph, and there is purpose and worth to each and every life.

That last line, of course, was used as the inscription on the wall at my father's gravesite at the Reagan Library. His hopeful outlook on life served to energize and motivate him throughout his leadership career.

My father's enthusiasm for the future provided a vivid contrast to the grim pessimism of Jimmy Carter and was a key factor in Dad's election in 1980. In the Reagan–Carter debate on October 28, 1980, Dad said, "For two-hundred years, we've lived in the future, believing that tomorrow would be better than today, and today would be better than yesterday. I still believe that."

Dad communicated hope and optimism during economic hard times. It took a couple of years for his fiscal program to gain traction and revive the economy, yet even before the economy turned around, people felt good about America because Ronald Reagan was president. In the wake of Vietnam, Watergate, the energy crisis, and runaway inflation, changing the mood of America was an enormous achievement. Just as Dad used to lift me up and carry me on his shoulders, he lifted the whole country on his shoulders with his infectious enthusiasm.

After leaving office, Dad reflected on the past and looked hopefully to the future in his speech to the Republican National Convention in Houston on August 17, 1992:

Here's the remarkable thing about being born in 1911. In my life's journey over these past eight decades, I have seen the human race go through a period of unparalleled tumult and triumph. I have seen the birth of Communism and the death of Communism. I have witnessed the bloody futility of two World Wars, Korea, Vietnam, and the Persian Gulf. I have seen Germany united, divided, and united again. I have seen television grow from a parlor novelty to become the most powerful vehicle of communication in history. As a boy, I saw streets filled with Model Ts. As a man, I have met men who walked on the moon.

I have not only seen, but lived the marvels of what historians have called "The American Century." Yet, tonight is not a time to look backward. For while I take inspiration from the past, like most Americans, I live for the future.

When my father spoke about America, we could all see our land through his eyes. He was like a child on Christmas morning—that's how he felt about his country. And Dad never tired of telling people how wonderful America is.

When you are full of hope and optimism, when you believe anything is possible in America, there's truly no limit to what you can achieve. My father proved the power of optimism throughout his acting career and his political career, and he worked hard to teach the power of optimism and enthusiasm to his children.

Leaders who envision a bright future and communicate that vision to their followers have a way of making their vision come true. That's how my father achieved so much in such a short span of time. That's how we can restore America again today.

If there's one subject Ronald Reagan could speak on with authority, it's leadership. In a speech before the Cambridge Union Society in England on December 5, 1990, Dad talked about the courage and confidence a leader must have in order to turn a vision into a reality: "A leader, once convinced a particular course of action is the right one, must have the determination to stick with it and be undaunted when the going gets rough."

Speaking at a Republican National Committee Gala honoring him on his eighty-third birthday, Dad said:

I have witnessed five major wars in my lifetime, and I know how swiftly storm clouds can gather on a peaceful horizon. The next time a Saddam Hussein takes over a Kuwait, or North Korea brandishes a nuclear weapon, will we be ready to respond?

In the end, it all comes down to leadership. That is what this country is looking for now. It was leadership here at home that gave us strong American influence abroad and the collapse of imperial Communism. Great nations have responsibilities to lead and we should always be cautious of those who would lower our profile because they might just wind up lowering our flag.

In recent years, we have desperately needed a leader like Ronald Reagan to keep America strong by keeping the government lean and the people free. America is drifting toward military unpreparedness and fiscal insolvency. America is losing respect abroad and becoming dangerously vulnerable to her enemies. It does indeed come down to leadership.

There will never be another Ronald Reagan, but you and I can learn the leadership lessons he has left for us. I can't think of a leadership role model more deserving of our study than my father.

He Set the Leadership Example for Us

Everyone is a leader in some arena of life. You may never run for president. You may not be a political leader or a business leader.

But you can still be a leader in your church, in your classroom, in your family, or among your peers. No matter what our leadership arena may be, there are lessons we can learn from the leadership example of my father.

Leadership must be bold, not hesitant or faint- hearted. My father established a simple policy: "We win, they lose." That policy is so bold that it instantly grabs your attention—and so concise that it is unforgettable. It was the theme of my father's foreign policy throughout the eight years of his presidency. In the end, Dad won—and the Soviets lost.

Boldness was a key element of my father's leadership style. He often said that leaders (especially Republican leaders) should wave "a banner of bold, unmistakable colors, with no pale pastel shades." By this, he meant that leaders should speak in terms that are daring and dynamic, forceful and arresting. Leaders should not appear hesitant, should not mumble uncertainly, and should not use weasel words. Leaders must proclaim, in terms loud and clear, the strong contrasts between themselves and their opponents.

We often hear people say that there's not a dime's worth of difference between the two political parties—and it's becoming increasingly hard to argue with that view. But whenever a leader offers voters a choice between "bold colors" and "pale pastels," boldness wins every time. Liberal Democrats never shy away from waving their bold liberal colors around. Unfortunately, all too many heirs of the Party of Reagan are wrapping themselves in pale pastels.

As I have studied Dad's approach to leadership, I am impressed again and again with his uncompromising boldness. He managed to communicate bold ideas and bold principles in a pleasing way. He mastered the art of being boldly charming, boldly engaging, boldly persuasive, and boldly likable. He made friends of his enemies and got them to buy into his leadership vision.

To be a leader, you must *by definition* be bold. There is really no such thing as a "timid leader." That would be a contradiction in terms. If you are not bold, you are not leading. If you are in a leadership position, but you're trying to wave a banner of pale pastels, then please get out of the way and let somebody bold take over. Leadership is for the bold.

Be a good listener—and a firm decision-maker. Great leaders invite information, views, and opinions from all sides. They listen carefully, encourage everyone to speak, weigh everyone's views—then they decide.

Leaders sometimes have to go it alone against the advice and opinions of others. They must sometimes buck the consensus in order to do what they believe is right. If a leader fails to exercise authority when authority is required, he or she will appear weak and indecisive. A leader who loses respect loses authority as well.

Great leaders don't punt their decision-making responsibility to a committee. A committee is, by nature, incapable of exercising bold leadership. In a committee, responsibility for the decision is distributed among all the participants. The mind-set of a committee tends to be cautious and hesitant. Bold, decisive courage is usually found in a single leader—not in an atmosphere of "groupthink."

When my father made the decision to fire the striking PATCO controllers, he made it clear that it was his personal decision, no one else's. He intuitively knew that it was important to demonstrate bold decisiveness. His decision to stand firm and keep his word got the attention of leaders in all the world's capitals, including Moscow.

Dad established early in his presidency that his adversaries needed to take him seriously. His decisive, uncompromising action at the beginning of his presidency gave him a lot of leverage in dealing with all his other adversaries for the rest of his presidency.

To be a great leader like Ronald Reagan, be a good listener, be open to new information, be receptive to advice. When the time comes to decide, *decide*. Then stand by your decision and see it through to a successful conclusion.

Be a good delegator. Leaders don't do it all themselves—they recruit excellent people, and they empower those people to carry out the leader's strategy. Delegating is essential to leadership. If you are not delegating, you are not leading.

A leader can delegate tasks and responsibilities, but a leader cannot delegate accountability for the results. A leader is accountable for everything the subordinates do. Once we delegate tasks and responsibilities to other people, we have a duty to maintain communication, set standards, evaluate performance, and take the blame when the team fails.

Leaders who delegate well tend to succeed. A good delegator unleashes the talents, skills, and creativity of his or her people. As my father said, "Surround yourself with the best people you can find, delegate authority, and don't interfere"—that is one of the best prescriptions for great leadership ever spoken.

Leaders are communicators and leaders are readers. Newt Gingrich once told me a story about my dad's communication skills. Dad and Newt were both scheduled to speak at a GOP event. As Dad was waiting to be introduced, he reached into the left-hand pocket of his suit coat and took out his index cards for his speech—but he fumbled the cards and they fell on the floor in disarray.

Newt was worried for my father. The cards were jumbled and out of order. But Dad calmly picked up the cards, flipped through them, then tucked them out of sight. Moments later, he stepped up to the podium and wowed the audience with a brilliant speech.

"I realized then," Newt told me, "that your father could start anywhere in the speech, and he could go from there. He knew his own ideas so well that he could fill the time with brilliant thoughts and stories, and end exactly where he wanted the speech to end. How many speakers can do that?"

One reason Dad was such a great leader was that he was a great communicator. He knew what he believed, why he believed it, and how to communicate it powerfully and persuasively. And one reason he was such a great communicator was that he was a voracious reader.

I remember as a teenager walking into my father's personal library and being awed by the books that lined those walls. Those books weren't there to impress you. Dad read them all. He came from a generation before television, before smart phones, before social media. In his day, home entertainment consisted of radio and books. As a result, my father lived in a world of ideas. Unfortunately, we have so diminished our attention span that it's impossible for us to absorb ideas anymore.

Years ago, a friend shared a statement with me that I have never forgotten: *readers are leaders.* One reason my father led so well was that he was so well read. For all too many people today, "reading" consists of emails, texts, and tweets. But leaders read *books*. Leaders have the ability to focus and absorb the printed word. A great book can entertain us, instruct us, and change our lives. Read great books, and soon you'll be thinking great thoughts.

You can easily read a book a week if you try. How much would your knowledge expand if you read fifty-two books over the coming year? My father transformed the American economy because he had a deep knowledge of economics—and that knowledge came from books. He transformed the world because he had a deep knowledge of history—and that knowledge came from books.

By reading books, you'll increase your vocabulary, sharpen your thinking skills, deepen your knowledge, and broaden your horizons. Schedule a daily time for reading books, at least half an hour a day. Download a Kindle app to your smart phone, and you'll always have a book to read at the dentist's office, in the airport, or at the barbershop. An ebook is a great companion when you are troubled by insomnia. Don't kill time—*fill your time* with great books.

Learn from my father's example. If you want to lead, *read*.

Remember that the struggle never ends. We tend to think that evil and corruption are temporary problems to be solved. All we have to do is elect the right people, apply the right solutions, and everything will be fixed. Then we can go home and live happily ever after. I think a lot of conservatives assumed that the Reagan Eighties had fixed the world. We restored the economy, strengthened our military, and toppled the evil empire. The world was saved.

We became complacent. We fell asleep—and as we slept, evil emerged in the Middle East, in the form of Al Qaeda and ISIS. The nuclear menace grew in Iran, Pakistan, and North Korea. Our own government became increasingly corrupt and unresponsive to the people while ignoring the needs of our veterans. The national debt spiraled out of control.

Evil always grows when Americans sleep.

I went to Berlin in June 2007, shortly before the twentieth anniversary of my father's Brandenburg Gate speech. There I met with Alexandra Hildebrandt. She and her late husband, Dr. Rainer Hildebrandt, founded the Checkpoint Charlie Museum near the Berlin Wall, the most visited museum in Berlin. It chronicles the terrible history of the Berlin Wall with exhibits, artifacts, and photographs.

While I was at the museum, I chatted with a high school student. It was his first visit to the museum, and he had not had a chance to tour the exhibits. I asked him, "What do you know about the Berlin Wall?"

"Well," he said, "I know that the Americans built the Wall to keep the Communists out of their sector." Here was a young man who lived in Berlin but had no understanding of the Wall. The schools he attended were not teaching him his own history. Those who don't know their own past are at risk for the future.

We Americans view problems in history as having a beginning, a middle, and an end. But world problems don't really have an end. Evil doesn't have an end. It is always at work, always scheming, always trying to subvert civilization. We need to understand that history is an ongoing, never-ending struggle between freedom and tyranny. We need to teach the next generation about the recent past if we want them to have a future.

My father understood that evil exists, it is not going away, and the job is never done. In his Evil Empire Speech in 1983, he said, "No government schemes are going to perfect man. We know that living in this world means dealing with what philosophers would call the phenomenology of evil or, as theologians would put it, the doctrine of sin. There is sin and evil in the world, and we're enjoined by Scripture and the Lord Jesus to oppose it with all our might."

So we must not become complacent. We must not go to sleep. We must fight. It's a good fight, and one worth waging—but it's a fight that will not be finished in our lifetime, or in the lifetimes of our children and our children's children. As long as evil exists, the struggle never ends.

Lead with optimism and enthusiasm. Optimists are far more likely than pessimists to reach their goals and achieve their vision. Why? Several reasons:

Optimists are confident, and confident leaders are decisive. People who lack confidence are hesitant and they pass up opportunities by failing to seize the moment. They dither and fret over decisions because they fear that any decision they make will turn out badly. Where pessimists see obstacles, optimists see opportunities.

Optimists are able to persevere through tough times because they believe better times are coming. Optimists believe in themselves, and this enables them to pursue challenging goals, welcome new experiences, bounce back from adversity, and work hard to achieve their dreams.

Whatever your leadership arena—your family, your company, your school, your nation—envision a bright and optimistic future. Then go out to your people and promote that vision, using inspiring word pictures and metaphors. Ignite the enthusiasm of your followers. Strengthen their courage. Persuade them. Motivate them. Then lead them toward the bright vision of the future you have planned for them.

When America desperately needed a leader with a bold and optimistic vision, Ronald Reagan stepped up. Now our families, our schools, our businesses, our churches, and our nation desperately need new leaders, bold leaders, enthusiastic leaders. It's your turn to step up.

My father set the example. Now it's your turn to lead.

12

Trust in God

MONDAY, MARCH 30, 1981, THE sixty-ninth day of my father's presidency, started out like any other work day.

I was in my office at Dana Ingalls Profile Inc., a small aerospace company headquartered in Burbank, California. It was about half past eleven in the morning, and I was meeting clients.

There was a quick knock on my office door—then Mike Luty, the Secret Service agent assigned to protect my family, opened the door and said, "There's been an assassination attempt on your father. One man is down, but your father is OK."

Before I could say a word, he shut the door and was gone.

For several seconds, I stared at my clients—then I said, "Did he say somebody tried to shoot my dad?" I stood up. "Excuse me."

I went out and found Mike Luty and had him repeat what he said. Mike repeated his message, and added, "Your father is headed back to the White House. As soon as I get more information, I'll let you know."

I went back to my office and concluded my business with my clients, then I turned on the radio. The radio news bulletin had the same information the Secret Service agent had given me, except that it was becoming clear that three men had been wounded, not just one—Dad's press secretary, Jim Brady; a Secret Service agent, Timothy McCarthy; and a D.C. policeman, Thomas Delahanty. The report said that my father was returning to the White House.

So I called the special number I had for the White House. I didn't expect to reach Dad, but I thought I could at least talk to Nancy. But when I got through to the White House, I learned that Nancy had just left.

That information gave me a cold chill. I instantly knew that something was seriously wrong. If Nancy had left the White House, headed for some other destination, then Dad had to be headed someplace else, too. Only one destination made sense: the hospital.

At that moment, I knew Dad had been shot, too.

I went and told Mike Luty, and he tried to reassure me. "I'm sure he went to check on Jim Brady and the others who were shot."

I shook my head. "I'd bet anything Dad was shot, too."

"That just can't be. I'm in touch with the command post, and they told me Rawhide is definitely not hurt."

Minutes later, however, Mike Luty received confirmation: "Rawhide" had in fact been shot. He was at the George Washington University Medical Center, fighting for his life.

"I'm Alive, Aren't I?"

At 2:27 p.m., Washington time, a disturbed young man named John W. Hinckley Jr. stood on the sidewalk outside the Washington Hilton Hotel. His right hand, thrust into his pocket, gripped a pistol loaded with explosive-tipped Devastator bullets. He watched as President Reagan emerged from the hotel with his aides and Secret Service guards. As the president paused by the limousine to waive to the crowd, the gunman pulled out his weapon and fired wildly, hitting Jim Brady, Agent McCarthy, Officer Delahanty—and my father.

The bullet that hit Dad was a ricochet. It glanced off the steel flank of the bulletproof limousine, flattened, and penetrated beneath Dad's raised left arm as he waved. The entry wound was a tiny slit, more of a buttonhole than a gunshot wound. Dad didn't even know he'd been shot.

In the next instant, the chief of the Secret Service detail, Jerry Parr, shoved my father into the backseat—Dad landed painfully on the transmission hump. Parr leaped in after him and shouted to the driver, "Go, go, go!"

The limo roared off in the direction of the White House.

"You broke my ribs," Dad complained as Parr lifted him off the floor of the car. Dad started coughing, and Parr handed him a handkerchief. When Dad coughed up blood, Parr ordered the driver to head for George Washington University Medical Center. Parr's split-second decision saved Dad's life.

(Here's an interesting sidenote, in 1939, Dad made a motion picture called *Code of the Secret Service*. He later called it "the worst picture I ever made" and was so embarrassed by it that he refused to attend a screening. In fact, Dad told Maureen and me that if we ever saw that movie, he would write us out of the will. Yet a young boy named Jerry Parr loved that picture, watched it multiple times, and was inspired by that movie to become a Secret Service agent. If Dad hadn't made that embarrassing movie in 1939, Agent Parr might not have been at Dad's side in 1981, ready to make that life-saving decision. God truly does work in mysterious ways.)

Dad walked into the hospital trauma unit on his own two feet, but he collapsed just after he got through the triple-glass doors of the ER. He gasped, "I can't catch my breath!"

Doctors would later discover that the bullet had stopped within a quarter-inch of Dad's heart. He fought for breath as doctors and nurses cut the suit off his body. His blood pressure was too low to register, indicating internal bleeding. He was going into shock.

The medical team gave Dad oxygen, IV fluids, and blood—the first pint of many. The doctors couldn't control the internal bleeding and Dad's left lung had collapsed.

The surgical team met with Dad and Nancy, explaining that they needed to perform exploratory surgery to remove the bullet and stop the bleeding. As the doctors prepared for surgery, Dad said, "Please tell me you're a Republican." One of the surgeons—reportedly a confirmed Democrat—replied, "Today, Mr. President, we're all Republicans."

After three hours spent exploring Dad's chest, the doctors were unable to find the bullet. It was frustrating because the X-ray showed right where the bullet should be. It was not uncommon to leave a bullet in a gunshot victim—but this bullet was close to Dad's heart and might even enter an artery, where it could kill him without warning.

Just as the surgeon was on the verge of closing up, he found the slug—flattened to the shape of a dime. Once found, it was easily removed.

Later, when Dad awoke from the anesthesia, he was weak but aware of his surroundings. He saw white-gowned figures moving in the room around him. He was unable to speak because of the tube down his throat. He motioned for something to write on, and a nurse handed him a pad and a pen. He scrawled, "I'm alive, aren't I?" For the next few hours, that pad would be his only way of communicating.

At that time, no one but the doctors knew how close the world came to losing Ronald Reagan. All the accomplishments of the next eight years, including the revived economy and the end of the Cold War, were compressed into a quarter-inch space between a madman's bullet and my father's heart.

Miserable with Worry

Meanwhile, in California, Colleen and I were practically impris-
oned in our home, as an army of reporters swarmed around our
neighborhood. Our friends, Don and Dottie Price, were with us,
helping us maintain our sanity. At one point, Don took our son
Cameron for a walk. (News reporters snapped their picture, and
the photo was published the next day, misidentifying Don as a
Secret Service agent.)

After a while, the lead agent on our security detail, Cliff
Baranowski, entered the house. In a dry, businesslike tone, he
said, "A plane will be waiting for you. When you get on the plane,
they'll give you a blanket, earplugs, and a box lunch. Takeoff is
at six tonight. You'll get into Washington late, stay overnight in
the White House, and tomorrow you'll go to the hospital to see
your father."

"Why will I need a blanket and earplugs?"

"The only plane we could get is a C-130 transport. It's not a
comfortable airplane, so dress warmly."

All the Reagan children except Ron boarded the flight at
LAX—Colleen and Cameron; Maureen and her fiancé, Dennis
Revell; and Patti—along with our Secret Service agents. (Ron,
who was with the Joffrey Ballet, flew to D.C. from Nebraska.)

A C-130 is a cavernous aircraft without any insulation. We
soon discovered that when the heater was on, it was an oven.
The moment the heater snapped off, the airplane became a deep
freeze. The scream of the engines penetrated the aluminum airplane skin like it was paper. The flight from LAX to Washington
was noisy and we were miserable with worry about Dad.

Out of all of us, Patti seemed the hardest by the crisis. She
had struggled the most with Dad's politics and with living in the
shadow of his fame. But as the plane took off and climbed into
the sky, she seemed more frightened and broken than the rest of
us. Patti and I had not been close for years, but during the flight,

she leaned against me for support, and I put my arm around her. It was good to know that, whatever our differences in the family, we were united in a crisis.

As the plane made its descent toward Washington, we wondered: Would Dad be conscious? How would the assassination attempt affect his presidency? Would he serve out his term?

We arrived late that night and stayed at the White House. Colleen and I stayed in the Lincoln bedroom. We rose early the next morning, had breakfast, and rushed to the hospital. Nancy's children, Patti and Ron, were allowed to see Dad first—which infuriated Maureen and me. But we used the waiting time to visit the other wounded men, Brady, McCarthy, and Delahanty.

James Brady had been shot in the head, and it broke my heart to see his wife Sarah hovering over him, pleading with him to live.

After visiting the other patients, Maureen, Colleen, and I stayed in a holding area. We waited and waited—and waited some more. Finally, a Secret Service agent came to the holding area. I thought he was going to usher us in to see Dad. Instead, he said, "The doctors don't feel the president is strong enough to see the rest of the family right now. Come back in twenty-four hours."

In my usual diplomatic way, I said, "That's stupid! Let me talk to the doctor."

"The doctor is not available."

When the agent left, Maureen said, "Michael, you've got to be my bird dog. You've got to sniff out a way to get us into Dad's room."

"Leave it to me."

I went out and poked around until I found an unlocked door. I opened it and found myself face to face with a doctor. I said, "I'm Michael Reagan. Why are you keeping my sister and me from seeing our father?"

The doctor stammered incoherently—and I knew we were in. Soon, Maureen, Dennis, Colleen, and I were led into Dad's room. The window shades were closed for security reasons, but the room was brightly lit. Dad looked tired from his ordeal, and he was in pain. Yet he was alert, and his face lit up when he saw us. His wit was in typical Reagan form.

"Michael," he deadpanned, "if you're ever shot, make sure you're not wearing a new suit."

"Excuse me?"

"You know, that was a brand-new suit I was wearing yesterday. First time I ever wore it. Michael, do you know what happens when they bring you into the emergency room of the hospital? They don't go to you and say, 'Please remove your suit, Mr. President.' No, they take a pair of scissors and cut your clothes right off of you! The last time I saw that suit, it was sitting in a corner of the emergency room, completely shredded."

"I can see how that would be upsetting, Dad. But at least they did save your life."

"Yes, the doctors and nurses here are great. You know, I hear the parents of the fellow who shot me live in Denver. His father's in the oil business, I think. The least they could do is buy me a new suit."

"I think they owe you that much, Dad."

The Power of Prayer

The assassination attempt had a profound spiritual impact on my father.

After the attempt on his life, Dad had to forgo one of his great pleasures in life—spending time with God's people in church. He never got over seeing his longtime friend, Jim Brady, writhing on the ground, his face in a pool of blood. Dad always blamed himself for that. It affected him deeply to know that three men took bullets intended for him. He never wanted to put bystanders in harm's way again. And he never wanted to see that scene played out in a church. So he reluctantly avoided church for the next eight years.

The assassination attempt also moved him to recommit his life to God. While he was still in the hospital, he told me, "Michael, I've thought a lot about the events of that day, and how close I came to death. Not only would my earthly life have been over, but everything I wanted to do for the American people would have ended. God controlled every circumstance. I believe He spared me for a purpose. Michael, I want you to know I've decided to recommit the rest of my life and my presidency to God."

Cardinal Terence Cooke of New York visited Dad during his recovery. "Mr. President," he said, "you surely have an angel sitting on your shoulder." There may have been more truth to that statement than even Cardinal Cooke realized.

Days after the assassination attempt, Patti talked about the incident with a friend who was a hospital nurse. Patti mentioned that Dad had seen people clad in white when he came out of the anesthesia. The nurse said, "Are you sure your father said the people wore white?"

"Yes," Patti said. "He was definite about that."

"It's odd," said the nurse. "No one in a recovery room or intensive care wears white. They all wear green scrubs."

Patti then called Nancy and told her about her conversation with the nurse. Nancy said, "You're right, all the hospital personnel wore green, not white."

Who were the white-gowned figures Dad saw in the recovery room? Might they have been angels? Patti and Nancy think so. I'm inclined to agree.

It wouldn't be surprising to find that my father was surrounded by angels in that moment of crisis. He was a man of quiet but profound faith. For as long as I can remember, Dad has been on good speaking terms with the Lord.

Dad often talked about the spiritual teaching he received from his mother, Nelle—and that, of course, is why Dad used to take

Maureen and me to stay with Nelle on Sundays. He wanted us to receive the same Christian instruction that he received when he was a boy. He decided for Christ and was baptized when he was twelve years old. From that time forward, prayer was an essential part of his life. During the Great Depression, he prayed not only for his family, but for the healing of his country from its economic woes.

When he was on the Eureka College football team, he prayed before going out on the field. No, he didn't pray to win the game. He prayed that there would be no injuries and that he would do his best and have nothing to regret at the end of the game. Dad kept his prayers to himself, fearing that his teammates might ridicule him. But one day he mentioned in a team meeting that he prayed—and all his teammates said that they prayed, too. He concluded, "That was the last time I was ever reluctant to admit I prayed."[1]

Dad experienced a dramatic demonstration of the power of prayer while governor of California. Soon after he was inaugurated, a doctor diagnosed him with an ulcer. For the next year, he carefully followed the doctor's advice, watching his diet and downing large quantities of Maalox. He also prayed for healing, but the ulcer continued to trouble him. In fact, the pain in his stomach grew continually worse as the pressures of the office weighed on him.

One morning, he got up and went to the medicine cabinet to take another dose of Maalox to start the day. A thought occurred to him, *You don't need this stuff anymore.* He decided to skip the Maalox and see what happened.

He went to his office—and realized that the pain in his stomach was gone. He took his first appointment for the day—a businessman from Southern California. As their meeting was drawing to a close, the businessman got up to leave and said, "Governor, I just want you to know that I'm part of a group of people who meet every day and pray for you."

"Well, thank you," Dad said. "I put a lot of stock in prayer. Please thank the others for me."

Later that day, Dad met with another businessman. Once again, as their meeting was ending, this businessman said that he and his prayer group were meeting daily to pray for Dad.

A few days later, Dad went to the doctor for his annual checkup—and the doctor was surprised to find no sign of an ulcer. Dad was healed—and he was certain he was healed by the power of prayer.

Dad deeply believed in the importance of praying for the nation. In his first inaugural address on January 20, 1981, he said, "I am told that tens of thousands of prayer meetings are being held on this day, and for that I am deeply grateful. We are a nation under God, and I believe God intended for us to be free. It would be fitting and good, I think, if on each Inauguration Day in future years, it should be declared a day of prayer."

The prayers of other people meant everything to Dad when he was wounded by a would-be assassin. "It's a remarkable feeling to know that people are praying for you and for your strength," he once wrote. "I know firsthand. I felt those prayers when I was recovering from that bullet."[2]

Breaking the Curse

Dad viewed prayer as a key ingredient in healthy relationships. I know he prayed daily for each of his four children. As president, he prayed that his political relationships would work smoothly so that he, his allies, and his opponents could work together for the good of the nation. Speaking before the National Prayer Breakfast on February 4, 1982, he said, "In one of the conflicts that was going on throughout the past year, when views were held deeply on both sides of the debate, I recall talking to one senator who came into my office. We both deeply believed what it was we were espousing, but we were on opposite sides. And when we finished talking, as he rose, he said, 'I'm going out of here and do some praying.' And I said, 'Well, if you get a busy signal, it's me there ahead of you.'"

On January 29, 1985, Dad proclaimed a National Day of Prayer. In his proclamation, he said, "Today our nation is at peace and is enjoying prosperity, but our need for prayer is even greater. We can give thanks to God for the ever increasing abundance He has bestowed on us, and we can remember all those in our society who are in need of help, whether it be material assistance in the form of charity or simply a friendly word of encouragement. We are all God's handiwork, and it is appropriate for us as individuals and as a nation to call on Him in prayer."

Near the end of his second term as president, he delivered his final address to the United Nations in New York. After the assassination attempt, he had committed his presidency to God, and God had blessed his efforts. The United States and the Soviet Union had just reached an agreement to dramatically reduce their nuclear stockpiles, so it was a time of real hope and optimism for the world. Near the end of that speech, which he delivered on September 26, 1988, my father said, "When we grow weary of the world and its troubles, when our faith in humanity falters, it is then that we must seek comfort and refreshment of spirit in a deeper source of wisdom, one greater than ourselves."

That was how my father lived his life—and that was how he conducted his presidency. As Cardinal Cooke said, Dad must have had an angel guarding him when that gunman opened fire on the sidewalk outside the Washington Hilton Hotel. There's ample precedent in the Bible for a belief in guardian angels. "For he will command his angels concerning you to guard you in all your ways," wrote the Psalmist.[3] And the New Testament tells us, "Are not all angels ministering spirits sent to serve those who will inherit salvation?"[4]

I believe angels were overseeing the surgery on my father when doctors, on the verge of giving up, found the bullet lodged close to his heart. And angels must have been at his side during his talks with Tip O'Neill and Ted Kennedy and other congressional opponents as they hammered out a plan to restore the American economy. Angels probably whispered in Dad's ear during his summit meetings with Mikhail Gorbachev. Angels undoubtedly gave him strength and wisdom to comfort the nation when the crew of the space shuttle *Challenger* perished shortly after launch.

And I believe the presence of angels is preceded by prayer. My father was accompanied by guardian angels because he prayed and because others were praying for him. Amazing things happened during my father's presidency because he was on speaking terms with the Creator of the universe. Let me tell you about one of those amazing things.

You may find it hard to believe. In fact, I'm not sure I believe it myself. However you choose to interpret the facts, these facts cannot be denied:

For more than a century prior to my father's election as president, there was a regular twenty-year "death cycle" among American presidents. Beginning with William Henry Harrison in 1840, every president elected or reelected in a year ending in zero died in office. Many people believe that this twenty-year cycle was due to "Tecumseh's Curse," a curse that (according to legend) was invoked by a Shawnee prophet, Tenskwatawa, brother of Chief Tecumseh. Tenskwatawa conjured this curse as a punishment against William Henry Harrison, who defrauded the Shawnees while governor of the Indiana Territory, and who killed many Shawnees at the Battle of Tippecanoe in 1811. Harrison was elected president in 1840 and died after just one month in office.

After Harrison, the "curse" supposedly claimed Abraham Lincoln (elected 1860), James A. Garfield (elected 1880), William

McKinley (elected 1900), Warren G. Harding (elected 1920), Franklin D. Roosevelt (reelected 1940), and John F. Kennedy (elected 1960). Dad was aware of the "curse" when he ran for president, but he laughed it off as a silly superstition when he ran in 1980. Yet he came within a quarter of an inch of being the next victim of Tecumseh's Curse. Some believe that when my father survived the assassination attempt, he broke the "curse" on the presidency (to the relief of George W. Bush, who was elected in 2000).

If you don't believe in curses, I understand. I'm frankly not sure what to believe. But I'll tell you this: if a Shawnee prophet actually could call down a curse on the American presidency, I'm sure we would need a president of deep Christian commitment and prayer to break that curse.

This Blessed Land

I'll never forget Thanksgiving 1985.

The entire Reagan clan was gathered around the dinner table at Rancho del Cielo, Dad's Santa Barbara ranch. Now most people know that if you want a pleasant and serene holiday dinner, don't ever bring up politics or religion. Of course, our two favorite subjects in the Reagan family are (what else?) politics and religion.

As we were passing the turkey and mashed potatoes, Patti began talking about her Buddhist beliefs. Naturally, my brother Ron chimed in next, explaining why atheism is the only rational worldview.

I had committed my life to Christ and was baptized on Father's Day 1985, so I was a new Christian. In a private conversation, I had told my father about my newfound faith. So as the discussion of religion swirled around the table, Dad leaned toward me and quietly said, "Michael, I've been praying that Ron would accept Christ like you and I have."

Why didn't Dad mention Patti? I'm not sure, but I think he probably thought that Patti, at least, was on a spiritual path that might bring her back to the faith. Dad worried that Ron, an atheist, was in greater spiritual danger.

I lived with Dad and Nancy from the time I was fourteen until I got out of high school. Every Sunday morning, Dad, Nancy, Ron, and Patti would get dressed up and go to Bel Air Presbyterian Church. They always left me behind.

Years later, I took Dad aside and said, "I'd like to know why you never invited me to go to church with the family after I moved in."

"Your mother raised you Catholic. I didn't want to upset her."

"That makes sense," I said, "but I wish you'd explained it to me earlier."

I have heard Dad's critics say that he wasn't a serious Christian. They claim he only talked about religion to get votes. After all, he didn't attend church while he was in the White House, so he couldn't have taken the Christian faith very seriously. But Dad could not have been more serious about his faith.

Before Easter weekend 1988, I flew with him to California aboard Air Force One. I had appeared on the Larry King show to promote *On the Outside Looking In,* and had spent the night at the White House. As we approached the airbase at Point Mugu, I noticed Dad counting on his fingers. "November . . . December . . . January," he said. "Nine months."

"What are you doing, Dad? Nine months until what?"

"I'm counting the months until I can attend church again."

"Why can't you attend church?"

"I stopped going to church after I was shot," he said, "When I saw those men lying wounded on the sidewalk, it really shook me up. I never want something like that to happen when I'm in church. When I leave office in January, I won't be such a target anymore, and I can start attending church again."

"Why don't you go this Sunday? I think you should."

"Well, I'll think about that."

Dad did attend church that Easter Sunday. Nine months later, after leaving the White House, he never missed a Sunday morning service until he became too ill to attend. After that, the pastors would come to the house. On one occasion, Dad's pastor told me, "I came to minister to your father, but he ministered to me."

Like most Americans of his generation, my father understood that America was built on the firm foundation of Judeo-Christian morality and values. Faith in God is central to our history and our philosophy of government.

That's why my father spoke so frequently and passionately about our American tradition of religious freedom. Yes, atheists are free to be atheists. And as the First Amendment requires, we do not have an established state church. But we do have the constitutionally protected freedom to pray and to express our religious beliefs—not merely in private, but in the public square, in our schools, in our military, in our halls of government.

If my father were alive today, he wouldn't ask why there's no prayer in school. He would ask why there's no prayer in the home. I once spoke at a Christian event where about four hundred people attended. I was introduced as the son of Ronald Reagan, a president who supported prayer in school.

I began my talk with the question: "How many people here have children in school, grades K–8?" A lot of hands went up. "How many of you pray with your children before you send them off to school?" No hands went up.

"The problem," I said, "is not that there's no prayer in school, but that there's no prayer in the home. Too often, we want to blame the government or blame society. When it comes to prayer, I think we need to accept responsibility for our own failure before we fix society."

My father often said that America has a special place in history—a divinely appointed place. At the National Prayer Breakfast in 1982, he said, "I believe this blessed land was set apart in a very special way, a country created by men and women who came here not in search of gold, but in search of God. They would be free people, living under the law with faith in their Maker and their future."

And in the Reagan–Carter debate on October 28, 1980, he said:

I've always believed that this land was placed here between the two great oceans by some divine plan. That it was placed here to be found by a special kind of people—people who had a special love for freedom and who had the courage to uproot themselves and leave hearth and homeland, and come to what, in the beginning, was the most undeveloped wilderness possible. We came from a hundred different corners of the earth. We spoke a multitude of tongues. . . . We built a new breed of humanity called an American— a proud, independent, and most compassionate individual.

My father was a defender of America's founding freedoms. He knew that we are all endowed by our Creator with certain inalienable rights. And he believed that our government must never make any law abridging the freedom of religion.

How to Live, How to Die

As people of faith, we depend on God for many things. We ask God for strength in difficult times, wisdom in perplexing times, protection in times of danger, comfort in times of loss, and courage in times of fear. There are few things we fear more than death itself. My father was no different. There was a time in his earlier life when death was a mystery that troubled him, and filled him with questions and anxiety.

In 1941, Dad was in New York when his mother called him with the news that his father, Jack Reagan, had passed away. Hearing the sorrow in his mother's voice, Dad said, "I'll be there right away." Nelle asked him not to take an airplane because she thought airplanes were dangerous. Dad agreed to take the train, and Nelle delayed the funeral until he arrived.

Arriving home, Dad went to the funeral chapel and spent hours sitting beside his father's casket, thinking about death. But Dad later said that, after he had grieved and brooded over his father's death for a number of hours, he felt a strange peace wash over him. He sensed his father saying, "Don't worry about me, son. I'm doing fine here."

Dad said he was never troubled by the fear of death again.

In November 1994, after he was diagnosed with Alzheimer's disease, Dad wrote a letter to the American people. He disclosed his illness and wrote of his love for America and his hope for the future—and he talked about the end of his life, "When the Lord calls me home, whenever that may be, I will leave with the greatest love for this country of ours and eternal optimism for its future. I now begin the journey that will lead me into the sunset of my life. I know that for America there will always be a bright dawn ahead."

Almost ten years later, on Saturday, June 5, 2004, my father passed from this life and into the presence of his Lord. He was ninety-three years old. My sister Patti later said, "If a death can be lovely, his was." It's true. For days, as he was dying, he had not opened his eyes. But on the last day of his life, as breathing became very difficult for him, my father opened his eyes and he looked up at Nancy. The last earthly vision he beheld was the face of the wife he loved.

And the next vision he beheld was the face of his Lord.

There are many passages of Scripture I could cite to characterize his life and his faith in God. But I can think of no more appropriate verse than the words of the apostle Paul, written near the end of his life to his spiritual son Timothy, "I have fought the good fight, I have finished the race, I have kept the faith. Now there is in store for me the crown of righteousness, which the Lord, the righteous Judge, will award to me on that day—and not only to me, but also to all who have longed for his appearing."[5]

Most of the lessons my father taught me were about how to live my life—how to live with faith in God and with love for my fellow human beings. But he left me one last lesson, and when the day comes, I hope and pray that I have learned it well.

He taught me how to die.

A Close Encounter

I was midway through the writing of this book when everything nearly came to a screeching halt. It was Sunday, October 11, 2015. Colleen and Ashley had run in the Long Beach Marathon. After the run, I took my wife and daughter home, then I went out to pick up our dogs and bring them back to the house.

I picked up the dogs without incident and was on my way home. Colleen called me on my cell phone and said, "Michael, I just wanted to make sure you're OK. You didn't look well when you left, and I was concerned about you."

"I'm fine," I said. "I'll be home soon." We chatted for a few moments.

Then it hit me—hard. I felt I had to throw up. I pulled over, got out of the car, and leaned over—but I couldn't throw up. I had heard that nausea and dry heaves were often a sign of a heart attack. That scared me. I still had Colleen on the phone, and I told her what was happening to me.

"Michael," she said, "where are you? Ashley and I will come get you."

I knew where I was—but I couldn't tell her. I couldn't name the cross streets. There were street signs nearby—but I couldn't read them.

At that moment, I knew it wasn't a heart attack. I was having a stroke.

I got back in the car and started driving. I was about four miles from our house. I kept my phone on and kept talking to Colleen. Meanwhile, Colleen told Ashley to call the paramedics, then they each took a car and went looking for me.

Colleen and I continued talking, though I don't remember anything I said or how I got home. I remember driving down one street and realizing I had just passed my front gate. I told Colleen I was at our house. Then I backed up, opened the gate, and parked the car perfectly. Moments later, Colleen pulled in behind me. She helped me out of the car and sat me down in the garage.

Minutes later the ambulance pulled in, followed by Ashley. The paramedics bundled me into the ambulance and rushed me to St. Joseph's Hospital in Burbank. There I was evaluated and they told me I had suffered a mild stroke. The doctors wanted to keep me overnight for observation. They thought I'd be able to go home the following day.

But at 11:30 the next morning, I had a seizure and another stroke. My heart went into atrial fibrillation and flutter, and the doctors used the paddles on me three times to get my heart back into its rhythm. They then put me into an induced coma for two days.

When I came out of the coma, I had visitors—my dear friends Bob Neal; Bob Scullin; their wives; and my birth brother, Barry Lang, with his wife, Sandy. I had first met Barry in 1987 during my search for my birth mother. At one time, he was a writer for the sitcoms *Happy Days* and *Laverne and Shirley*, but he had left California because of the drugs and corrosive culture of Hollywood. Barry now runs Waterbeds 'n' Stuff in Columbus, Ohio. He had flown out to be with me after Colleen told him about my stroke.

A woman came in who introduced herself as a therapist who worked with stroke patients. She would show me different shapes—squares, circles, triangles—but I couldn't tell her what they were. I could speak, and I had no paralysis, but I couldn't recognize words or shapes.

As Barry and I visited, I remembered something he had told me soon after we met in 1987. He had come out to California before my first book came out, and he said to me before he left town, "Just to let you know, because of our family genetics, you will either die before you're sixty-nine, or you'll live to be in your nineties. It all depends on which kind of heart you got."

In fact, Barry needed a quadruple bypass at age forty-three and has had eleven stents put in since then, though he is otherwise in great physical shape. After Barry told me about my genetic history, I talked to my doctor, and he put me on low-dose Bayer aspirin. I've gone to the doctor every year, gotten regular checkups, and I've done everything my doctor told me to. I go to the gym three or four days a week, my resting heart rate is 41, and my doctor tells me I have the heart of an athlete.

My doctor said, "This stroke is ultimately the result of your genetics, not your lifestyle." When the doctors did an angiogram, they found that the blood vessels going to my heart were more than 90 percent clogged. I needed a quadruple bypass.

They scheduled the surgery for November 2. As the anesthesiologist was preparing to put me under, the surgeon said, "Do you have anything to say before we begin?"

Any last words? I hadn't expected that question. I realized that this was as close to death as I was likely to get and still live through it—if I lived through it. I didn't know if I would survive open-heart surgery. The odds were good—but the reality is that not everyone makes it.

I looked at the surgeon and said, "When I wake up, I want to see my wife and family—not my parents."

The anesthesiologist and the surgeon both chuckled—then they proceeded to put me under. I found out later that, after the surgery was completed successfully, the surgeon went out and told Colleen, Cameron, and Ashley what I had said.

The surgery went well, but afterward my heart refused to beat properly on its own. So three days later, the doctors installed a pacemaker.

I stayed in the hospital from October 11 to November 9—twenty-nine days—and I had the greatest doctors and nurses on the planet. During my stay, Bob and Cathy Scullin came to the hospital on Thursdays and Sundays to read Scripture and serve me Communion.

My cognitive therapist thought she would need to work with me for about a year. But after three months, she said I was functioning well. I could read (though not as easily as before the stroke, due to a blind spot in the upper right corner of my vision), and my cognitive abilities were back to normal.

We told very few people that I'd had a stroke. Because of the work I do, I didn't want to give anyone the impression that I was incapacitated and couldn't do my job.

I feel extremely blessed. I had suffered two strokes and a seizure, but I had no paralysis, my speech was not affected, and within a short time I was back at work, giving speeches and working on this book. I wasn't able to drive for a while, but that was a minor inconvenience.

In the midst of the writing of this book, I had a close encounter with death. I didn't want to die—but if death came, I was ready. I didn't want to leave my family—but I knew I would see them again.

I was afraid when the stroke first hit me and I didn't know if I could find my way home. I was afraid when they were about to put me under and open my chest. Though I fear the *process* of dying, I'm not terrified of death itself. When the time comes, my faith in God will carry me through the doorway of eternity.

That, too, is one of the lessons my father taught me.

Epilogue

A Lesson Dad and I Taught Each Other

M Y SISTER MAUREEN WAS one of the most selfless people I've ever known.

After Dad was diagnosed with Alzheimer's disease, Maureen organized fund-raisers, gave media interviews, testified before Congress—anything to find a cure for the disease. Her only thought was for Dad and all the other people suffering from the disease.

She was so wrapped up in the cause that she neglected her own health needs. After skipping checkups and ignoring the warning signs, she was diagnosed with advanced melanoma. Even after she knew her illness was terminal, she never thought about herself. She only thought about Dad, about Mom, about her husband and daughter, about me. Maureen was a mother hen, and she was watching over everyone but herself.

In December 2000, Colleen and I went to visit Maureen at St. John's Hospital in Santa Monica. She was receiving biochemotherapy treatments at the John Wayne Cancer Institute there. When we arrived, we visited awhile with Maureen, her husband Dennis, and her daughter Rita. Finally, Maureen said, "Everybody out! No, not you, Michael. You stay."

When it was just the two of us, she said, "I know how busy you are, Michael. You've got your radio show, your writing, and your speaking—but I want you to do something for me. I've been hoping and praying I would beat this cancer. But if I don't make it, I want you to promise me something."

"What's that?"

"Promise you'll carry on the work I'm doing. Promise you'll leave radio, and you'll devote yourself to preserving our father's legacy."

"I promise."

Eight months after that conversation, on August 8, 2001, my sister stepped into eternity.

Her funeral mass was a beautiful celebration of her life and an expression of her faith. Ron, Patti, and I took part in the service. Though I was only supposed to give a Scripture reading, I departed from the script and talked about Maureen and all she had meant to me over the years. I said a heartfelt "thank you" to her for breaking open her piggy bank and giving her savings to the nurse—all ninety-seven cents of it. Maureen brought me into the Reagan family, and I'll always be grateful.

I wasn't sure if it was okay to go off script like that. But Mom hugged me and thanked me for sharing that personal story of Maureen, and I knew I had done the right thing.

After Maureen's death, I took up the causes that she had championed. I joined the board of the John Douglas French Alzheimer's Foundation (jdfaf.org), which does an outstanding job of funding Alzheimer's research. My father's longtime friend Art Linkletter served as chairman of the board for more than twenty years; after he passed away in 2010, I was named honorary chairman of the foundation.

I was elected to the Board of Trustees of Eureka College in 2006—another cause that was dear to Maureen's heart. She was elected to the board in 1999 but passed away before she could complete her term.

To fulfill my promise of maintaining my father's legacy, I founded the Reagan Legacy Foundation (reaganlegacyfoundation .org). Among the foundation's projects are the Ronald Reagan exhibit at the Checkpoint Charlie Museum in Berlin; funding for the Ronald Reagan French-American Conference Center at the Normandy Museum in Sainte-Mère-Église (the first town liberated by the Americans on D-Day); and a student exchange program, Liberty Education Tours, which introduces future leaders to the accomplishments and ideas of President Reagan.

My favorite project of the foundation is the educational scholarship program for personnel who serve aboard the USS *Ronald Reagan*. Because of my father's illness, he never got to see the aircraft carrier named for him. The USS *Ronald Reagan* is the flagship of Carrier Strike Group Five—and on March 15, 2016, I will visit the ship at its home port in Yokosuka, Japan, to hand out more Reagan Legacy Foundation scholarships to deserving sailors, airmen, and their families.

We also obtained permission from the government of Berlin to place a plaque in the ground at the Brandenburg Gate, commemorating my father's "Tear Down This Wall" speech in 1987.

I work with the Young America's Foundation (YAF), the organization that maintains my father's ranch, his "cathedral in the sky." I often speak at YAF events. The Young America's Foundation is doing an excellent job, inspiring the next generation of Reagan conservatives and upholding the values and principles my father fought for.

As I have traveled the world, in country after country, people tell me, "Please tell the American people to get it right. The world cannot afford for America to fail." As my father so often reminded us, America is that "shining city on a hill." Oppressed people around the world look to America as a place of refuge and hope. We have to keep the lights burning in this shining city. We mustn't let its light go dark.

A Time for Choosing

My father launched his political career with a televised speech on behalf of Barry Goldwater on October 27, 1964. That speech was called "A Time for Choosing." In that speech, my father laid out the essential principles of what we now know as Reagan conservatism: limited government, lower taxes, free market economics, the inalienable rights of the individual, and the preservation of the Constitution. It was more than a speech about conservative principles—it was a speech about *American* principles. He said:

> You and I are told increasingly we have to choose between a left or right. Well I'd like to suggest there is no such thing as a left or right. There's only an up or down—up to man's age-old dream, the ultimate in individual freedom consistent with law and order—or down to the ant heap of totalitarianism. And regardless of their sincerity, their humanitarian motives, those who would trade our freedom for security have embarked on this downward course. . . .
>
> The Founding Fathers knew a government can't control the economy without controlling people. And they knew when a government sets out to do that, it must use force and coercion to achieve its purpose. They also knew, those Founding Fathers, that outside of its legitimate functions, government does nothing as well or as economically as the private sector of the economy.
>
> So we have come to a time for choosing.

Though Barry Goldwater lost in a landslide, that speech had a profound impact on the nation. Soon afterward, GOP leaders and average citizens were urging Ronald Reagan to run for governor of California. And the rest is history.

One of the last official acts of Dad's career was his speech at the 1992 Republican National Convention in Houston, Texas. These two speeches—"A Time for Choosing" in 1964 and the convention speech in 1992—are like bookends to his political career. In his final great speech, he returned to the grand themes he first proclaimed in 1964 and embodied throughout the Reagan Eighties. He said:

> While I take inspiration from the past, like most Americans, I live for the future. So this evening, for just a few minutes, I hope you will let me talk about a country that is forever young.
>
> There was a time when empires were defined by land mass, subjugated peoples, and military might. But the United States is unique because we are an empire of ideals. For two hundred years we have been set apart by our faith in the ideals of democracy, of free men and free markets, and of the extraordinary possibilities that lie within seemingly ordinary men and women. We believe that no power of government is as formidable a force for good as the creativity and entrepreneurial drive of the American people. . . .
>
> We have arrived, as we always do, at the moment of truth—the serious business of selecting a president. Now is the time for choosing.

He closed that speech on a note of farewell. "My fellow Americans," he said, "good-bye, and God bless each and every one of you, and God bless this country we love." It truly was my father's farewell to the nation. Exactly two years after delivering that speech, he was diagnosed with Alzheimer's disease.

In November 1994, he handwrote a letter to the nation, saying, "I have recently been told that I am one of the millions of Americans who will be afflicted with Alzheimer's disease. . . . I now begin the journey that will lead me into the sunset of my life. I know that for America there will always be a bright dawn ahead."

That's my Dad—as optimistic as ever. But will there always be a bright dawn for America? It depends on you and me. It depends on the choices we make, day by day.

Every day is a time for choosing.

The Greatest Lesson of All

After my father was diagnosed with Alzheimer's disease, my sister Maureen would visit Dad at the house and work jigsaw puzzles with him. At first, they would work the big 500-piece puzzles. But as his disease progressed, Maureen would bring a 200-piece puzzle, then a 100-piece puzzle, and finally a 50-piece puzzle.

We would take my son Cameron, who was a teenager, to visit his grandfather. Cameron enjoyed taking books from the shelves of my father's library and looking at them. He'd sit next to Dad and they would look at the books together. One of Cameron's favorite books to thumb through with Dad was written in Chinese characters. They would look at the beautiful pictures in the book, then laugh because neither of them could read the writing.

Ashley, who is five years younger than Cameron, would sometimes have lunch with Dad at his thirty-fourth floor office suite at Fox Plaza in Century City. At Christmastime in 1995, Colleen and I took Ashley to the office and we had a wonderful lunch with Dad. After lunch, some of Dad's staffers announced that they had put together a program of Christmas music in the conference room.

It was about a year and a half after my father was diagnosed with Alzheimer's, and by that time he was having some good moments and some bad moments. For most of our time together, Dad seemed much like his old self. But after lunch, the Alzheimer's seemed to really kick in. Colleen and I decided we would not stay for the Christmas program, so we hugged Dad good-bye. At that moment, he really couldn't communicate with us except with a hug.

Then Dad looked at twelve-year-old Ashley and it was as if everything came into focus for him and he was his old self again—he truly seemed as if he had never had Alzheimer's a day in his life. "Ashley," he said, "would you like to join me and listen to some Christmas carols?"

The transformation was startling. Dad wrapped his arms around Ashley and gave her a big hug, and she put her arms around Dad and squeezed him tight. As they hugged, Dad looked at me with that Reagan twinkle in his eye. "You know why I'm hugging Ashley?" he said.

"No, Dad—why?"

"Because she's a *she*."

That's my dad—always a ladies man. We walked into the conference room and enjoyed the Christmas program. But before we left, the curtain of Alzheimer's had come down again over my father. But it had been wonderful, if only for a moment, seeing how a hug from Ashley brought back the old Ronald Reagan we knew and loved.

He was a wonderful father and grandfather—but he wasn't always a "huggy" kind of guy. He came from a generation in which men didn't express emotions. In his foreword to the paperback edition of my book, *On the Outside Looking In*, Dad wrote, "Being a father forty-five years ago was a much different role than it is today. . . . Fathers didn't spend the amount of quality time with their children that today's fathers do, and they weren't always free to hug their sons or say I love you."[1]

Dad didn't realize how I struggled with the emotional distance between us. He didn't understand that all four of his children felt unsure of his love for us. Despite how much we admired him and respected him, despite his kindness and gentleness as a father, we struggled to feel close to him. In my own case, after carrying the burden of my childhood secret for so many years, I came to believe that if Dad didn't hug me, it was because there was something *wrong* with me.

And for years, I felt bitter and angry because of that.

One day, while I was in prayer, I felt God speaking to me: *Mike, when was the last time you hugged your dad?* And the answer, of course, was that I had *never* hugged my dad. He didn't initiate any hugs—and neither did I.

That was a moment of clarity. I realized that the problem was not all him. At least half of it was me. So I decided that, the next time I saw my father, whether we were alone or in public, I would give him a hug.

In early 1991, my father came to San Diego to appear as a guest on my Radio KSDO talk show. It was one of the proudest days of my career, interviewing my father about his book, *An American Life.* After the show, Dad and I walked out to the lobby—and it hit me: *This is it. This is the day I give my father a hug.*

There were Secret Service agents, reporters, and station personnel all around. I didn't care. I reached out, wrapped my arms around my father, and hugged him. And how did my father react? He tensed up! He wasn't ready for it, he was embarrassed by it, and he wasn't sure how to react. But I hugged him tight.

And after an awkward moment or two, he returned my hug.

In that moment, something changed. Our relationship was never the same. From then on, whenever my father and I said hello or good-bye, we hugged each other. And very often, to my surprise, *he* was the one who initiated the hug!

And here's the amazing thing: it turned out that Dad wanted a hug as much as anyone—he just didn't know how to go about it.

Three years after that first hug, Dad told the world he had been stricken with Alzheimer's disease. Time passed, the disease progressed, and it gradually stole my father's memories from him. The day came when he no longer remembered my name.

But he still recognized me. He knew who I was. I was the guy who hugged him.

When he would see me, he would open his arms and wait for me to give him a hug. And I would always reach out and pull him close to me, hug him tightly, and say, "I love you, Dad."

And he'd look me in the eyes, and he knew me.

One time, Colleen and I went to visit him. He and Nancy sat together in the den, and Colleen and I spent most the time conversing with Nancy, while including Dad as much as possible. Finally, it was time to go. Colleen and I said good-bye to Dad and Nancy, and we left.

But there was something I had forgotten to do—something I had never forgotten before. I forgot to give my father a hug.

Colleen and I were in the driveway, walking to our car, when Colleen touched my arm and said, "Michael—you forgot something."

"What did I forget?"

"Turn around."

I looked—and there was Dad, standing at the door, arms outstretched, waiting for his hug. I ran back and hugged him and said, "I love you, Dad. I love you."

I'm glad I finally stopped resenting the distance between my father and me and started bridging the distance. That was a lesson Dad learned from me, and I learned from him: Take the initiative. Put your arms around someone you love. Say "I love you," before it's too late.

That's the greatest lesson of all.

Notes

CHAPTER 1

1 Maureen Reagan, *First Father, First Daughter: A Memoir* (New York: Little, Brown, 1989), 70.

2 Ronald Reagan, foreword to *On the Outside Looking In*, by Michael Reagan (New York: Zebra Books, 1989), 8–10. Citations refer to the paperback edition.

3 Ryan Sanders, "The Father Absence Crisis in America [Infographic]," National Fatherhood Initiative, November 12, 2013, http://www.fatherhood.org/bid/190202/The-Father-Absence -Crisis-in-America-Infographic.

CHAPTER 2

1 Kiron K. Skinner, Martin Anderson, and Annelise Anderson, *Reagan in His Own Hand: The Writings of Ronald Reagan That Reveal His Revolutionary Vision for America* (New York: Simon & Schuster, 2001), xvi–xvii.

2 Kevin Duncan, "Americans Paying More in Taxes than for Food, Clothing, and Shelter," Tax Foundation, May 3, 2012, http://taxfoundation.org/article/americans-paying-more -taxes-food-clothing-and-shelter.

3   Janet Bodnar, "Economist: We're Taxing the Wrong Things," *Kiplinger*, May 7, 2015, http://m.kiplinger.com/article/business/T019-C021-S003-economist-we-re-taxing-the-wrong-things.html.

4   Mike Rowe, "Why 'Work Smart, Not Hard' Is the Worst Advice in the World," *PopularMechanics.com*, August 14, 2013, http://www.popularmechanics.com/technology/a9333/why-work-smart-not-hard-is-the-worst-advice-in-the-world-15805614/.

5   Martin Luther King Jr., *I Have a Dream—40th Anniversary Edition: Writings and Speeches That Changed the World*, ed. James M. Washington (San Francisco: HarperSanFrancisco, 1992), 20.

6   Michael Moroney, "The Myth of Working Hard vs. Working Smart," *Entrepreneur*, December 27, 2013, http://www.entrepreneur.com/article/230527.

CHAPTER 3

1   Ronald Reagan, *Speaking My Mind: Selected Speeches* (New York: Simon & Schuster, 1989), 14.

2   Katherine Mangu-Ward, "Kerry on Reagan," *The Weekly Standard*, June 7, 2004, http://www.weeklystandard.com/kerry-on-reagan/article/5421.

3   Shannon Bream, "Reagan Gets the Shaft in Textbooks," *Tricky Politics* (blog), March 11, 2010, http://trickypolitics.blogspot.com/2010/03/expert-reagan-gets-shaft-in-textbooks.html.

CHAPTER 4

1   The University of Virginia's Miller Center of Public Affairs, "President Reagan: First Press Conference, January 29, 1981," YouTube video, 5:57, transcribed by the author, posted by "MCamericanpresident," April 6, 2011, https://www.youtube.com/watch?v=xGaN_qjih08.

2   Dinesh D'Souza, *Ronald Reagan: How an Ordinary Man Became an Extraordinary Leader* (New York: Simon & Schuster, 1999), 9.

3   Kiron K. Skinner, Annelise Anderson, and Martin Anderson, *Reagan: A Life in Letters* (New York: Free Press, 2003), 747-748.

4   Ibid., 800.

5   Ronald Reagan, *An American Life* (New York: Simon & Schuster, 1990), 715.

6   David Cross, "The Evil Empire Speech," *Following the Presidents* (blog), February 25, 2013, http://followingthepresidents .com/2013/02/25/the-evil-empire-speech/.

7   Natan Sharansky, "The View from the Gulag," *The Weekly Standard*, June 21, 2004, http://www.weeklystandard.com/ article/5446.

8   Ibid.

9   Leslie Stahl, *Reporting Live* (New York: Touchstone, 1999), 113.

10 William E. Pemberton, *Exit with Honor: The Life and Presidency of Ronald Reagan* (New York: Routledge, 1998), 69.

CHAPTER 5

1   Ronald Reagan, *The Reagan Diaries*, ed. Douglas Brinkley (New York: HarperCollins, 2007), 6.

2   Ibid., 12.

3   Child Trends Databank, "Births to Unmarried Women," Child Trends, March 2015, http://www.childtrends.org/?indicators =births-to-unmarried-women.

4   1 Corinthians 13:4-8a, 13 (New International Version).

CHAPTER 6

1   Max Boot, "Reagan Vindicated: Missile Defense Works," *Commentary*, November 18, 2012, https://www.commentary magazine.com/american-society/military/ronaldreagan -vindicated-missile-defense-works/.

2   2 Chronicles 7:14 (New International Version).

3   Ronald Reagan, "Primary Resources: Iran Arms and Contra Aid Controversy," *PBS*, http://www.pbs.org/wgbh/american experience/features/primary-resources/reagan-iran-contra/.

CHAPTER 7

1   Paul Kengor, "That Wall," *National Review*, June 12, 2007, http://www.nationalreview.com/article/221231/wall-paul-kengor.

2   Williamson Murray and Richard Hart Sinnreich, *Successful Strategies: Triumphing in War and Peace from Antiquity to the Present* (Cambridge, UK: Cambridge University Press, 2014), 412.

3   Jack Nelson and Eleanor Clift, "But 'Star Wars' Remains a Contentious Issue: Two Leaders Try to Charm Each Other," *Los Angeles Times*, November 22, 1985, http://articles.latimes.com/1985-11-22/news/mn-990_1_star-wars.

4   Robert Knight, "Reagan's Rollback of Communism Is a Model for the Tea Parties," Townhall.com, February 8, 2011, http://townhall.com/columnists/robertknight/2011/02/08/reagan%E2%80%99s_rollback_of_communism_is_a_model_for_the_tea_parties/page/full.

5   Paul Kengor, "That Wall."

6   Igor Korchilov, *Translating History: Thirty Years on the Front Lines of Diplomacy with a Top Russian Interpreter* (New York: Scribner, 1997), 156.

7   Ronald Reagan, *An American Life* (New York: Simon & Schuster, 1990), 706-707.

8   Peggy Noonan, *What I Saw at the Revolution: A Political Life in the Reagan Era* (New York: Random House, 2010), 149.

9   Ronald Reagan, *Speaking My Mind: Selected Speeches* (New York: Simon & Schuster, 1989), 199.

10 Mark 9:35 (New International Version).

11 Donald T. Regan, "Death of a Boy's Goldfish and Other Summit Events," *Sun-Sentinel*, May 23, 1988, http://articles.sun-sentinel.com/1988-05-23/features/8801310656_1_goldfish-first-lady-villa-fleur-d-eau.

12 Thomas L. Friedman, "How to Get a Job at Google," *New York Times*, February 22, 2014, http://www.nytimes.com/2014/

02/23/opinion/sunday/friedman-how-to-get-a-job-at-google
.html?_r=0.

CHAPTER 8

1 Steven F. Hayward, *The Age of Reagan: The Fall of the Old Liberal Order, 1964–1980* (New York: Three Rivers, 2001), 101.

2 John Meroney, "Here's the Rest of Him," *Claremont Review of Books*, May 24, 2001, http://www.claremont.org/crb/article/heres-the-rest-of-him/; Lou Cannon, *Ronald Reagan: The Presidential Portfolio: A History Illustrated from the Collection of the Ronald Reagan Library and Museum* (New York: PublicAffairs, 2001), 40.

3 Ronald Reagan, *An American Life* (New York: Simon & Schuster, 1990), 153.

4 Ronald Reagan, *Speaking My Mind: Selected Speeches* (New York: Simon & Schuster, 1989), 163.

5 Carl Sandburg Home, "Lincoln Biographer," National Parks Service, http://www.nps.gov/museum/exhibits/carl/lincoln Biographer.html.

6 Matthew 6:1 (New Living Translation).

CHAPTER 9

1 Ronald Reagan, *The Reagan Diaries*, ed. Douglas Brinkley (New York: HarperCollins, 2007), 12.

2 Matthew 6:12 (New International Version).

3 Patti Davis, "Saying No to Daddy," *Town & Country*, January 2012, 77.

4 Patrick B. McGuigan, "Ronald Reagan at 103: A Reporter Recalls Face Time with the President," Watchdog.org, February 6, 2014, http://watchdog.org/127553/memory-reagan-at-103/.

5 "Child Molesters," Yello Dyno, http://yellodyno.com/Statistics/statistics_child_molester.html.

6 Matthew 18:1-9; 19:13-14; Mark 9:37, 42; 10:13-16; Luke 17:1-2; 18:15-16.

CHAPTER 10

1 Ronald Reagan, *An American Life* (New York: Simon & Schuster, 1990), 109.

2 2 Timothy 1:7 (New King James Version).

CHAPTER 11

1 Paul Kengor, "Where Have You Gone, Bill Casey?," *American Thinker*, February 26, 2009, http://www.americanthinker.com/articles/2009/02/where_have_you_gone_bill_casey.html.

2 Ronald Reagan, "Remarks and a Question-and-Answer Session with Reporters on the Air Traffic Controllers Strike," Public Papers of Ronald Reagan, Ronald Reagan Presidential Library & Museum, August 3, 1981, http://www.reagan.utexas.edu/archives/speeches/1981/80381a.htm.

3 Marshall Loeb, Lee Smith, and Ann Reilly Dowd, "Cover Story: Reagan on Decision-Making, Planning, Gorbachev, and More," *Fortune*, September 15, 1986, http://archive.fortune.com/magazines/fortune/fortune_archive/1986/09/15/68051/index.htm.

CHAPTER 12

1 Ronald Reagan, *An American Life* (New York: Simon & Schuster, 1990), 56.

2 Ronald Reagan, *Speaking My Mind: Selected Speeches* (New York: Simon & Schuster, 1989), 135.

3 Psalm 91:11 (New International Version).

4 Hebrews 1:14 (New International Version).

5 2 Timothy 4:7-8 (New International Version).

EPILOGUE

1 Ronald Reagan, foreword to *On the Outside Looking In*, by Michael Reagan (New York: Zebra Books, 1989), 8. Citations refer to the paperback edition.

Bibliography

Bodnar, Janet. "Economist: We're Taxing the Wrong Things." *Kiplinger*, May 7, 2015. http://m.kiplinger.com/article/business/T019-C021-S003-economist-we-re-taxing-the-wrong-things.html.

Boot, Max. "Reagan Vindicated: Missile Defense Works." *Commentary*, November 18, 2012. https://www.commentarymagazine.com/american-society/military/ronaldreagan-vindicated-missile-defense-works/.

Bream, Shannon. *Tricky Politics* (blog). http://trickypolitics.blogspot.com/

Cannon, Lou. *Ronald Reagan: The Presidential Portfolio: A History Illustrated from the Collection of the Ronald Reagan Library and Museum*. New York: PublicAffairs, 2001.

"Child Molesters." Yello Dyno. http://yellodyno.com/Statistics/statistics_child_molester.html.

Child Trends Databank. "Births to Unmarried Women." Child Trends, March 2015. http://www.childtrends.org/?indicators=births-to-unmarried-women.

Cross, David. *Following the Presidents* (blog). http://followingthepresidents.com.

Davis, Patti. "Saying No to Daddy." *Town & Country*, January 2012.

D'Souza, Dinesh. *Ronald Reagan: How an Ordinary Man Became an Extraordinary Leader*. New York: Simon & Schuster, 1999.

Duncan, Kevin. "Americans Paying More in Taxes than for Food, Clothing, and Shelter." Tax Foundation, May 3, 2012. http://taxfoundation.org/article/americans-paying-more-taxes-food-clothing-and-shelter.

Friedman, Thomas L. "How to Get a Job at Google." *New York Times*, February 22, 2014. http://www.nytimes.com/2014/02/23/opinion/sunday/friedman-how-to-get-a-job-at-google.html?_r=0.

Hayward, Steven F. *The Age of Reagan: The Fall of the Old Liberal Order, 1964–1980*. New York: Three Rivers, 2001.

Home, Carl Sandburg. "Lincoln Biographer." National Parks Service. http://www.nps.gov/museum/exhibits/carl/lincolnBiographer.html.

Kengor, Paul. "That Wall." *National Review*, June 12, 2007. http://www.nationalreview.com/article/221231/wall-paul-kengor.

———. "Where Have You Gone, Bill Casey?" *American Thinker*, February 26, 2009. http://www.americanthinker.com/articles/2009/02/where_have_you_gone_bill_casey.html.

King, Martin Luther, Jr. *I Have a Dream—40th Anniversary Edition: Writings and Speeches That Changed the World*. Edited by James M. Washington. San Francisco: HarperSanFrancisco, 1992.

Knight, Robert. "Reagan's Rollback of Communism Is a Model for the Tea Parties." Townhall.com, February 8, 2011. http://townhall.com/columnists/robertknight/2011/02/08/reagan%E2%80%99s_rollback_of_communism_is_a_model_for_the_tea_parties/page/full.

Korchilov, Igor. *Translating History: Thirty Years on the Front Lines of Diplomacy with a Top Russian Interpreter*. New York: Scribner, 1997.

Loeb, Marshall, Lee Smith, and Ann Reilly Dowd. "Cover Story: Reagan on Decision-Making, Planning, Gorbachev, and More." *Fortune*, September 15, 1986. http://archive.fortune.com/magazines/fortune/fortune_archive/1986/09/15/68051/index.htm.

Mangu-Ward, Katherine. "Kerry on Reagan." *The Weekly Standard*, June 7, 2004. http://www.weeklystandard.com/kerry-on-reagan/article/5421.

McGuigan, Patrick B. "Ronald Reagan at 103: A Reporter Recalls Face Time with the President." Watchdog.org, February 6, 2014. http://watchdog.org/127553/memory-reagan-at-103/.

Meroney, John. "Here's the Rest of Him." *Claremont Review of Books*, May 24, 2001. http://www.claremont.org/crb/article/heres-the-rest-of-him/.

Moroney, Michael. "The Myth of Working Hard vs. Working Smart." *Entrepreneur*, December 27, 2013. http://www.entrepreneur.com/article/230527.

Murray, Williamson, and Richard Hart Sinnreich. *Successful Strategies: Triumphing in War and Peace from Antiquity to the Present*. Cambridge, UK: Cambridge University Press, 2014.

Nelson, Jack, and Eleanor Clift. "But 'Star Wars' Remains a Contentious Issue: Two Leaders Try to Charm Each Other." *Los Angeles Times*, November 22, 1985. http://articles.latimes.com/1985-11-22/news/mn-990_1_star-wars.

Noonan, Peggy. *What I Saw at the Revolution: A Political Life in the Reagan Era*. New York: Random House, 2010.

Pemberton, William E. *Exit with Honor: The Life and Presidency of Ronald Reagan*. New York: Routledge, 1998.

Reagan, Maureen. *First Father, First Daughter: A Memoir*. New York: Little, Brown, 1989.

Reagan, Ronald. *An American Life*. New York: Simon & Schuster, 1990.

———. Foreword to *On the Outside Looking In*, by Michael Reagan, 8–10. New York: Zebra Books, 1989.

———. "Primary Resources: Iran Arms and Contra Aid Controversy." *PBS*. http://www.pbs.org/wgbh/americanexperience/features/primary-resources/reagan-iran-contra/.

———. *The Reagan Diaries*. Edited by Douglas Brinkley. New York: HarperCollins, 2007.

———. "Remarks and a Question-and-Answer Session with Reporters on the Air Traffic Controllers Strike." Public Papers of Ronald Reagan, Ronald Reagan Presidential Library & Museum, August 3, 1981. http://www.reagan.utexas.edu/archives/speeches/1981/80381a.htm.

———. *Speaking My Mind: Selected Speeches*. New York: Simon & Schuster, 1989.

Regan, Donald T. "Death of a Boy's Goldfish and Other Summit Events." *Sun-Sentinel*, May 23, 1988. http://articles.sun-sentinel.com/1988-05-23/features/8801310656_1_goldfish-first-lady-villa-fleur-d-eau.

Rowe, Mike. "Why 'Work Smart, Not Hard' Is the Worst Advice in the World." *PopularMechanics.com*, August 14, 2013. http://www.popularmechanics.com/technology/a9333/why-work-smart-not-hard-is-the-worst-advice-in-the-world-15805614/.

Sanders, Ryan. "The Father Absence Crisis in America [Infographic]." National Fatherhood Initiative, November 12, 2013. http://www.fatherhood.org/bid/190202/The-Father-Absence-Crisis-in-America-Infographic.

Sharansky, Natan. "The View from the Gulag." *The Weekly Standard*, June 21, 2004. http://www.weeklystandard.com/article/5446.

Skinner, Kiron K., Annelise Anderson, and Martin Anderson. *Reagan: A Life in Letters*. New York: Free Press, 2003.

———. *Reagan in His Own Hand: The Writings of Ronald Reagan That Reveal His Revolutionary Vision for America*. New York: Simon & Schuster, 2001.

Stahl, Leslie. *Reporting Live*. New York: Touchstone, 1999.

The University of Virginia's Miller Center of Public Affairs. "President Reagan: First Press Conference, January 29, 1981." YouTube video, 5:57. Posted by "MCamericanpresident," April 6, 2011. https://www.youtube.com/watch?v=xGaN_qjih08.